Praise for *Carolina Blood*

"Hood's knack for painting richly nuanced characters, weaving fine tapestries of intriguing plots, and dousing us with rich Appalachian history makes his storytelling not just compelling, but enriching and important, as well. From the first page the novel intoxicates no less than the moonshine that washes through the narrative."

—Win Neagle, author of *Smoke and Gravity*
and *Full Count*

CAROLINA BLOOD

BOOKS BY RICHARD HOOD

Regret the Dark Hour
Carolina Blood

RICHARD HOOD

CAROLINA BLOOD

Down & Out Books
3959 Van Dyke Road, Suite 265
Lutz, FL 33558
DownAndOutBooks.com

Cover design by Eric Beetner

ISBN: 1-64396-146-2
ISBN-13: 978-1-64396-146-0

For Jan, who makes the sun shine.

PRELUDE

1973

The black-and-white Ford police car lurched upward, passing a huge granite outcrop, where the steep, muddy track switched back, climbing the dark mountain. A light autumn rain had begun to fall and the bobbing headlamps sent back bright streaks dissolving instantly into the night, like sparks from a fire. As the car labored upward, the flashes of rain thickened into silvery gobbets, promising real snow farther up the mountain.

A grizzled, one-armed man fought with the steering wheel, spinning and grasping at it to catch the recoil, wrestling the car up the mountain. He peered through narrow, varmint's eyes at the darkness ahead. He was wearing a police cap that was too large, pulled down to cover his heavy brow line. A thick, blue-leather glove was pulled onto his one hand, and he wore a similarly oversized police jacket, the empty sleeve wrapped and tied around the stump of his left arm. Otherwise, he was dressed like a farmer, in overalls and thick-soled Brown's boots. Beside him rode a younger man in a loose khaki shirt and blue jeans, wearing identical heavy leather gloves, and gazing through the windshield with the same slitted, weasel eyes as his father. Now and then the young man would lean slightly and let a gob of tobacco juice fall into the darkness at his feet.

"When's the last time they cindered this fuckin road?" he growled. "Whyn't you let me drive and stop twistin at that wheel like it's a goddamn phone dial?"

The driver said nothing, intent, jerking and catching the rebounding wheel. The other man rose a bit, steadying himself on the shoulder rest, and, reaching into the black well of the back seat, drew forth the shotgun. Its two short-sawn barrels gleamed dully in the greenish dash light. He tilted the gun along his body, the stock dropped between his legs.

"We hit the right jolt on this here road, that'll go off, turn you into a goddamn door screen," the older man said, wrenching hard at the steering, as the road climbed yet more steeply and turned right, lapping onto itself. "Jesus," he said, holding the wheel with his knee and downshifting, gunning the engine, as the track rose before them like a sheer wall. The car veered and skidded a moment, then surged, its lights swinging upward into an immense blackness flashed with the thickening rain.

The road straightened and humped, and the young man with the gun said, "There, Pawp. Right there." The driver pulled at the wheel and the car nosed down into a shallow pull-out lined with rotting saw logs and hedged by tree limbs and brush.

They sat still a moment, listening to the tick of the cooling engine. Then the older man, Pawp, lifted a quart mason jar, tucked it between his legs and whorled open the lid. He shut his eyes and took a long pull, then handed the jar across the seat. His son dipped his head, running his thin pink tongue all the way around the glass rim. Then he lifted the jar, pouring a stream of the white whiskey into his throat, letting it fill his open mouth. He made a few gulping, glottal sounds, coughed once, and handed the liquor back to his father, who finished it and threw the empty jar over his shoulder into the back seat.

"All right," the son said. "Get them things and let's move, god damn it." He leaned sideways, pointing his shotgun at the passenger door, and kicked it open.

"Since when was you the boss of this here show?" said the

older man, leaning into the rear to fetch a hatchet, tucking a flashlight and a pair of wire cutters under the stump of his left arm.

Five minutes later, they were some forty feet above the pull-out, at the side of the curving lane, where they snipped and hatcheted at an ancient rusted barbed wire fence. As the fat, wet snow began to fall, their gloved hands dragged free three locust posts and the trailing snarl of wire, pulling it through the underbrush and out onto the lane, where they stretched fenceposts and tangle across the narrow roadbed.

"Let's get hid," his father said. "Where's that blowbellows of your'n?"

"I got it," the boy said, lifting the sawed-off shotgun, and watching two plump snowflakes slap onto the barrels. "Don't you worry none about me."

A moment later, they heard the motor above them, and saw the beam of headlights sweep the treetops. They waited, one on each side of the lane, for the car to make the final switch and head down to where the tangle of wire and posts blocked the way. The older man leaned down and tugged and twisted a gnarled, cutoff rhododendron trunk. The thick stump came away with a dark, tearing sound, and he held up the root, thick and jointed at the center, like a man's elbow. He *hmmmd*, a low, mirthless laugh, and stood, a dark, grotesque figure, grasping the club in his single hand, like some mythical beast that had torn off and wielded its own arm for a weapon.

The descending vehicle, in odd congruence with the scene below, also held an older and a younger man, though, in this case, it was the younger man who drove. He wore a scrupulously laundered white shirt and a pair of corduroy slacks, like a town-dweller, though his steering was paradoxically steadier, as though he were accustomed to driving on the mountain. Watching the lane through large, expressive eyes, he swung the wheel smoothly through the switchbacks, his hands graceful and sure. His companion was middle-aged, like the man called "Pawp," and had a growth of salt-and-pepper stubble on his weathered face. The car descended slowly, deliberately, its headlamps waving rather than jouncing, until they lighted on the barbed barrier.

The car eased, stopped, then rolled tentatively forward and stopped again, a few feet from the wire. The younger man opened his door and stepped out, running his hand along his hair, puzzling.

Swiftly, as though this had been a signal of some sort, a dark figure in a policeman's jacket loomed forward, swinging his crooked club and striking the young man across the face, loudly snapping the bridge of his nose, and dropping him to the wet road, his face spurting blood, his shirt front already soaking.

Meanwhile, Pawp's son had tapped his shotgun against the passenger window, motioning for the older rider to come forth. The door opened slowly and the young man made lifting gestures with the gun barrel, beckoning his prisoner out into the lane, where he looked across at his son, lying on the road making wet, sobbing sounds. Rising slightly, the hurt man raised his hands, tentatively touching his broken nose, and gasping, "What..."

"Sunbitch," said Pawp, kicking viciously through the man's hands, sending up a spray of thick, dark beads and pitching him backward onto the muddy lane, where he lay, groaning quietly.

"Let's go." Pawp dropped the root, bent and grabbed his man by the collar, dragging him upward and forward, into a lurching trot, the hurt man dropping to his knees, then stumbling upward again to wobble a few steps, then falling, rising, tripping, pulled along too quickly, while, across the way, the other man was waved in the same direction, down and to the right, into the darkness of tangled growth beyond the road.

They came to the remains of barbed-wire fence, where Pawp dropped his bleeding prisoner and grabbed a gloveful of rusted wire. His son slammed the gun stock into the older prisoner's belly, doubling him over, while Pawp bent and wrapped a turn of wire around the gasping man's neck, then downward in a loop, trapping the hands, the man crying out sharply when the coarse barbs stabbed his flesh. Pawp spun the wire, his single arm dexterous and sure, wrapping the barbs three more times around the arms and body, which was now shuddering and jerking against the scouring cuts of the wire. The man moaned as he fell back, next to his son, who lay bleeding, his eyes wide and frightened.

The sawed-off shotgun swung lazily, pointing first at one man, then the other, then back again.

"Which of you Hamptons sons of bitches wants to die first?" Pawp said.

PART ONE

JAMES

Saying I need an image to make the world
I went back home and held my eyes on the hill
And it said You need a word deeper than I
—Shelby Stephenson

ONE

Jim Thorwait had never thought much about origins. He'd always scoffed at the genealogical charts his mother constantly drew up and revised, the ones showing them to be direct descendants of John Paul Jones. "Why is it everybody finds great, heroic ancestors when they go into discovering their family trees?" he would ask her. "Why don't they ever find out it was John Wilkes Booth?" he said. "Or who was that guy that slaughtered children after his orgies? Gilles de Rais?" And his mother would say, "You're terrible," though he could tell she liked this joshing, liked the slight taste of the forbidden, found it all amusing. After she died, ten years ago, he found he missed the banter about those carefully constructed charts, and he secretly rolled one of them up and kept it at his place.

Now, the family trees and all that research into lines of descent appeared like some part of an enormous ironic joke; now that he'd discovered the adoption papers, now that he knew he wasn't descended from anybody on those charts, and particularly not those he was most sure of…the recent ones.

The call came when he was working on a prewar L10 guitar, adjusting the bridge, doing the complex, four-way measurement necessary to getting the guitar set up correctly. Most players just eyeballed this sort of thing, but he knew it was the fit of the bridge, as well as its perfect match to the arched top, that made the difference between a valuable collector's instrument—which would be worth the same ten thousand dollars whether or not it was set up correctly—and a true musician's guitar, one that spent its time working instead of hanging on a wall. He was good at this kind of task: he'd found the fine groove between science and art, where the music lived in these old instruments, he knew how to coax it forth, and he had plenty of clients from all over the country who would have the tools of their trade—mandolins, banjos, guitars—in no other hands than Jim Thorwait's. So, he was sighting carefully, sliding the bridge slowly along the curved spruce top, edging it into place, when the phone jangled.

"Damn" he said, giving up the task and heading for the telephone. He'd have to start all over, and so his voice was a little edgy when he snatched up the receiver to hear that his father had died, that morning, of a massive coronary.

Thus began the strange journey into his own past. The entire weekend seemed unreal from the start, too much like a plot out of grand opera and, at the same time, completely farcical, absurd, one of those foolish old songs, like "My Brother Bill Got Shot," that are so funny because they make no sense. He must have looked pretty comic, he thought later, leaning over his father's desk with a knife, jimmying the file drawer because he couldn't find the key anywhere in his father's dark paneled office, among the medical books and journals. And then, of course, there was the irony of circumstance that seemed to operate throughout that weekend, because he said "Damn," to the drawer, just as he had to the phone, and, again, he was met with the shock of a lifetime. The drawer sprang open, and, almost without looking, he reached in and drew out, from all the identical-looking files, a thin manilla folder marked "James."

He felt a twinge of guilt, felt sneaky, like a little boy poking around in secret while the adults were away, until he opened the folder and found that he had not been the one acting in secret, found that nothing had been as he had thought—not even himself.

He found her name at last, tracking backward through the papers from the file, the legal forms and scribbled notes that had come to him only now, after his father—a nervous, intelligent man with deep blue eyes—had let up his vigil forever, like a sentry falling asleep at the post. The blue eyes had almost been a part of the trick, Jim thought now, for his own eyes were blue, large, and expressive, and people had often said, "He has his father's eyes," when, he now discovered, this was simply impossible.

Because this transaction, thirty-eight years ago, this adoption of a child from a poor young woman by a kindly old physician, would mean, had meant, that he—Jim—would be, had been, raised the only child of a wealthy couple, a society mother and an esteemed doctor. This had determined that he would live, had lived, the sort of life he had. He'd been "raised well," and "well educated," though he'd also had the circumstances that allowed him to turn his back on college education and follow his yen to work with acoustic instruments. And though he knew there was plenty of inherent talent in his hands and ear, he knew, too, he'd been raised with the kind of solicitude and leisure that allowed him to learn to play and understand musical instruments. He'd been able to travel and watch the master craftsmen and the virtuoso players. And now, owning his business, working when he wanted to on only the best instruments for the finest musicians, at top prices. He saw immediately that, were it not for this flimsy file of papers, he would most likely have lived a life of struggle and exigency, laboring with calloused hands, or perhaps cleaning the workshop of the esteemed craftsman he had, instead, become. *Maybe allowed to string up the instruments after Mister Thorwait had finished.*

So he had to absorb all this at once and find some place in the midst of his grief for the father—*who was never my father*—for the outrage and anger that had no outlet, because the man, the pseudo-father, was dead (the "mother" dead, as well), while this woman, the real mother, as far as his experience could say, had never existed at all. He couldn't fathom the *why* of it all. Why they hadn't ever told him he was adopted, why they had kept these papers locked away. He realized that he would never have known had his father not died so suddenly, unexpectedly, before he'd had time to protect the files from the eyes of a surviving son.

So it made no sense. But there was the truth, *the God damned fact of it.* And he felt himself *wronged*—because he had been tricked, fooled, for so along—and *wrong*, himself—because he was not the person he claimed to be. And he found himself seething, boiling, wondering, *Why? Why? Why didn't they tell me? Who were they protecting by not telling me the plain truth of who I was?* But, of course, they had escaped the accounting, both of them, the serene, soft-spoken woman he'd called "Mother," and the driven, gifted physician he'd called "Father." And meanwhile, the three words, repeating ceaselessly like a trivial ditty, some pointless jingle stuck in his head: *I was adopted, I was adopted, I was adopted.*

Her name was Allie Morelock, and the papers said she had been seventeen years old when his father, the doctor, arranged to adopt her son. Jim had been about a year old, though he would never be quite certain whether the date typed to the crisp birth certificate (stating—proving—that he was the son of Dr. and Mrs. George Thorwait) was as spurious as the document itself, or whether he had, in fact, been born on February 10, 1973. *I don't even know my real birthday,* he thought, and then, *I don't even know my name*, staring at the certificate, realizing he would never know whether the woman, Allie Morelock, had called him "Jim" or some other name, whether the doctor had chosen a new name to mark the startling change of direction this baby's life would take. *I only know who I am, and shouldn't have been. I've never been given the chance to know who I was, and should have become.*

A note in the file told him she had worked in his father's house—probably the cleaning woman or the cook—and had come from a place called "Shaleen Prong," in Jefferson County, North Carolina. She hadn't signed the legal document—probably, he decided, because she didn't know how—but there was the initial, M, laboriously drawn, rather than written, like a child's first printings. Beneath the initial, the full name, *Allie Morelock*, was crisply typed. Further down, he saw the physician's familiar signature, and then the attorney's. The document itself was strange, not a court order or a paper generated by any public or private agency. It was a single agreement, more like a contract, between this poor, illiterate mother and the wealthy physician. So Jim could see that the adoption had been arranged through a lawyer, all of it privately and quietly, almost like a sale of some illicit substance, or of stolen goods. He realized this sort of thing—the secret adoption—could not have happened even a few years later. But, to a leading citizen of Roalton, Tennessee in the early seventies, the negotiation with a powerless, poor young woman, and the intervention of an influential attorney sworn to confidentiality—the manipulation of whatever papers and identities had to be created to make him, *James Thorwait*, into a person—would all have been handled smoothly, discreetly, noiselessly, and, finally, wrapped up neatly and cleanly in this thin sheaf of papers, and the fraudulent birth certificate.

After several days of seething, raging, wondering, he began to consider more directly who this young woman (he had whispered the word, *Mother*) had been, how she had come here, why he had been recreated as the son of Doctor Thorwait, even, perhaps whether she still existed. *If she does, she would know my name and my birthdate, wouldn't she? She knows it right this moment, somewhere back in those mountains, perhaps. Perhaps she's thinking of it right now, wondering how her son is.*

On a Thursday morning, two weeks after the discovery, he was sitting at his bench working out costs and materials for restoring a 1926 F-4 mandolin that he had discovered in an estate sale near Asheville. He had a nose for finding these rare instruments, a combination of luck and something of a hunter's instinct. Once he could think of an instrument as "a fact," he looked upon the rest: whereabouts, ownership, the necessity to negotiate a sale, as a mystery to be solved, and it was this feeling of mystery that urged him to eventual success. On this day, though, the will that had driven him to dig up the rare mandolin became entangled with his curiosity about the woman on the papers—Allie Morelock—and he found himself losing track of the figures on his work notes, because he was, instead, counting back the years. He realized with a start that she would only be fifty-six years old, today, and, at that moment, she became to him a real person, someone out there who could, in fact, be found, dead or alive.

So he hurried to finish up the work that was pending. He got the instruments back to their owners, contacted his major clients, told them he was not taking any jobs for the next few weeks, and went to work to track down whatever he could of *Allie Morelock* with the same single-minded sensibility he'd directed at finding and repairing instruments.

It didn't go quite as well, though. He spent a day looking through records in Roalton, searching for some reference to Allie, Allison, Alice, Morelock. He found both too little and too much. There were plenty of Morelocks in East Tennessee, and three A. Morelocks in the phone book, though each call led to a dead end.

He tried looking on maps. Jefferson County, North Carolina was easy enough to find. But he couldn't find Shaleen Prong anywhere, on a road map or a USGS topographical map, or even on older maps from dusty volumes in the library. Nor could he come up with anything helpful on the internet. He found no trace of her, or her place, beyond the adoption papers. It was as though she had borne him, handed him to the doctor, and evaporated, her identity as shadowy as that of the child he might have become had he remained in her life, she in his.

But at last he had the fact of her. He had something to look for.

* * *

His search had revealed the Jefferson County seat, Glade, easily enough, and the Glade Public Library, which he had phoned, asking some questions about local records, and eliciting only wariness and suspicion. Finally, he decided to look for a newspaper, and found one on a web listing of North Carolina weeklies. The *Mountain Gazette* was published in Glade, and, though there was no web page, there was a phone number. So he called, wondering how to ask the questions that might evoke response rather than mistrust.

"*Mountain Gazette*, this is Sam," the full, genial voice said. "What can I do for you?"

Jim told him, stumbling a bit, that he was looking for information on a person named Allison Morelock, who had been from that area and had spent some time in Roalton, Tennessee.

"She owe you money?" the voice said, not unfriendly, joking perhaps. "Because if she owes you money..."

"I'm an adopted child," Jim said, feeling the curious discomfort of having to say this, hearing himself speaking the words, identifying himself this way to another person for the first time. "I was adopted, that is, thirty-eight years ago, and I've found the name of my mother was Allie Morelock and she's from your area. And I'm calling to see if you might be able to tell me where to start looking."

"I believe there's ways to do that," said the man. "Aint there? Through the state? I believe there's even folks that'll help you work through the records, the adoption records, with the agencies. Aint they?"

"This wasn't exactly done through the state," Jim said. "Or through an agency. It was a bit more oblique, a private matter."

"So they went around the state," said the man. "Well, that weren't all so unusual, I reckon, back then. Folks'd just go ahead and do it, maybe pay a little money, fix it all up between the two of em. That sort of thing?"

"That sort of thing," Jim said.

There was a pause at the other end. Jim heard the sound of a door opening, a woman's voice. Then the muffle of a hand over the receiver.

"Well, that's a interesting story, sounds like," the man finally said. "You comin up thisaway to look around?"

"Well, yes," Jim decided. "I think I am."

"I don't mind if you want to stop in here to the paper, though I aint too sure what you could want from us. You tried the library?"

"Yes," Jim said. "They weren't too eager to talk with me. Like I was prying into their business."

Lofton chuckled. "You aint from around here, are you?"

"Well," Jim said, "I think maybe I am."

Again the soft chuckle. "You been away, let's say. I can tell already they aint a lot of mountain folk in you, at least not right out front where folks can hear it. And people round here can be a little backward in talkin to strangers. Specially strangers asking questions. You know?"

"What else can I do but ask questions?" Jim said.

"Sure now, I reckon that's true," Lofton said, the voice quiet, friendly, reassuring. "Tell you what: you come on down here and come over to my house, maybe I can help get you started around here. We might could figure out something."

"That would be a great help," Jim said. "Would you rather I came to your newspaper office?"

"Cousin," Lofton said, "you can come to one or the other and you'll still be standin in the same place. Same address, same phone. Where you callin from?"

"Roalton," Jim said. "How far is it?"

"You can get from here to Roalton in a hour and a half, if you drive the way I do," said Lofton. Jim liked the tone of amiable cynicism in the man's voice. He found himself, strangely, wanting to befriend this man who knew about the adoption and who was from that place, and who might help, with that same easy ironic good nature.

"And how long would it take me to get up there from Roalton, driving the way I drive?" Jim asked.

"Well, now, that's harder to say," Lofton said. "You might never get here."

TWO

On a bright day in September, the man who knew himself as Jim Thorwait wheeled his green Mazda Protegé up the twisting, steep road from Cheat Hollow. Route 45 was a "Tennessee Scenic Highway," running alongside a rocky, tumbling mountain stream, crossing and recrossing the furious water at tight bends, as it worked its way up the hollow toward Needle Gap at the top of the ridge, and the state line, which ran from mountaintop to mountaintop, like stitches, on the contour map. The day was clear and cold for late September, the trees and thick bushes bright green and full, until. As his car ascended and the air thinned, the leaves began to color and turn to bright autumn foliage. At the gap, the maples, hickories, and oaks blazed orange, red, and yellow, then he crested the grade and began to descend into North Carolina and drop toward the deep greens of late summer, again. *Time travel*, he thought.

Gradually the grade lessened, the land began to open, where small garage-like shops sold sourwood honey and wood carvings. Further down, he passed a Dairy Queen and the Mountain Rest motel, a hungry-looking place with one car in its parking lot. A half mile further along, he entered the town of Glade, tucked into a wide bowl of open ground, and crossed by parallel, one-way main streets, each about a mile long, ending, on the eastern end, in a courthouse square. Along these main roads stood a café, a school, a library, a police station, a dollar store, hardware and drug stores, even a small hospital, all tucked into the curved bottom of the basin, whose sides were the looming mountains. Spreading back from the center was a small grid of side streets that held clapboard and brick houses, each quietly showing its white-railed front porch to the others. On the edge of these residential blocks, a few tiny farms clung to the rising slopes, the broad, ugly tobacco plants looking too big for the narrow, sloped fields, the unpainted curing sheds showing black-stripped gaps, like the porches in negative, between pale, narrow, gray planks. Even on this clear day, Jim felt a settled sense of darkness about the entire town, as though it had never gotten enough light. Now, still only late afternoon, the sun hovered close to the western rim of mountains; it would sink behind the wall of rock and woods, leaving the town in cold shadow, while daylight still shone in Roalton, or even in the gap he had just crossed. And the town, too, had a lonely air about it, he felt, as though it had been tossed carelessly into this unlikely hollow and forgotten, abandoned. He wondered whether this explained his own almost instinctive solitude, the reason he left school and learned on his own, in order to gain a skill where he would work alone. Perhaps it came from this place, the huddled isolation, the dark looming mountains rising on all sides. Perhaps his mother had carried this solitude within her, embodied it, after generations of mountain time, had implanted in his very heart and blood this dark seclusion, so that he really was *of* this place, even though he had never been here before.

The thought unsettled him. He turned on the radio, but could only find hoarse voices telling him about Jesus and Jeremiah, and the end of time.

Sam Lofton had given Jim sketchy directions and said, "Just ask once you get into town; anybody can tell you where I am." Now that he was here, though, Jim felt reserved, almost bashful. He'd always been most comfortable talking to another musician in the shop, both sets of eyes focused on the instrument set between them. Here, he wondered about having to speak with any of the people he saw on the street, either the two women he'd seen in longish print dresses, chatting and laughing in front of the dollar store or the men he'd seen coming out the bay door of a fifties-style filling station dressed in dark, oil-stained overalls. So he didn't ask his way. He drove up and down the two main roads, until he spotted Blackberry Lane, where he turned and rolled slowly along, looking for the right place.

His telephone conversation with Sam Lofton had made it clear that the paper was a small-time operation, probably only the one man, and perhaps a secretary. Still, it seemed a good place to start: find the local newspaper and enlist some help with county records, local history, whatever might lead him to the person or place he sought. And now, here he was, in the deep mountains, driving slowly around this lonely town, looking for number 210, Blackberry Lane. He found himself trying to think through his shyness, telling himself about the shabby darkness of the town, trying to feel arrogant and superior: *Sylvan Glade? Blackberry Lane? All these nice, quaint country names. And then you look around and find yourself in a godforsaken little place like this. Were they hoping they could name their way out of this isolation, hoping if they called things by a cheery enough word maybe the loneliness might go away? Well, it doesn't work. I guess I know that much already.*

Spotting the number, 210, painted on a big black mailbox, he drew up and parked in front of a clapboard house whose decades-old white paint glowed dully through a layer of red grime and dust. A hanging signboard, newer and brighter than the house itself, announced, *Mountain Gazette*, in stark black type. Jim gathered his papers and eased out of the car. An irregular stone walkway passed through a shabby, loose-gated picket fence and between two stringy forsythia bushes to a thickly painted green front door on which hung a heavy, oversized brass knocker in the shape of a bear's head. He studied the knocker a moment: it seemed outsized, far grander than the door or the house, or the sign. He shrugged, lifted the brass ring, and let it fall.

"Yeah," came a voice from inside.

Jim hesitated a moment, then opened the door and stepped into a vestibule, giving onto a larger room to the right.

"Just keep comin," said the voice, and Jim turned into a room, confronting a chaotic turmoil of papers, books, grocery bags, folders, handbills, glossy ad inserts, scattered in piles upon the warped, groaning pine floor, stacked onto tables and flung indiscriminately into corners. On one wall was a huge topographical map, in pale greens and tans, covered in spidery black lines. To the left rear was a swinging door. On the far right, a narrow, open stairway led upward.

At the center of the room, a full-faced bearded man in spectacles sat behind a battered desktop, talking on the telephone. He raised his eyes at Jim and gestured toward a pale green couch against the wall to the left. It appeared to be the only clear surface in the room.

"Okay, buddy," the man said to the telephone. "We got an order to run you for three more months at the same price. Fair enough?" He grinned and made a cutthroat sign to Jim. "Well, now, I aint sure about that," he said. "Look, I got somebody here. How about I holler at you tomorrow? Okay? Bye now."

"Howdy," the man said, hanging up the phone.

"Sorry to interrupt," Jim said.

"Are you kiddin me?" the man answered. "I hate to think what I owe you for doing me the favor of interrupting that phone call." He waved a hand at the couch again. "Have a seat."

Jim approached the man and stuck out a hand. "James Thorwait," he said. "I called you, yesterday morning?"

"Yeah," the man said, grasping the proffered hand and giving a cursory shake. "Yeah. Sit down," he said, motioning once more to the couch. "You want a cup of coffee? It's pretty bad, but it's a fresh pot, I can say that much for it."

"Thanks," Jim said, sitting on the couch while the man swung around and bustled about a cabinet, upon which an old alumi-num coffeemaker sat. "Bet you haven't seen one of these perco-lators in a while," the man said. "Everybody has them new Mis-ter Coffee things. White plastic. But this here—Momma's old percolator—it was the newest thing since electric light when she brought it home. It took her a year to get Daddy to drink coffee outen the thing. He wanted the big old speckled hen, the enamel pot on the stovetop, you know? That you could carve the coffee out of, it was so strong? You know? But Momma, she figured how to make this here perc taste even meaner than the old egg-shell stuff, so Daddy took to it. I reckon I did, too," the man said, pouring a thick pool into two big blue mugs. "You take any-thing?"

"Sounds as though I'd better," said Jim.

The man laughed. "I take it with a pile of creamer on the top," he said. "It don't taste any better, but it looks a mite prettier. I got sugar here, somewheres, if you want it regular."

"No," Jim said. "Creamer is fine."

"Got some aspirin iffen y'all practice preventative medicine," the man said, his drawl thickening. "Or some whiskey, iffen you want to go holistic."

"Not just yet, thanks," said Jim.

The man picked up a cardboard cylinder and shook a cloud of powder into each mug. He shuffled around the tabletop, found a big tarnished spoon, and worked at each cup. "That'll do her," he said. "I ought to make you sign a legal waiver before I give you this, but I reckon I'll just have to trust you." He laughed. "You look as though you're strong enough to get through it."

Jim smiled and accepted the proffered cup. Sam Lofton had a broad, pleasant face, intelligent eyes, unruly brown hair and beard. Jim liked the man, liked the leisurely loquacity, the tinge of irony he'd first heard on the phone, the folksiness that, he al-ready sensed, was a mask, hiding a sharp and perceptive intelli-gence.

"Am I presuming right?" he asked the man. "You're the editor of the paper?"

"Oh, hell," the man said. "I'm sorry. I always forget to introduce myself. Hell, I'm the editor and publisher and reporter and advertising department and compositor and paste-up artist. He gestured to indicate the chaotic piles of paper around the room. "I reckon I'm every damn thing except the cleanin woman." This time, he stuck out his own hand. "Sam Lofton," he said. "Mighty pleased. Now, where can we start on all this? That's the first question."

Jim told Sam Lofton the story, opened the file and showed him the forms, the covenant whose terms were his entire life. And now, hearing himself speak the actual syllables of Allie Morelock's name, telling this man the story, watching the man hear her name—now, suddenly—she became a woman, a creature, who breathed and moved, the way an instrument is only glued wood, like a chest of drawers, until you string it up and touch the first pulsing note. And now Jim had spoken his mother into truth by telling the story, speaking her name, *Allie Morelock*, four syllables, soft as brushstrokes. And the thought frightened him.

"I don't know who she is, beyond the name, Allie Morelock, and I can't even find the place where she belongs," he said, trying, perhaps, to relegate her to the abstract, again. "She's not really anything but a name on paper, since even the location doesn't seem to exist. Except the county, Jefferson County. At least I found that."

"Yessir," Sam said. "This here's Jefferson County. And, if it helps any, they's a heap of Morelocks around here. So you've found kin, that's for sure, even if you aint found her."

"Perhaps I could track her down by talking to kin folks," Jim suggested.

"Might be," Sam said. "But I'd say there's too many of them. There's Morelocks all over the place. My sister's married to a Morelock, the no good sonofabitch. God, I hope you aint close kin to him. Anyways, you wouldn't know where to start, if you just was to look for Morelocks. Like trying to describe somebody by saying, 'Well, let's see…she has two eyes and a nose…' That's about where you'd be starting, around here, when you say, 'Well, let's see…she's a Morelock…' Because who the hell aint?"

Jim shrugged, a gesture followed by a long silence. Sam leaned back and sipped at his coffee, watching, saying nothing. At last, Jim decided that he needed to go about this thing the way he sought out rare, missing instruments. He began in exactly the same way he'd ask around about places and people. *You don't just barge in, grab someone, and say, 'Where is that herringbone D-28?' You ask for background, history—'Did anybody play good music around here, back in the thirties?' And you enlist their aid, since they already know more than you do. And people want to help, mostly.*

"I was hoping, I suppose, that maybe you could give me some assistance," Jim finally said. "That you would know your way around any public information from the past. Or you might have some files, here, or something, anything."

"I don't mind lookin," Sam said. "That's what I do. And I'm one of them fellows that just kindly has to know, once somebody wants to know, if you catch my drift. I guess that's what makes me a newspaper man. Besides, if I aint huntin up your momma for you, I'll spend the week with the obituaries and the lost dogs and the church supper. You might say you're the balm in Gilead. And once you start pokin around into families and history, so to speak, they's no telling what you might turn up back here that might could be of some interest, if you was a newspaper. So I'll try to do some lookin around, won't cost you nothin." He leaned forward, scanning through the paper, the adoption agreement, he held in his hand. He studied the page a moment. "I bet I can help you some, right now," he said. "Looky here."

Sam laid the paper flat on the desk, pointing a stubby finger. "See there? It says she's from Shaleen Prong?"

"Yes, I know," Jim said. "It doesn't exist, anywhere. A least not anymore, it seems. I've looked on topo maps, road maps, even old maps from the thirties. It doesn't exist."

"Does, too," Sam said. "Come over here."

He beckoned Jim to the huge wall map and traced a finger up a long arrow of contour lines in the northwest corner of the sheet. "Look here." His finger stopped on a line of print, curving along the path where the contours came to sharp points. Jim cocked his head and read, aloud.

"Chasteen Creek."

"That's right, but it's wrong," Sam said. "It's spelt right, C-H-A-S-T-E-E-N. But folks around here call it *Shaleen*, don't matter how it's spelt. *Shaleen*. Your momma likely couldn't read, or hadn't never seen the name in print. So she told your daddy—or probably the attorney feller—she was from Shaleen, and he wrote down what he heard, since he never heard her say, 'Chasteen.' Got to be. They's plenty of places down here like that: if you was to look them up on maps, or in a courthouse, you'd never know they was the same place, because the spelling don't have a hell of a lot to do with the name. They's one up here a little more East that's spelt H-A-M-S-T-O-N Cove. But if you was to ask around where Hamston is, nobody'd be able to tell you. Because, here, you'd call it Farsten Cove." He laughed. "A whole lot of difference between what the writers say and what the sayers say, aint it? Now looky here…"

His finger moved slightly higher, to a point above the "Chasteen Creek" legend where the contour lines diverged, a smaller, steeper series of points, indicating a stream bed, squiggling to the left. There was no name printed on the map.

"Shaleen Prong," said Sam, tapping his finger on the notched lines. "Don't reckon any of the map folks ever paid no attention to the prong. But there she is, I reckon. Now mind, I don't know that for sure. But a *prong*, well, that's the higher reaches of a creek, or it's a spur line, kindly." He ran his finger up the course of the creek.

"So if you find Shaleen Crick, you look up the slope and you'll likely find Shaleen Prong," he said. "You see? It'd be a rill that runs off the flank of the mountain away up there. Just runs down from a big spring, I reckon, like all these high cricks. Shaleen Prong, feeds into Shaleen Crick. You can see how it widens out and gets flat enough to where folks could put up buildings on the branch. But, now, today, this whole piece of water, the bigger stream, too, is just called 'Shaleen.' That's where your momma's from."

Jim felt gooseflesh on his skin as he gazed at the thin zigzag of blue ink, rising out of the larger stream. He could make the close, sinewy contour lines into landscape, seeing the steep valley of the big creek and the wide, level meadow where the prong came in, the dark, rocky ravine above, out of which the water tumbled. His eyes followed the big stream down the valley, as it twisted and turned its way toward the main road, where the river, Snake Laurel, ran.

"It's way up that mountain, isn't it?" he said. He tried to imagine himself, a little boy sitting on a rock by the tumbling stream, watching his mother carry water.

"It's back up there, sure enough. It's about as far back into the coves as anyone gets. Or got, I reckon."

"So I could start by talking to Morelocks up there, couldn't I? That wouldn't be too difficult, would it?"

"Wouldn't if you could find any Morelocks up there anymore. But there aint," Sam said. "It's all federal land, now." Sam opened his hand and brushed it in a wide circle over the surface of the map. "All this in green. All of it's Forest Service land. Don't nobody live way up there no more. Not unless they're croaching: livin' on public land despite, because even the federal folks don't go up into there more than once in a blue moon. You might find someone up there, croaching. But I'd doubt it. They wouldn't want to be found, of course, and I aint sure how much of that goes on anymore, anyhow. I doubt you'd find anyone actually livin' that far up on Shaleen. They's one or two Morelocks still livin further down the creek, just off the high road, though. My sister lives up there, with her Morelock husband. But that's about all.

"Still, it aint a dead end. Shaleen, that's a kindly historical place around here." Sam paused and sipped his coffee. "We was always afraid of the place, growin up," he said.

"Afraid of it?" said Jim.

"You know, everywhere you go, there's a neighborhood, kindly, that's 'bad,' where you ain't supposed to go, because it's full up with mean, nasty people. I bet you got a few of those back over to Roalton, don't you?"

"Beech Creek."

"See? Now they aint no explanation, really, for why any particular area has got a premium on big bad fellers who want to fight, but it has. You could say it's poverty or booze, or what have you, but then you look around and you see a plenty of other places where folks is poor and even where they might drink a lot, dull the pain kindly. And those places ain't mean at all. Sad, maybe. But you ain't afraid to go there. Unless you're just afraid to look at sad folks. You know?

"And you know what it is? It's tradition. A mean place grows folks up mean, just like a place that's full of good banjo pickers or fiddlers will raise up a lot more good uns. It's like the feller says in the song, 'It's a family tradition.' You know?"

"So here I am, looking for my background," Jim said. He laughed. "And it turns out I may belong in a barroom fight."

"You don't look like one of them Morelocks much to me," said Sam. He smiled. "Don't look nearly mean enough."

"Well, thanks," Jim said, wryly.

"Anyways, our nasty place was always Shaleen Creek. Folks up there—Hamptons and Morelocks, mostly—they kindly liked to make whiskey and shoot one another. You know about feuds, I reckon. Well, they really was some pert nasty feuds up in these hills. And so we all grew up afraid of Shaleen. 'Don't let me catch you up to Shaleen, or I'll tar you.' You can hear folks sayin that to their kids, can't you? Of course, that can make the kids want to get up there as fast as they can. Like my sister, who wound up getting herself married to one of them Morelocks. Lord help her." Sam shook his head.

"So, anyways, you might have a momma who's from that mean line of Morelocks," he continued. "It wouldn't be too hard to find out about them, being as how everybody was afraid of em. Celebrities, you might say."

Sam finished his coffee and rapped the cup down hard against his desktop. He raised himself and walked around from behind the desk. He headed for the swinging door at the back of the room, saying, "That's enough of coffee. You want a beer?"

"It's a little early, I guess," Jim said.

"I didn't ask you what time is it, I asked you iffen you wanted a beer." Sam's smile was friendly, a little ironic, *the smile of a warm-hearted cynic*, Jim decided. *And a drinker.*

"Why not?" Jim said.

"Atta boy," Sam said, disappearing through the swinging door into what Jim could see was a small kitchen.

A few seconds later, Sam returned, handing Jim a sixteen-ounce can of Old Milwaukee.

"That's a beer and a half," said Jim.

"Well you can only drink two-thirds of it, iffen you're a stickler for accuracy," Sam said, winking. "It beats the hell out of the coffee. I can guarantee that." He returned to the desk chair and sat, rocking back a bit.

"Trouble with mean neighborhoods is everybody don't stay away from them. They's some young folks that are kindly drawn to that. Their folks tell them, 'You stay the hell away from Shaleen,' and that's the first place they want to go. And young girls, they sometimes get caught up on finding a outlaw, you know? What's that Waylon tune? 'Ladies Love Outlaws.' Somethin like. Well, my sis was just right to get drawn into that crowd. She was young for her age, if you know what I mean. And she got kindly rebellious. You know.

"Anyways, my sis, she married Paul Morelock; he's from them Shaleen Morelocks. Still lives up there, on the old Morelock place, surrounded by that federal land, now. He's no goddamn good. Ever month or two, sister turns up here with a black eye or marks on her face, where that sonofabitch has slapped her around. She comes in here and recovers for a few days. I try to get her to stay here, but nothin' I say makes any difference. Two, three days later, she'll go back to the bastard. What makes a woman do that, I don't know. She's a smart kid, and she could've done a hell of a lot better than to marry Paul Morelock. But you can't never tell a young gal nothing, can you?"

Jim shrugged. "I never had a sister. That I know of."

"If you're from up this away," Sam said, "I bet you a hundred dollars you got sisters and brothers like you got teeth." He raised his beer, toasting Jim, and taking a large swallow. "Anyways, we can take a run up toward Shaleen, and meantime I can ask around, get some background. And I'll talk to little sister, see if she learnt anything from that snake about the Shaleen branch of the family. Lord help."

"Okay," Jim said. "So let's nose around a little with an eye on Shaleen Prong."

Sam smiled. "That's the place to start, I'd say, if I was a newspaperman."

"All right," said Jim. "Let's go up there."

"Well sure, but let's not get to the blacksmith's before the horse. Let's let me check around a little first, see what I can find by way of background. You get settled in. Where you stayin? You can't be stayin with your people because you aint got any yet, so to speak."

"I saw a motel on the way in," said Jim.

"Gracie's," Sam said.

"No," said Jim. "It was called Mountain Rest."

"Yes," said Sam. "Like I said: Gracie's. I'm not too sure Gracie is open for business overnight anymore. But let's us both run up there and I'll see if they'll put you up. Gracie, she aint up there no more. She's got it run by her nephew and his gal. At least she thinks they're running it. They're a mite lowdown, you might say, and I'm not right sure motellin is really what they do to make a dollar. I believe they might be involved in more of a side business is my hunch."

"Surely you don't mean drugs, up here?" asked Jim. "Surely not prostitutes?"

"I aint ready to say. But I believe they're sellin something out of there, either 'for here' or 'to go,' if you catch my meaning. But they might be interested in puttin somebody up for a day or two, if I go along and ask em. They want to stay in good with the local investigative reporter, wouldn't you think?" He smiled. "And, by the way, don't never think drugs aint a big thing around here. This here is one of the drugginest places in the country. We got the perfect spot to be handlin drugs, when you think about it. It's not likely you'll see anybody nosin around here fixin to fight the war on drugs, is it? And plenty of folks with nothin to do."

Sam took another long pull on his beer. "That's what makes folks into drug users, you know that? Boredom. And lonesomeness, which might just be the same thing. And they get started on the drugs because they don't have nothin to do and they don't have a best friend. So the drug kindly becomes the best friend. You know? And we got a history of findin best friends up thisaway, what with moonshine and rabbit tobaccer and whatnot. They's been plenty of good old marijuana come out of these hills. Nowadays, it's meth and pills, opioids. But I aint certain about what these two is up to at Gracie's. Whether it's 'for here' or 'to go,' like I said. And after all, like you said, the sign says 'Motel.' So let's run up there. You might have to shoo the chickens out of the tub, but it's a place to stay. Could be."

Sam pulled his Toyota pickup out from the alley behind the house, and Jim followed in his own car, trailing Sam out of town. The bed of Sam's truck was so rusted Jim could look right through any number of ragged gaps in the panels or the gate, and the truck gave out a series of loud clatters—like a loose load of steel pipe—whenever it hit a bump.

At the plain sign Jim had seen before, there was still only one car in the lot. They pulled in and parked in a rank, next to the long, yellow Chevrolet.

"Wipe your feet," Sam said, winking, as they entered the shabby office. The room bore a sharp, dirty chemical smell that Sam sniffed at, pointing his nose into the air and snuffing loudly, like a hound. He turned, nodded knowingly to Jim, winked again, and whispered, "That's the 'to go,' right there."

Behind the counter a door opened, and a young woman emerged, followed by a squalling, naked girl of about three. The woman appeared to be about twenty and might once have been quite pretty. But she had already gone puffy, her face round and listless, her body soft and defeated. She wore a huge cotton jersey, like a nightshirt, beneath which her large breasts moved—sloshing too loosely—fat nipples pushing against thin fabric. Her hair was unkempt, running in wet, narrow streams straight back to fall over her hunched shoulders.

"What you want?" she said. She sounded both hostile and fearful at the same time.

"Want a room, iffen you got one," said Sam. Jim noticed Lofton's accent had suddenly become thicker and slower than before. Sam pulled out his wallet and waved it. "We're payin cash, ma'am."

The naked child, still crying loudly, tugged at the woman's nightshirt.

"Didn't I tell you to shut up?" said the woman, by all indications still talking to Sam.

"We're just a lookin to find—"

"We aint got a room," the woman said.

The little girl sobbed, and the woman raised an open hand, threatening.

"I told you to cut out that cryin," she said, sounding angry and nervous.

"Looks like they's plenty of vacancy," Sam said, sweeping his arm in an arc, taking in the empty lot and the long line of rooms.

"We're remodelin," said the woman. Jim felt uncomfortable, tense. The child squalled. "Aint you that newspaper feller?" the woman asked suspiciously. "What you want with a room?"

"Every dern room being remodeled?" Sam said. He craned his neck trying to see past her into the back. The woman reached down and shook the crying child by the shoulder.

"Shut up, I said." The woman's voice had risen, exasperated, still sounding both dangerous and frightened.

"I don't mind an unfinished room," Jim said. "I imagine I've slept in worse."

"Shut the fuck up," the woman said. At first Jim thought she was talking to him. But then she slapped the child, hard, across the face. The little girl's head snapped back just before the woman struck her again, pushing her thin little body backward, her head thumping the wall. The child wailed. The woman hit her again.

"Stop that," Jim shouted, reaching out a restraining hand. The woman stared at him uncomprehendingly, her broad hand drawn upward, the curved palm reddening.

"Let's just go," Sam said, grabbing Jim's sleeve and pulling him toward the door.

"No," Jim said jerking his arm free, "God damn it. You can't just..." He turned back toward the woman to find she was gone, she and the child disappearing into the back room.

"Come on," Sam said. As they left the room, they heard another sharp smack of skin against skin.

In the parking lot, the two men faced each other without speaking. Both were breathing hard. From the interior of the building they could hear muffled shouting and the thin, high wail of the girl.

"Jesus," Jim said at last. "Why did you stop me? God, I hate to see that. Why did you stop me? Who is that woman? Jesus."

"You come stay with me," Sam said.

"Jesus," Jim said, again. He took a deep breath, calming

himself. "I can find a place," he said at last.

Sam didn't answer. He waved Jim a *follow me* gesture and turned toward his truck. Then he stopped, turned back, and peered narrowly at Jim.

"Just how sure are you about wantin to find that momma of your'n?"

THREE

When she had spent her fury on the little child, Lindee Macleen walked past the girl, who was weeping soundlessly now. She went through the back doorway, passed through a small, cluttered room and into a small bedroom, where she peeled off the shirt and flopped, naked, onto the dirty sheets, reaching across to the end table for a cigarette.

Minutes later she picked up the phone and dialed, shouting at the doorway, "I'm on the phone. Keep quiet, you hear?" She waited through the craddle of the ring, wondering whether Trapper's cell phone would have any sort of signal through the mountains. It often didn't. But then she heard the recorded message, the single tone. And she spoke.

"Trapper. You comin home sometime today?" she said. "Or you goin to be gone over the night? This goddamn kid is driving me nuts. Anyways, I aint heard nothing from Paul about the money, so I reckon we're okay. You be careful, though." She drew hard on the cigarette. Her voice lightened into a little girl's tease. "Come on home, honey. I want to play with you," she cooed, her hand snaking down to touch herself.

She had met Trapper Mason a year ago in Roalton, where she had appeared one night, with the little girl in tow, at Pink's

Country Grill, out on Route 45. Trapper had come along just in time, too, she often told herself, just when she'd run out of places to go, just when she needed a man to take her in. The child—her name was Caroline—was the fruit of an earlier relationship, Lindee's first, in fact, after running away from the coal field shanty, across the line in Virginia, where she'd been raised. By now, her recollections of home had faded to a background memory of the numbing work, the harsh shouting, and the continual beatings her older brother—the closest thing to a parent she'd known—had administered between occasional sexual onslaughts. She'd preferred the molestation to the beatings, had taken a degree of pleasure in knowing she could make a man stiffen and moan and, at least for the moment, could secure a margin of safety and security by offering her body to the man's touch, rather than to his fists.

But, in the long run, it was all the same thing: the furious brother taking charge, taking her over, conquering her either way. So she had run off, headed for town, where she believed she could find work and independence. What she found was a series of other men, some of whom hit her, too, but all of whom, at least, took her in, cared for her, and offered her the soothing balm of alcohol and drugs in exchange for the gift of her young body.

She believed Trapper would be the last one. He treated her better than most, treated the daughter better than she did, herself. He was sufficiently aware of Lindee to respond to her most importunate needs and was sufficiently indifferent to her activities not to bother catching her with Paul Morelock when Trapper was on a run. Paul, in his turn, only wanted her on this basis, a once-a-month fuck, and so he never interfered with the ongoing household situation, the closest thing to a real family Lindee had ever experienced. Because, though they lived in a seedy motel, using it as a cover for the drug operation, and made their money illegally, always on the edge of the dark violence attendant on this sort of life, still they slept together, arose and ate toast, orange juice, and coffee, called each other "sweetie," and shared the good and the bad times, almost like an old married couple. Almost like a real family.

The motel had been her idea. It belonged to an aging aunt of Trapper's, Aunt Gracie, and had become something of a white elephant to the old woman. So Lindee had talked Trapper into offering themselves as "managers," taking the place off her hands, and paying for her to rent a trailer in Deke Hollow, over the way. The drug manufacturing operation had paid Gracie's bills, as well as their own and left them some to save up for her future dream: a move back into Roalton, in a house of their own, in one of the better parts of town. "No more of these shithole apartments," she would say, the negative encompassing the entirety of her desire: the house and yard and nice things, the normal life.

She didn't like hitting Caroline, but sometimes the kid just wouldn't shut up, and there was nothing for it but to teach her to mind. She knew that there were episodes when she got carried away, like today. *It was those others, the two men come in and left so quick, made me do it*, she decided. Because Caroline embarrassed her with all that crying, making her feel exposed and foolish, and this forced her to strike out at the little girl.

She pondered a moment, wondering about the two men. Maybe she should tell Trapper. *That newspaper man weren't up to no good.* And she decided she wouldn't hit Caroline again. And other times, she loved the little girl so much, and wanted to give her everything. *No, I won't do it again, especially after we can get out of this shithole, get into a nice house in town. If only the kid would keep quiet once in a while.*

Paul Morelock was a short, stocky man with big hands and the usual narrow, glinting eyes that announced he was a Shaleen Creek Morelock. Today, though, he was in Roalton, parked out front of a sprawling, nondescript plank-sided building near the tracks. The translucent plastic sign swinging over the building's door said, "PINK'S," then showed a red-and-silver beer label, and said, in smaller print, "Bottles and Cans."

It was a slow, empty, late summer morning at the bar, too early for any but the most habitual drinkers, a time when the room itself seemed to settle into a sort of breathless heart failure, huddled gloomily against the cold drizzle outdoors.

Pink's had been a "dry hall," in the old days, when alcohol was outlawed throughout the county. Most of its expanse had been a dance floor, and country or hillbilly bands had held forth on a small stage, while crowds of dancers swirled or clog-stepped on the booming wood floor. The liquor had been sold surreptitiously, out from under a long soda-and-snack bar in the side room.

Now, though, the side room was the entire focus of business. The big, open dance hall was dark and dusted now, a junk space, and the snack room had been converted into a full-scale bar, Pink's Grill.

The room was a high-ceilinged tunnel deepening away from one largish, dirty window at the front. The walls were green checked plaster above, running to a chair rail that had been painted so many times it looked like it was made of clay. Below that, a similarly shapeless wainscot smeared its way down the length of the room. The bar running along one side glowed dully, the diffuse indigo of dark wood stained with smoke. Three skin-colored Formica-topped tables, their cigarette burns flecking them like moles, ran along the other side, along with a shuffleboard machine, its hollow plastic bowling pins hanging like knuckle bones. The darkness collected at the end of the long room, puddling around a defeated pool table.

Two older men sat at the far end of the bar, hunched over beers and shot glasses, studying them. Though the men sat close together, they did not speak, gave no indication of knowing one another. Excepting the mere fact of physical proximity and the exact similarity of posture, they might have been complete strangers, in the way of old drinkers who belong together only because they've long ago worn out whatever loves or friendships they may have had, and so now are left with each other, like stale heels from a bread loaf.

At the near end sat Trapper Mason, alone, toying laconically with a half-full beer bottle, tipping it and rolling the neck with his fingers, tracing ellipses with the bottom across the small, sodden napkin on the bar. The bartender, in a soiled white shirt and wool slacks, stared, unmoving, at the flickering square of the television propped high on the top shelf, among the kewpie dolls and bowling trophies. On the screen, an audience whooped and screamed at an obese woman seated in a chair, talking to a thin, styled man in a tan suit.

Paul Morelock pushed through the door, shambling and determined, a bear through canebrake. He stood for a moment, accustoming himself to the dark, then turned and moved straight toward the young man at the bar, who set his beer down and stepped back, one hand held forward, a placative gesture.

"Now, Paul, don't worry," Trapper said, defensively. "I'm workin on the money. I brought the stuff in my own self because I'm workin on the money, and I wanted to get in here, get it done before you had to. But them dirty bastards didn't have it neither. Honest. I was a going to tell you. I'll have it by Tuesday, like I said. It aint but a few days late."

Morelock sucked a tooth. "Don't get scared, now." He smiled thinly. "I aint a going to hurt you, Trapper. I just come in to say hey, and find out what you done with the batch. Hell, I just wished you'd told me you was bringin it in on your own, you know? It aint no way to do business."

"I was fixin to tell you, Paul," Trapper said, still wheedling, afraid. "I didn't know how to find you down here. Didn't know you'd be able to find me without you havin to run around too much. So I was tryin to get shed of the batch myself, get money you wanted, maybe make up some extry on my own and give all the money to you is all. Honest to God."

"Well, now, don't you worry, Trap," Morelock said. "I aint fixin to do nothin to you." He grinned. "What you got there? A

Old Mil?" Still moving deliberately, quicker now, he reached the bar and snatched up Trapper's bottle of beer. He held it sideways, letting the beer running slowly out onto the floor. "You going to buy me a beer?" he said.

"Sure, Paul, sure," Trapper said. "I'll get you one right now." He dug into his pockets, both hands scrunching deep, searching. "Let me just..."

He was still talking when Morelock swung the bottle, shattering it against the bridge of his nose, blowing white foam and blood upward and out, as Trapper pitched backward, hands still in his pockets, his body a limp, crumpling rag. Morelock looked at him a moment, then set the shard of bottleneck carefully on the bar. He reached down, turning Trapper over roughly, snaking a hand into the jacket pocket, pulling forth a fat roll of bills.

"Shit," he said. "The little shit."

Peeling a twenty off the top, he tossed it on the bar and shouted, "This feller wants one of your upstairs rooms. Throw him up there and let him sleep this off, hear?"

He turned and walked out into the October drizzle while the bartender and the two old men watched curiously. There was no need to bother much: they'd clean the young man up and get him upstairs. They knew Paul Morelock. *Anyways, folks at Pink's is about as like to call the police as I am to take up figure skatin. Not very damn likely.*

An hour later, he hollered into a cell phone the edge of a half-empty parking lot, his shoulders hunched against the falling rain as he shouted into the receiver.

"Money, Pawp. I got the money. The somofabitch sold some produce on his own. But I got the other groceries and I got what he had on hisself. Looks like a mite fair roll."

He paused, listening.

"Well, sure, Pawp, don't worry none about that. He aint going nowheres, tonight.

He listened again.

"Don't worry about that. I'll get it outen the girl," he said. "I'll run over there and squeeze it outen her, nice and juicy. Besides, it'll put her in better, she won't wonder so much where her sweetheart spent the night, I reckon…"

He paused.

"Okay, okay." he yelled. "I'll stop and take care of her and then I'll run the pills up the crick to Granpawper, tomorrow." He paused, again. "Yessir, Pawp. This afternoon." He spat onto the wet pavement. "All right. Let me get outen the fucking rain and get them pills. I want out of this town before dark." He rang off, shook himself, like a shaggy animal, and shambled across the street to his truck.

Inside the cab, he reached behind the seat and pulled out a can of beer. He cracked it open, catching the swell of foam on his tongue, licking in a slow circle all the way around the rim of the can, the way his Pawp always did, then tipping the can up and letting the warm, fuzzy liquid slosh down his throat.

"I've got a guest room, upstairs we'll put you in," said Sam, after he and Jim had returned to the newspaper office. He held up a hand to stifle any objections. "Don't worry about it. It'll be nice to have some company around here that aint a sister that's been beat up by her no good husband. So don't you worry. Come on up and let's get you settled.

"You live here, too?" Jim said.

"I do," said Sam. "This here is a multipurpose building. Newspaper office, home, battered gal's shelter." He paused a moment. "Now I reckon it's a detective agency. Or maybe a missing persons bureau, hey?"

"The question, I'm afraid, is which person is missing?" said Jim. "Am I, or is my mother?"

Sam made a short, *hmhm* laugh.

"This used to be the police station, away back. They shut it up about thirty years ago, I believe, and put the county deputies in charge, down by the courthouse. Not that they're worth a damn. But this was it. There's even two little jail cells in the back, down behind the office. Full of papers, now. I've got keys for em, somewheres."

He led Jim up the stairs to a small room with a sloping ceiling and a big dormer window. The room was remarkably clean and orderly, compared to the office downstairs, and was dominated by a beautiful antique double spool bed with a faded quilt. There was a small oak chair and a square bedside table. The walls were bare except for a photograph of an elderly man peering out of a large oval frame, a faintly amused expression on his face, as though he knew he'd been relegated to the spare room. Jim recognized Sam's ironic mien in the old man's face. "A relative?" he pointed.

"Great uncle," said Sam. "I never knew him much, but somehow I wound up with the picture."

"He looks like you," said Jim.

"That's what Leela says. I reckon so."

"Leela?" Jim asked.

"Little sister. My usual guest. She comes here once in a while when her beloved husband gets a mite too rough. I've tried to get her to call him in, tried to do it myself, but she won't let me. Of course, the police is relations to him, anyways. Aint worth a chewed plug to call them. They'd just do nothing, except likely tell him you'd complained, and he'd smack her around for that, too. But I'll never figure out why she goes on back to him a week later, every time. I reckon they say that's the way it is with women who get trapped in with bastards like that. Part of the trouble, I guess: she'd rather have the problems she's used to than be out on her all-alone, findin problems she didn't even know could be there, much less be used to. You suppose you can get used to anything like that to the point where you're afraid to try somethin else? I don't know.

"And every time she stays here she comes down on the first

night, after she's put her things up here. Comes down and points up, as though we could see that photo through the ceiling, and says, 'Uncle Sy looks just like you.' And I always say, 'You mean I look just like Uncle Sy.' And she smiles, every time, even if she's standin there with a black eye or bruises all over her arm. It's enough to make you cry."

"Maybe you should tell her to stay home and send the husband here," Jim said. "You could lock him in one of your cells."

Sam stopped and looked at Jim. "I believe you're starting to sound like hill folks already, cousin Morelock," he said. He gestured, a sweeping arm, taking in the interior of the room. "There aint a dresser in here, so you'll have to live out of your suitcase. Or you can use the closet down the hall. It's got hangars and a few drawers in the back, you can have them, if that's better. That's what Leela does."

"This is fine," said Jim, setting down his suitcase. "I'm very grateful. I'm not sure what it would have been like, staying back there at that motel."

"That weren't much fun to watch, was it," said Sam.

"I've never seen anything like it," said Jim.

Sam looked at him, musing. "No, I don't reckon you have," Sam said. "What'd you say you did, down in Roalton?"

"I didn't say," Jim answered. "I'm an instrument repairman and dealer. I guess that's one connection to these mountains."

"How's that?" said Sam.

"Mostly I work on acoustic instruments. A lot of them are from bluegrass musicians. You know, banjos, guitars, mandolins."

"Well, there you go," said Sam. "And you've just now found out that you come by it honest, hey?" He turned and led Jim out of the room. "Anyways, that poor kid you just saw get beat up, she'll likely grow up and marry some shiftless bastard and they'll go to whooping their kids. Aint a hell of a lot you can do about it."

"Call Children's Services? Make a complaint?" Jim asked.

"Depends on whose side you're on, I guess," Sam said.

"What? Whose side? Mother or child? Is there any choice?" Jim felt the anger, saw the little girl's head thumping the wall. "Jesus."

"Not mother or child," Sam said. "That's not what I meant." He waved a hand. "Never mind. You don't understand. You'd have to be from around here, I reckon."

Wearing her oversized shirt, and holding her daughter's tiny hand, Lindee stood in the sad, darkened lobby of the Mountain Rest motel, watching through the slatted shade for Trapper's truck to appear in the pebbled lot, thinking, *Where is he? It's getting on toward evening, the sun already behind the mountains.* She didn't like this part of the day, that strange lapse of time when the entire hollow was swathed in deepening shadow, while the bright blue sky blazed overhead, as if the land itself didn't know whether it was broad day or deep dusk. Everything took on a strange, thin coloring, that made her feel as though her insides had changed, as if she were dizzy, or disappearing. She always prayed when she found herself alone during this eerie hour, prayed to God to help her hide in the shadows and not let her go floating up into that bright blue emptiness, where everyone would see how she was disappearing.

She squeezed Caroline's damp little hand. Where was Trapper?

She was worried about the two men who had come. She blamed herself for having let them walk off without identifying themselves, worried about what Trapper would say, worried that the men may have smelled the meth fumes, and that they had definitely watched her hitting her daughter. It was like this more and more, she knew. Something would happen, right in front of her, and she'd just let it go. Until it was too late. And then she'd get anxious about it and would worry herself into a state, feel like it was all her fault that it had happened in the first place. Now it was those men. What had she been thinking, letting them walk in, sniff around, watch her hit Caroline, and walk out again? They must have been looking for the drugs. And even if they weren't, they'd surely go to the county about the whipping. She'd seen the expression in the man's wide eyes, the thinner man, who looked to her like he must be from outside of here, from a city, somewhere. He looked so shocked, so scared. Horrified. *Hasn't he ever seen anybody hit their kid before? Well, for sure, he'll call the county. And the newspaper will carry it. And then they'll come in and find all the meth business and then everything will fall to pieces.*

Why didn't I tell Trapper about the men? It hadn't even occurred to her when she'd left that message. It wasn't until later that she'd even thought about those men being trouble. *Why do I always forget until too late?*

She let go of Caroline, wrung her hands. *Where is Trapper?*

A moment later, she brightened, straightening up and running a hand through her strings of hair. A vehicle had turned into the lot. She could hear the skirling gravel. But it wasn't Trapper's green Ford. It was Paul Morelock's paneled truck. She felt a flutter in her stomach.

Morelock's big form swung out of the cab and moved toward the office, shambling.

"Here's Uncle Paul, honey," Lindee said to Caroline. "Go on back to your room and play with your teddy bear." Caroline turned obediently and glided silently away, through the rear.

The door swung open and Morelock entered, immediately grabbing at her, pushing his sweated body against her, talking low, not waiting, running his hands over her large, slack breasts.

"How's my big baby?" he mumbled, licking her ear, reaching under the long shirt, cupping a big hand between her legs, his snaky fingers feeling for her.

"Stop it, Paul," she pleaded. "Where's Trapper?" She struggled listlessly, a weak gesture of resistance. "Where's—"

"Trapper's up in town, for somethin or nother," Paul said. "They say." He pushed Lindee to arm's length and looked at her. "You know where he went and what for?"

"No, Paul," she said. "Honest, I don't. I didn't even know he was in to town."

He laughed at her. "You sure of that, honey?"

"No, I thought it was him right now," she said. "I don't…"

"Don't you worry about Trapper Mason," Paul said, pulling her back close. "He aint comin back tonight. Let's give Uncle Paul some of this, honey." He surged the cotton shirt upward, her arms raising as he pulled it off, baring her, fondling her while he pushed her backward toward the rear, through the hallway, into the bedroom.

He pushed her onto the sheets and stood over her, watching her naked body, while he unclasped his belt, let his pants down, exposing himself to her, proud of his arousal.

"You want a yard of this?" he said, straddling her, sliding his weight over her breasts, moving himself upward. "Whyn't you slop the hog a little, big baby?"

Out of the corner of her eye, Lindee saw Caroline standing in the doorway, clasping a soiled stuffed bear, staring.

Paul pressed himself to Lindee. She closed her eyes and took him.

Later, she asked him how he knew where Trapper was, and she told him about the two men.

"Nevermine Trapper," he said. "He's all right. Just stayin into town." He played absently with her nipple. "What about them two men, though? They aint up to no good," he said. "Whyn't you tell me before?"

"You were a mite busy," she said. "You know, you shouldn't ought to do that in front of Caroline. You should've let me get her outen here."

He waved a hand. "She left in a minute. Don't worry about it none. If that's the worst thing she's a going to see."

Lindee began to protest, but he cut her off, putting a damp hand across her mouth. "Shut it," he said. "What about them two?" he said. "Tell me about them. I don't like it. Not a damn bit."

FOUR

Jim awoke next morning to bright sunshine streaming through the small bedroom window. He had been dreaming, the usual hazy, formless dream without story or meaning, and he awoke feeling emptied in a way that had become so familiar he'd decided it must just be how things were. Although he knew there were people who didn't awaken to this feeling of something missing that had never been, he felt it was as much a part of himself as the deep blue color of his eyes. And so he figured those other people must simply have different mornings, the way they might have a different eye color. For him, it was this loneliness, so that his days became struggles to fill the vacancy with tasks—refretting a fine old Weymann five-string, or the sheer movement of going out in search of another prewar Martin guitar, before night could fall and empty the place, again.

And here he was, deep in the mountains, searching, this time, for another self, one that had never been: Jim Thorwait, *no, Jim Morelock*, he told himself, because he, Jim Thorwait, had been conceived not by the union of a man and a woman but by some confluence of attorney, money, and sheer willfulness. So perhaps it was no wonder he felt this loneliness at his very core. And perhaps it was no wonder he sought the woman—Allie Morelock—who, as a name written on a page, only confirmed the sense of abstraction he felt at his center. He thought of a great musician who had told him once that the essence of musical genius was a feeling for "the space between the notes," and he felt that he understood this instinctively. It was why he was so good at handling these instruments: he knew that the sound doesn't come from where you place a bridge; it comes from where you don't place it. And he believed this sensibility came from the same feeling of isolation that made his evenings and mornings so lonely.

So perhaps if he could find, or at least place, this Allie Morelock, the discovery would give her a face and a body, and so perhaps he could finally recognize the space around her as his own. And then he might feel the music vibrating, filling that blank core, and giving him both peace and purpose. At any rate, here he was, and he rose in the shaft of sunlight beaming through the window, wondering, *what day is it?*

He dressed, feeling the emptiness in the house and went downstairs to find the confirming note, scrawled on scrap paper and taped to the desk lamp, hanging like a forgotten ornament.

JIM—COFFEE'S ON. THERE'S STICKY BUNS IN THE FRIDGE. MAKE YOURSELF AT HOME. I'M OUT SNOOPING AROUND ON YOUR MAMMA'S BACKGROUND.

There was a scrawled *S.* at the end.

After a very sweet cinnamon roll and a cup of the fearfully strong coffee, Jim determined to go for a walk and look over this place, county seat, at least, to his mother's home, a town she must have seen, even walked around in. It was possible, he told himself, with something of an inner thrill, that he would see her on the street, *this very day.* He wondered if there would be some glimmer of recognition, in either of them, and, as he closed the front door and came onto the street, he found himself looking for people, looking for a middle-aged woman, half afraid of finding her.

He turned toward the southernmost of the main streets, walking beneath trees just beginning to fade into autumn. This side street was quiet, empty of people, and a little shabby. He passed a vacant storefront, then a barber shop. The red-and-white-striped cylinder turned above the door, but he saw neither barber nor customers through the big plateglass window. There were chairs lined up, backs to the window, the usual counters and shelves, a large, engraved cash register of greening brass, but no equipment: no clippers or vials of tonic, none of the usual paraphernalia, except a stack of magazines and newspapers by the big, cream-colored barber's chair.

The barber shop was bounded by a row of storefronts—small businesses and offices—and, at the corner, a two-story brick building, giving onto the main street. Reaching the corner, Jim saw this was a hardware store. As he passed the open front door, he smelled the familiar leathery odor, wondering, *What makes that smell?* He stopped for a moment, sniffing. It was the smell of every hardware store he'd ever been in, but it didn't smell of wood or metal. He wondered. *It smells like shoe polish. Why doesn't it smell like nails, or glue, or something that ought to go with hardware?* But anyone would know this smell, and would say, "Hardware," even though the smell seemed entirely disconnected from the essential thing, the hardware, itself. *It's a bit like the Shaleen Creek thing. That the adoption paper spelled 'Chaleen,' but everybody around here knows that it's not.*

Oil. Maybe that smell is oil. He decided it was and walked on.

The next building was a café. "Orrie's," the sign proclaimed, in weathered blue. Jim decided to go in. *Have a cup of real coffee and some pie*, because he thought that would be what local people would have, and he felt himself wanting to be taken for a local. But the impulse was followed by hesitation, and he decided he'd had breakfast already and it was pointless to go into a place just to pretend he was someone he wasn't. He turned and walked on.

In the distance he saw the filling station he'd noticed driving into town, and he determined to go there and buy himself a coke. It would be easier than having to enter the enclosed space of

Orrie's, more like dipping your toe in the water than the kind of immersion he'd just retreated from. *Or a Dr Pepper*, because he had a vague understanding about mountain people preferring Dr Pepper. "Covites," they'd called these hill people, back home, the reference being to mountain coves and hollows, though he'd known and used the epithet long before he ever understood the derivation. He wondered about it, now, realizing that he'd always known it was a slur, a derogation, based upon the self-satisfaction of knowing you'd never work in a gray uniform with your name on the pocket, and the folks around Roalton who did were likely displaced persons, covites, who belonged elsewhere and were here on sufferance, to do the work that needed doing. He realized with something of a shock that he was walking around among covites this morning, hoping to be taken for one of them.

The gas station was a remarkable place, another instance of time travel, this square white building with the two bay doors, a car up on one of the lifts, even the old flying horse sign lined in neon tubing, the round-shouldered gas pumps without slots for sliding credit cards. The red tin wiper-blade box with the slanted top perched by the door.

The only thing missing was the coke machine.

He stopped, wondering, *how can a place like this not have a coke machine?* Then he realized the interior had been turned into an approximation of a "food mart," like the gas stations everywhere else, and he told himself this was good: he would have to speak with someone, even if only to say please and thank you. So he crossed the corner street to the station.

Entering the store, he found three men sitting on stools along a tiny counter topped with coffee pots and a hot dog machine. One of the men was in the process of dropping peanuts into his bottle of coke, and he stopped, his curled hand suspended, to watch Jim walk in and by them, toward the racked soda pop coolers at the rear.

Jim felt the silence, that particular kind of stillness that told him he was its cause. The men, showing the whites of their eyes, following him, staring with a kind of impersonal disapproval, as though he were a strangely colored scrap of paper blown in through the front door, stained with a light brown smear. Jim felt a rush of irritation at the implicit hostility, and he tried to turn it all into sarcasm, thinking, *Is this the biggest thing that's going to happen to them today, watching a stranger buy a soda pop?*

He pulled a can of Dr Pepper from the rack. Down the counter, the men had stopped watching him and had begun talking again. *Well, at least I'm not too entirely fascinating.* As he passed back by the men, he heard one of them saying, "I don't give a good god damn if they do. Whose town is this, anyhow?" The man swiveled his stool and stood up, stepping back just enough so that Jim would have to turn his body to pass in front, toward the counter, while the man watched him with broad eyes that squinted when they met Jim's.

"You aint from around here, hey?" he said.

"No," Jim said. "I'm not, exactly."

"I didn't think so," the man said, smirking. "Best watch your step." The others laughed.

Jim felt the anger rise, again, but he laughed too, and said, "Thanks, I will. I wouldn't want to step in something that stinks, would I?"

The big man moved an inch closer, glowering, and said, "You don't like it around here, what'd you come for?"

"You, Chinch," said the woman behind the counter. She was thin and had a long, wrinkled face; her colorless hair was tied back in a lank ponytail. "Cut it out."

The big man turned himself on one heel and walked out, passing too close, so that Jim had to step back. When he was closest to Jim, almost touching, the man turned and shouted back, "See you fellers again," as though Jim wasn't even there, not even an obstruction to be stepped around. "Don't step in nothing that stinks," he called, as he barged out the door.

Jim paid for his Dr Pepper, trying to feel, or at least act, relaxed and unmoved. Inwardly, he discovered, he felt shamed, and, oddly enough, his feelings were hurt. He was angry, too, but with the anger of the man who is the butt of a joke, exposed and embarrassed, with no recourse but to think about what he *should* have said.. He felt the hot rush up his neck, the seethe of despairing fury, because he knew there wasn't even anyone to respond to. He knew, too, that this burning reaction itself added to the power of the other one, the joker, who could see Jim's frustration and irritation in his flushed face, and who could keep up his own swagger just by barging away, through the door, without even bothering to see Jim's response, or even remember he'd said this thing to Jim.

The tired-looking woman at the counter slid him his change. "Anything else?" she said, in a toneless, bored voice.

"No," Jim said. "Thank you."

"Come back now," she said flatly.

Jim nodded his head and turned, fast, out the door, the men, again, swiveling to watch him go, while he felt, again, the burning flush of exposure, or shame, or anger, whatever it was. He was half disappointed and half relieved to see that the other man, the big man who had spoken to him, was not outside, and he walked quickly across the concrete apron and away.

It surprised him that this feeling stayed with him all that morning, ebbing and rushing, in waves, as he returned to the house and tried to read. He tried to shrug it all off, but he kept thinking about it again and again. It mattered, he decided, because he had wanted to feel a sense of belonging, had come here to find his place, in a matter of speaking, and had been rebuffed on his first trivial walk through town. He felt foolish that the rebuff was bothering him so much, and so the emotion fed on itself, sustaining itself into midday, when Sam returned, full of hearty friendship. Jim told him about the scene at the cafe, hoping for a partner, who might say, *Don't worry about it*, or, *Well, that guy's an asshole.* Instead, Sam said, offhandedly, as if it was the clearest thing in the world, "Well, he's right. You aint from around here, are you?"

"I was thinking maybe I was," Jim said, ruefully. "At least until everybody set me straight." He wanted, at least to find Sam, also a man from this place, responsive, able to recognize how he Jim, at any rate, *or at least treat me nicely*, he thought, feeling foolish at the very idea. "You know," he said, trying one last time, "it made me feel about as welcome as a fly at a picnic."

"Or a hippy at a hoedown?" Sam said. He smiled. "Look. Don't worry about it. You can't just go into Cal's, where the boys sit around and do nothing, without expectin to be looked over, at least. They likely to have felt the same as you would if some stranger came in and sat down in your TV room." His eyes narrowed. "Or would it be your library?" He watched Jim a moment, then smiled. "I'm sorry," he said. "I reckon you have to get used to us and us to you."

"It's not a lot of fun to feel as though you have to fight someone on your first day in town," Jim said.

Sam's eyes softened. He patted Jim on the back. "Look," he said. "Don't worry about it. It'll be okay."

That same morning, Paul Morelock rolled over toward Lindee and slid his hand across her breasts, throwing his thigh across her legs and sucking her neck.

"Let's have a little more red eye gravy," he crooned, nuzzling her. He took her hand and brought it downward, curling her fingers around his taut member. He growled at her touch and raised himself between her spreading legs. "Oh baby baby," he whimpered, sliding into her.

When he had finished and rolled heavily off her slack body, he said, "I reckon I'll wash this down with a beer. You want one?"

"It's not yet noon," Lindee said.

"It's a holiday," Paul said. "You got a night off from Trapper, got to spend it with me."

He was right, Lindee thought. She felt good having Paul stay here this long. Usually he was in a hurry, coming into the room and taking his pleasure, sometimes not even taking off his clothes, and leaving before the sweat had cooled on her spread body. Last night, he seemed to enjoy taking his time, lying on the bed after she'd pleasured him the first time, talking to her about the two men who'd come, telling her he'd take care of it. And he'd stayed the night—this was a first—stilling her worries about Trapper, saying, "Don't you worry none about him. He's took care of," and when she asked what he meant by that, saying, "I said hush yourself. We'll talk about Trapper by and by. He's got business. I reckon you know more about that than I do."

She had been a little uneasy about this answer, knowing that Paul would be murderous if he knew where Trapper really was, knew that Trapper had run a batch into town on his own, that they had held back some of the money to buy enough ingredient for two extra batches, this time. So she was in part relieved by the very fact that Paul was here and in a good mood. It meant he didn't know anything, didn't it?

It had been her idea. They needed to get some money put away and if Trapper just kept working for Paul Morelock, she could see them spending the rest of their lives in this shithole motel, breathing hot manure and lacquer—that was what cooking meth smelled like to her—like back home when her brother was putting linseed oil on the floors on a hot summer, when the stink from the barn mixed with that lacquer—so you smelled it on the back of your throat and up into your nose, like vomit. So, just as she'd talked him into taking over this motel in the first place, now she urged him to do extra to move along, get out of here, start working toward that house in town. Just go out on his own for a run or two extra.

Trapper had immediately demurred. "He wouldn't like that a hell of a lot," he said.

"What's he got to know for?" she had said. "Why should he

give a shit, as long as you run what he tells you to run and give him his goddamn money? What's he got to say about how you spend the rest of your time, if you want to run fifteen batches after you done his?"

Trapper had laughed sardonically. "Yeah. Right," he said. "He'd like to take my head off and stuff it up my ass."

But she had talked him into it by suggesting that he skim a little of the extra back to Paul in the form of pills. "Not too much," she said. "Not enough to make him think you're doing anything more than getting a better price, you know?"

Trapper liked that. "He'd be tickled if I was to turn up with fifty or sixty grams more of pills for free. I reckon he would."

"Tickled enough that he'd give you some slack and stop watchin you so hard. So you could just slip off now and again and sell some of your own," she had said, rubbing against him, using everything she knew to persuade him. "And none of the switchin for pills or nothing. Just cash." She licked his ear. "Come on, honey. Think what that money'd do for us. And for Caroline."

Caroline was the trump card. Trapper loved that little girl as if she'd been his own. He worried about the way she hit the girl, sometimes and tried to talk to her about it, saying, "It don't do her no good to keep a whaling on her, honey." And every time, Lindee vowed she'd never hit Caroline again.

And each time, she really believed she was telling the truth. It disturbed her because she hated people who couldn't control themselves, their drinking or drugs. She looked down her nose at the kids who used the stuff Paul and Trapper sold. And yet she would find herself drawing back an arm to aim a blow at Caroline without even having thought about it, in spite of her latest vow to stop. So it wasn't like she'd forgotten or lost control. It was just something that seemed to happen. And after, again, she'd hug the girl and swear never to hit her again.

But she thought maybe money would be the solution, thought maybe if she had her own place, their own life, she might not feel whatever it was—frustration, shame, grief, rage—that made her hit her little girl. Maybe.

So Lindee always responded to Trapper by bringing up her idea about the house. "I know it, Trap, and I try not to hurt her. But she just won't behave. I believe she's as unhappy in these dumps as we are. If we could get us a place, a nice place, I'd feel better and so would she and I wouldn't have to get after her all the time like I do."

"All right, hon," he had finally said. "Let's try it this once and see how it works. We'll use what we got here and make up the difference next week. I'll just buy twice as much shit." He had fretted a bit. "Jesus, baby, if that feller catches me, he'll tear me into pieces."

"Don't worry, Trap," she had said. "I'll keep him occupied while you go on to town." It was the first time she'd openly referred to the sexual encounters with Paul, and she watched Trapper to see how he'd respond. To her surprise, he seemed relieved.

"Yeah," he said, almost eagerly. "That'll be good. Keep his mind as far from town as you can."

She'd managed it fine the first time, going up to the filling station where she knew Paul would be in the morning and giving him the look that meant, *Trapper's gone.* And he had come over. She had tried to keep him for a while, but he had left pretty quickly, zipping up his fly and saying, "That's some hot gravy," or something, like he always did.

But this week she'd not gone looking for him. Then he had turned up just when she had expected Trapper to be getting home. He'd spent the night with her and had told her not to worry. And this was exactly what had made her uneasy.

Still, she had been soothed by the lazy morning Paul was spending with her, lying in the bed and talking—he'd never done this before—and caressing her before he took her again. She told herself it was all working better than ever if Paul was this relaxed and friendly with her.

So now, when Paul said, "Don't worry about Trapper," she

didn't feel anything beyond a mild unease. Perhaps Paul had indeed bumped into Trapper on his way out of town yesterday. Or, more likely, Trapper had called him on the cell phone to say he was busy in town for the night and wouldn't pick up the rest of this week's run until tomorrow. That was it. It wasn't all that uncommon for Trapper to stay overnight in Roalton. Likely Trapper was looking for a better price, or had found a new outlet, a safer one. And Paul had come straight over, knowing Trapper was engaged for the night in town. That was it.

"You want a beer?" Paul said, again, getting up and walking, naked, out of the room.

"I'm okay," she said. "I'll have me a sip of your'n"

"You already done that," he said, laughing coarsely.

He returned with the beer and opened it sitting next to her on the bed. He licked around the rim of the can and tipped it up for a long pull. She leaned toward him and he wrapped his arm around her neck, like a head lock and poured some of the beer into her open mouth. He tightened his grip very gradually, still pouring the beer, and it was a moment before she felt the squeeze and the pain. She choked, then moaned, trying to say, "Don't," but his arm had tightened on her throat, and she couldn't speak.

Just as the pain began to be really frightening, he let her go, flopping her onto her back. She gasped and coughed, looking at up him, her eyes wide.

"That hurt, Paul," she whined.

"Sorry, baby," He said. He took another deep drink of beer. "You want some more?"

He tipped the bottle slowly, spilling cold beer over her breasts and belly.

Lindee jumped, "yowing" at the cold wetness, flinging her feet over the side of the bed, getting up. But as she rose, Paul grasped her hair and yanked hard, snapping her head backward and pulling her over onto the mattress. He kept hold of her hair and lowered his own face, so he was looking straight into her scared eyes.

"Now just what the fuck do you and that sonofabitch think

you're gettin away with?" He jerked her hair. "Hey?" He pulled again, so hard she thought her scalp would tear. "Hey?"

That evening, Sam and Jim ate a supper of cold beans and sliced ham, Jim sitting at the couch balancing a chipped plate on his lap, a can of beer on the floor, while Sam swept clear a space on the corner of his desk, perched his plate there, and ate standing up, bending forward toward the plate for a forkful of food, then straightening and pouring down a large swallow of beer.

"We could eat in the kitchen like normal folks, I suppose," Sam said. "But tonight, I want to get past the first course and on to the second, what you might call 'main' course, as soon as we might."

"Just what did you have in mind for a main course?" Jim said, finishing his beans and ham, and taking a sip from the beer.

Sam moved behind his desk, saying, "Put down that beer can and let's get you started toward going native, what do you say?" He reached back behind the desk. "We'll get you a sup of stump-blower." He pulled out a large fruit jar filled with a cloudy tannish liquid. "And we'll talk over this stuff I found out."

"Stumpblower?" Jim said. "I'm afraid to ask."

"No, it won't hurt you none, if you take it easy." Sam winked. "Won't hurt you a hell of a lot if you don't take it easy, except temporarily, so to speak."

"Well, it doesn't appear to be moonshine, does it?" said Jim. "I know enough to know moonshine is clear. White lightnin, right?"

"You aint from around here, are you?" Sam said, winking. He opened a drawer and taking out two jam jar glasses, said "Moon-shine don't do a hell of a lot for me on its own. Tastes a lot like drinkin raw copper, seems to me. But as a base for something kindly sophisticated, like stumpblower, you got to have a jug of fine white liquor." He filled the glasses carefully, dipping his head as he poured, as if counting time. "So moonshine is overrated, I'd say." He slid a glass across to Jim. "Of course, to some, it's a way of life, even yet. And back in the old days, well, folks could live and die by it. That's what we're looking at here. The Shaleen Crick Affair, that was a moonshine war. Everybody says it was a family feud, and I reckon they're right, too. But down at the bottom, it was all about moonshine liquor." He held out a glass to Jim. "Now this here drink is puttin moonshine to good use."

"Good God," Jim said, eying the brownish stuff. "What's in it?"

"A part of moonshine, a part of apple cider, and a bag of them little cinnamon red hot candies. You throw that together and cap it up for a month, let that cider get workin, you got you a drink. Of course, you better unscrew her now and again, or she'll explode, kindly." He paused, thoughtfully. "I reckon that's where the name come from," he said, falling into his mountain voice. "Stumpblower." He held his glass up. "Here's water down the crick."

Jim clinked glasses and took a small sip. It was surprisingly good. He smiled. "I reckon I could cotton to this after a mite," he said.

Sam laughed. "We'll make a cousin outen you yet." He tossed back a swallow. "Except I never heard anyone from hereabouts say 'cotton to.' Except Jed Clampett. You got 'mite' right, though." He took another swallow. "Come on. Let me show you what I got."

They moved over to the couch and sat obliquely, facing each other. Sam spread his hands, an opening gesture, like a preacher greeting his flock.

"The Morelocks and the Hamptons both lived up the creek, all around the mountain there. Most of it's tore up today, but there's still some Morelocks down to the head of the holler. The Hamptons, god knows what's become of them. Oh there's Hampton kin all over the place. Me and Leela's Hamptons, you get right down to it. Loftons married a Hampton sometime back. But we're way-off cousins to these folks, the Hamptons I'm talking about. Shaleen Hamptons. They's only one of them left: Dicky Hampton, but he's a far cry from them original boys, you might say."

Sam tipped his glass and took a long drink. Jim could see the throat muscles working. "Jesus," he said. "I don't have to drink the stuff that fast to be your cousin, do I?"

"Anyways," said Sam, wiping a sleeve across his mouth, "This all seems to go back to Old Cuddy Morelock, who I reckon was the patriarch. He and his boys, all living together in a big old place up there that used to be the headquarters of a lumber operation. They had a double-ought steam sawmill working up there, up above the house a ways, until about nineteen and ten."

Sam took a scrap of paper off the desk and drew a large E. "Look here," he said. "This here's about what it's like up there, except the bottom and top arms of the E ought to be longer." He corrected his drawing, then drew a squiggled line rising diagonally across the letter.

"This twisty line, that's the crick, itself," he said. "It forks out, up the mountain, and that'd be the prong comin in. The bottom leg of the letter, that's the way up to where the sawmill was. Middle leg is the lane to Morelocks' home place. Top leg goes up to the Hamptons'. And these all come off the main road, which is the stem of the letter, kindly. Of course, they all twist and turn and curve back, really, like any a mountain track will. Might be some foot trails that links all these up. But these here, they're the main turn outs, they tell me. Don't know if they're even open no more. Except the middle one. That's where Paul Morelock and my sis lives. And his daddy, Johns Morelock.

"So after about nineteen and ten, like I said, they stopped millin. I reckon they were timbered out. This whole country was cut down and sawed up and shipped out, all the poplar and oak and chestnut. So there they were, the whole clan, and even old Cuddy probably couldn't remember how to farm, much less the boys, who'd likely grown up working timber all their lives."

"So they took to making whiskey," Jim said. He took another

small sip on his drink.

"Like ducks to water, it would seem. Anyway, and here were the Hamptons. They were in the same spot. They were doing the cutting and dragging, taking trees out of the high mountains with big steel cable and bringing them in to Cuddy's mill with ox teams. Morelocks sawed em up and run the lumber to town in mule wagons. So they were kindly partners, in the old days.

"Might be we could take a drive up there, up to the prong itself, see if they's anything left. Probably not much. But I bet we could find the old track up there and get there on four-wheel drive.

"Anyways, I found a picture."

Sam got up and moved back to the desk. He picked up a notebook and shook it until a large photo fell out.

"Look here," he said.

The creased and faded photograph at first looked like a picture of chaos, until Jim made out timber, piles of spilth and sawn boards lying in various haphazard stacks around a clearing embraced on three sides by steep slopes, themselves held close by tangled undergrowth. In the foreground stood two flatbed wagons, each drawn by a team of yoked oxen, standing by a pile of boards, the fresh-cut surfaces blazing and blurring in over-exposure. Dimly scattered through the hollow were ten or twelve men in slack, single-brace overalls, and as Jim's eye moved from figure to figure, he began to pick out shape and order: an enormous log drawn up against a notched blade, larger than a man, two black belts snugged onto big fly wheels at the blade gears and slung back into the hollow to a humped steam engine, barely discernable in the darkness at the deepest point of the hollow. Next to the engine there appeared to be a lean-to or a rough cabin, built right into the sheer mountain. The men, holding hooks or poles or ropes, were posed in position according to the various elements of the operation: feeding scrap wood into the engine, clinching and rolling timber, or tending the ox teams. A tall, thin, bearded man stood still, facing the camera, at the very center of the picture.

He rose up atop a stack of wood, a long-handled scythe-like tool held to his side, like a standard. Even in the obscurity of the old photo, the man's narrow eyes seemed luminous, burning out of the picture as though lit from some interior source, looking at once fiercely proud and defensively challenging.

"That would be Cuddy," said Sam, pudging a finger at the central figure. "He looks to me a mite like Cap'n Ahab."

"He looks like Lucifer," said Jim. "And the whole thing, the whole scene looks like some sort of Boschean vision of hell."

"Huh?" said Sam, taking another long drink. "Is that up the road, or down the road?"

"Hieronymus Bosch. He painted weird monstrous pictures of the inferno, among other things. Visions of the damned."

"Reckon he'd ever been to a sawmill?"

Sam broke the spell, stepping away from the desk and grabbing up the jug. He poured a small dose into each glass.

"Some of them in that picture must be old Cuddy's boys. He had six or seven sons, at least that I can find out. Got a few names: Floy and Vernon, then Kinnie, then Claude. Vernon, he got killed in the Shaleen Crick thing. One of them got shot up some. And I reckon they's some Hamptons in this picture, and some of them might got killed.

"So there's Cuddy, and his boys, setting up a moonshine business to make up for the collapse of the sawmill business. Probably they'd all been making whiskey all their lives, up there. Because it wouldn't take none of them long to figure out you could get ten cents a bushel for corn on the cob and five dollars a quart if you put it up in the air. And that was the problem, weren't it?"

"Because the Hampton boys knew how to make whiskey, too," Jim said.

"Because, like I said, it's a family tradition. And yes, the

Hamptons had forgot how to farm, just the same, and they was clean out of the same wood the Morelocks was out of, so they're lookin for a new line of work, too. And probably they all did okay, Hamptons and Morelocks, both, probably worked together, now and again, and made just enough to keep on going up there, but never had to fight about who was going to run the whiskey, right?"

"Right. Until the Volstead Act."

"That's it, isn't it? Prohibition. Aint that the way? The prohibition comes in, and now there's plenty of demand for whisky, so you'd think they'd all be happy to share, since the sharin would be easier than ever. Both families could get rich. You want some more of that stumpblower?"

"Yes I do," Jim said. "It is pretty tasty. I suppose it gets tastier as you go through it, doesn't it?"

"It won't hurt you none. If you get enough of it." Sam got up slowly and rambled back to the jar. He slewed it open and brought it back to the couch, setting it on the coffee table. "This way we can just help ourselves."

"So, anyway," Jim said.

"So, instead, the Morelocks gets greedy. Aint that the way it always goes? The more mud you got, the more you want to be the only hog in the waller, so to speak. They had a big operation going by now, all the way into Roalton, and the Hamptons, they was just still runnin a little liquor into Glade, here. But the Morelocks, they wanted all of it. And anyways, like I told you yesterday, Morelocks was just meaner'n anybody else around the place. They'd take and get you out of the way if they even thought maybe they didn't want you around. Like some kind of hillfolk mob family, you know? So they took to shootin Hamptons, again."

"Again?" said Jim.

"It appears they'd been some kind of a feud going on all along. Or at least somethin that got started back in the sawmill days. Maybe the same thing: the Morelocks wantin to run the whole show. But it'd stopped, or at least settled some, until the moon-shine thing. When they had the big shoot-up."

"How do you know all this?"

"Glen, mostly. Oh, I went down into town and looked in the county records a little. Looked over the newspapers. But I didn't find a hell of a lot. So then I went and talked to Glen."

"Who's Glen? Is he a Morelock or a Hampton?"

"He's a she," Sam said. "Glen Crary. Owns a general store out on the east drag. They's been Crarys runnin a store since these mountains was potato hills. She knows everything ever happened around that way. She's kindly our local historian. We'll go up and see her in a bit, when we know more about what to ask.

"Anyways, they got to feudin over who controlled the moon-shine out of that hollow. Like I said, Morelocks, they were the big outfit, all along, even back in the sawmill days, so Glen reck-ons they had got most everybody out of the liquor business up there except the Hamptons. So they took to feudin. Glen says they's a lot of local legend about the feud, how it was all about who fought on what side in the Civil War, and about how one of the Morelocks fell in love with a Hampton—sort of Romeo and Juliet style, you know. But she says that's all booshwah. Says it was nothin but moonshine and money.

"But they was fightin it out as families, so I reckon 'feuding' is what it was. They had some gunplay right down here in town. I bet we could look that up, somewhere. Must be some record of a gunfight in town.

"And all of it ended up at the sawmill, in nineteen and twenty-two. Nobody knows much about what happened there, because neither family dezactly told the same story, and nobody ever got jailed for it. Somebody ambushed somebody, anyways, right at the mill. Killed a Morelock or two and some Hamptons. And then, two weeks later, Lon Hampton, he was the second oldest boy, was found wrapped up in barbwire and shot to death, up on the side of the mountain. This time the law got involved, though you couldn't say it necessarily got its man. One of the Morelocks done a hefty chunk of time for the crime, anyways. I reckon the law was a mite frustrated that it never got to arrest nobody before, in spite of all the shootin and hollerin, so when it finally got some evidence on somebody, it threw the whole thing at him.

"And that was that," Sam said, taking another long pull.

The door swung open suddenly and a woman entered, already talking. "I'm sorry, Sam, but I've got to try again. I'm…"

"Oh," she said, catching sight of Jim. "Excuse me." She was short and thin, with straight black hair. There was a kind of plain prettiness about her, enhanced by evocative hazel eyes. The left side of her face looked wrong: darkened and shaded like a clumsy charcoal sketch. He realized the darkness was a bruise, and the thought embarrassed him, as though he'd intruded on her, and not the other way around.

"Speakin of the devil," Sam said. "Jim, meet Leela."

Jim saw the resemblance between the two, though the contusion on Leela's face rather spoiled what might have been the same genial aspect as her brother's. Like Sam, Leela had a strong nose and slim lips, a broad forehead, though the aspect was slimmer, more delicate than her brother's broad face, and the straight hair framed her face, where Sam's wild brown hair made his broad face look even wider.

Sam beckoned the two together and Leela stepped forward extending a hand. Jim found himself awkward and a little bashful in the presence of the bruised, beaten woman. He felt as if he were somehow at fault, felt himself coloring as he touched the warm, hand. It was firm enough but seemed still to retain a kind of girlish softness, some touch of underlying delicacy, that made him feel worse.

"Pleased" she said quietly, decorously. *It was as though she was at a damn tea party*, he thought, later that night. *As though that big swollen bruise wasn't there on the side of her face, at all.*

I guess that's one way to deal with the shame, or the hurt, or whatever you'd have to call it when you said it to yourself. So you just shake hands and say, "Pleased to meet you," and maybe that big bruise won't really be there the next time you look in the mirror. I don't know.

"You runnin away from that sonofabitch again?" Sam said.

"Sam," she pleaded, her eyes glancing off Jim.

"Well, honey, if you're going to come bustin in to the chief editor and publisher's office of a newspaper, blurtin out your own troubles, you can't expect him not to spread the news, can you? Besides, Jim already knows somewhat about you. In the abstract, so to speak."

"Maybe I should leave you alone for a while," Jim said. He was touched by the troubled look on Leela's face, and he realized that her sudden, talking entrance had been an anomaly: that this was a quiet woman, one who had turned her pains inward for so long that she had difficulty turning any sort of face outward, to the world. *So there's more to it than just trying to erase everything with some sort of tea-party decorum. Because it's so hard for her; she would only have shown it to her brother of all the world. And she thought it was only Sam listening when she came into the room, already talking. And the god damn bruise is something hard and cruel she's carrying around with her, like it's her fault, and she is prohibited from telling anyone, anywhere—not even the brother, this time—the real feeling of the thing.*

She was quite good looking, he thought, with a thin, slightly long-waisted body, a little bottom-heavy, clothed in a clean, faded cotton shirt and jeans. He noted, too, that the hazel eyes showed intelligence and grace, somewhere beneath the awkwardness and sadness. He couldn't see any trace of the hell-raising, rebellious teen Sam had described. Of course, she was older, too. Early thirties, he would guess. He realized, too, that Sam's easy bantering was comforting to her, where, to another, it may have seemed cruel. She took assurance from the brother's easy ironic way, and this was why she came to him. He drew her out of herself, to a degree, within the shelter of his overarching easiness.

"Well, now, this presents a problem," Sam said. "We got what you might call a logistical difficulty, here. Leela, honey, I done already give your bed out to this feller." He gestured toward Jim. "Aint no room at the inn."

She said nothing.

"I suppose you could have the couch," he continued. "You want to bunk on the couch?"

"Are you...do you need to stay here?" Jim asked her. "Because I could always..."

"Or you could play turnabout, like the miners used to, one of em in the bed, nights, and the other, days, spelling each other on different shifts. How long you fixin to stay this time before you give up and go back to that miserable..."

"Sam," she said, again. Then she appeared to shake herself, a long pulse seeming to run through her body, as though she'd made a decision and was setting herself to the task. She spoke.

"I'm through with him, Sam. This time. I've got to find out how to do it, how to get away on my own. Maybe I should just go."

"Go where?"

"Get my own place. I can't keep running back and forth from him to you, can I?" She looked downward as she said this, avoiding eye contact, or trying to hide the contusion.

"Well," Sam said, "one step at a time." He stretched himself and stood up behind the desk. "Where's your things? Jim, being as how Leela's the lady, and has what you might call a prior claim on the spare bed, what about if you was to move out onto the couch and give her the room? Then we'll see what becomes of this. Honey, I got to tell you, frankly, I'll believe it when I see it. But if you're really gone for good, we'll help you set up in your own place. Let's just go a step at a time, huh?"

"That'll be fine," Jim said, eagerly. He felt he wanted to show her he was on her side, that he would happily do something to help her. He found himself wanting to please her. "Sure. The couch is great for me. Sure."

"You aint seen how ornery that couch can get around two, three in the morning," Sam said. "But if you're game for it, let's make the switch. Where's your things, sister?"

Leela motioned toward the door.

"Let's get you situated."

FIVE

Next morning Jim awoke on the couch to find Leela sitting at Sam's desk, wearing a terrycloth robe and making figures on a scrap of paper. The robe was loosely tied, showing a shadowed neck, the notch of her collarbone, a hint of breast in the closing vee. The bruise on her cheek showed like a second shadow on her down-turned face.

"I hope I didn't wake you up," she said. When she raised her head, the wound showed lividly, worse than yesterday, a deep indigo spreading to red and yellow edges. Her eyes were soft, two pretty islands in a sea of bruises. She adjusted the gapping robe, pulling it closer. "I'm trying to figure out whether I have any money," she said. "Or how much money I don't have, I guess. Trying to figure out what I need to get by."

"Maybe you can get money from him," Jim said. He got up and moved across the room, sitting on the edge of the desk. "Take him to court."

"Well, he's got plenty of money," she said. "Or at least his Pawp does. They've got scads of money. Not that they spend any of it. Fancy trucks is all. The rest of it is piled up somewhere. But they's plenty of it."

"Then get some," Jim said, sitting on the couch.

"That might be easier said than done." She smiled. "He aint exactly the type to put up with this without a fight." She touched the robe, again.

"Where did all that money come from?" Jim asked, watching her bare forearm toy with the pencil, tapping the desktop.

"I don't know, exactly," she said. "Paul delivers produce in Roalton, and he makes a lot at it. But I don't know. They've always been involved in one thing or another."

"Like the old days," Jim said. "Moonshine?"

"I don't know," she said. She smiled dryly. "A woman's place, you know."

"Can a man, a family, really keep that sort of thing from his wife?" Jim asked. When she dropped her eyes, he said, "I'm sorry," thinking he'd hurt her.

"Well," she said, "they kept an awful lot from you, didn't they? Your family?" Her eyes were soft, warm.

"You've talked to Sam," he said. "About me."

She smiled. "Sam says you're lookin to find someone up here and I'm lookin to get away from someone. Like mirror images, he says. Says he's runnin a halfway house."

"I like him," Jim said. "He's a good man."

"Yes, he is," she said. "He's a true Lofton, like Daddy was. Sam, he looks just like Uncle Sy Lofton. Upstairs?" Again she brought her hand to the vee of her robe, pulling it tight.

"Yes," Jim said. "I thought so, too. And now you know I'm looking for my relations, as well."

"For your mother," she said.

"God," he said. "Is it really possible that parents would never tell a son about his adoption? Why? Why?" he said. "Do people really do that? Adopt a baby and never tell him he's adopted?"

"Looks like maybe they do." She sighed. "Sometimes I think maybe the only way folks can live anywhere near each other is to not tell each other nothin. And maybe other folks don't want to know. Rather have it all just secrets, rather than to have to work out anything as complicated as the truth. You know? Anyways, maybe back then, the fact that they knew the mother is what made them not to tell."

"Why?" he said again.

"Well," she said, hesitating, "I wouldn't want to say."

"Are we going to start not telling each other? So we can be friends?" he said, dryly.

"Okay," she said. "Well, it could have been outright snobbery. Could be they believed that you was low-bred and wanted to erase all connections to the woman, so you would grow up nothing but a Thorwait, son of the eminent doctor. Could be they thought they were doing right by you, so you wouldn't have to struggle with feeling like low-born. Being a Thorwait, they probably thought, was the best thing in the world, especially if you was comin from what they call covites. You ever hear us called 'covites'?"

He said nothing.

"Am I hurting your feelings?" She touched his arm, lightly.

"No," he said, patting her hand. "No. You could be right, anyway. My folks, my parents." He stopped. "You know, my adoptive mother and father, they were high society. They raised me with 'all the benefits and opportunities of good breeding.' They actually said that to me, more than once, when I'd done something they didn't like. They didn't like my leaving school to go work with music, with instruments. 'How can you go off and waste your life, when you've had all the benefits and opportunities of good breeding?' So they were snobs, sure enough. That's part of the whole problem."

She got up and moved to the coffee pot. "You want some of this stuff Sam calls coffee?"

"Sure," he said.

"What do you mean, the whole problem?" she said, pouring the coffee and bringing it around to where he sat on the corner of the desk, legs dangling. She stood by him, her own legs lightly touching his. "I recommend cream and sugar," she said.

"Just cream is fine." As she went back around the desk, he said, "The whole problem is the fact that I've become a person who I would never have been if I hadn't been adopted. And yet,

I never knew that was the case. And so I've grown up a stranger to who I was."

"So you come up here to get acquainted with the one you were? Or what? What is it you're looking for? Do you know?"

"No," he said. He took a sip of the coffee and grimaced. "But what else can I do? I mean, what would you do if you found out today that your parents weren't your parents and your mother was from some other place, some other life than the one you'd led. That she was the kind of person you'd been taught to take for granted. The kind who picked up after you; the kind with no face, or real life, just someone you expected to be there, like paint on the walls. What would you do?"

She smiled and put her hand on his shoulder. "I reckon I'd do just what you're doing," she said. "But can you find something in a place you don't understand? Could I find something in Roalton that showed me who I am, especially when the whole problem is that I'd become someone who couldn't understand what I was looking at, like the wall under the paint?"

"So you think it's hopeless," he said. He tried to appeal to her with his eyes. He wanted to hear her say *no, not hopeless, because I'll help you*, wanted to hear her offer collaboration, as if she saw something deep and true in him, the way he wanted to see the same thing in her.

"I don't know," she said. "But you're a business owner, a city boy, a wealthy man, compared to here. Educated and settled. And you want to pull all of that down so you can walk into these mountains? And do what? Pretend you're not smart and established? When everybody here can take one look at you and tell you're not from around here?"

"I've already been told that," he said. She saw that she had deflated him, taken something away from him and she felt compelled to reassure.

"Don't worry," she said. "I'm not being fair. You're right: what else can you do? And you'll find her, at least. You'll find that much out, I'm sure." She touched his arm again. And then she said what he'd wanted to hear. "Maybe I can help you."

He smiled at her, and felt he had accomplished something, at least. He'd made her his friend, even if he was still a stranger, an outsider. He lifted his cup and they clinked a toast, smiling.

"I wish it was something besides coffee," he said.

She took a sip and grimaced.

"Lord," she said. "Maybe it is."

That same morning, Paul Morelock sat in his father's living room, drinking a beer. He set the can on the coffee table, where, on the shelf just below, sat an enormous gilded and leather bound family bible. On the wall were three old photos.

"He's runnin his own traps," said Paul. "The sonofabitch. Got into town whilst I was up to the place fixin up my own. I knew he was into something, and I got to him in Roalton, at Pink's. I give him warning. I'd say that."

This was the house his father, Johns Morelock, had been born in, the ancestral Morelock home, a few hundred yards up Shaleen Creek from the high road where the creek emptied into river. Above the house was nothing but wilderness—federal land— where Johns Morelock's grandfather had run the family sawmill. Now the pathway was faded, barely discernable, though Paul used another way up: down to the main road and up a rough, overgrown lane shadowing the creek all the way, until the track topped onto the broad meadow at the prong. In fact, he'd been up there yesterday, as he said, "fixin up" his truckload to take into town.

"You got the pills?" his father said.

"Well yes, I got the damn pills, what do you think? That aint the problem. It's that Trapper. We got a problem on our hands with him." Morelock got up and walked across the room into a small bathroom, talking over his shoulder. "That's the leak we got to plug, right there. Speakin of leaks."

"So who cares about that?" said Johns.

Paul entered the bathroom, leaving the door wide open, and

pissed noisily, shouting into the living room.

"We'd best care about it before it gets outen our hands," he said. "Them two don't even know what the fuck they're a doing, tryin to run stuff on my own lines. They'll mess up somehow and we'll have the state a settin in our laps quicker'n fleas on a fyce. And that aint all there is to it."

He buttoned his fly and walked back into the room, wiping his hands on the seat of his pants.

"Where's them pills?" Johns said.

"Would you forget about the goddamn pills?" Paul said. "I got the fuckin pills. Forget the damn pills."

"Don't talk to your Pawp like that," Johns said, angrily, reaching out a foot and kicking over Paul's beer can. It rolled to the floor and lay there, burbling fluid.

"Shit Pawp, I didn't mean nothing," Paul said. "I reckon this is got me riled."

"All right," said Johns, mollified. "All right."

"And like I said," Paul added. "That aint all there is to it." He wagged a finger. "That newspaper feller, Leela's brother. He's snoopin around Gracie's for some reason, with a stranger from out of town. Don't know who the stranger is, but he don't appear to take too kindly to anything that's a going on at Gracie's. So now we got Trapper a runnin off on a tangent and Sam Lofton nosin around in the same place where Trap and the gal is makin the product, and we got a feller from out of town we don't know what the hell he's after."

"Sam Lofton!" said Johns. "What in hell is Sam Lofton got to bother us with? He aint got the gumption of a pussycat. Iffen he did, he'd been over here after you, kindly protectin his sister." The man laughed. "She's gone again, aint she?"

"Never mind that," said Paul. "She'll be back. Sometimes, I swear I got a mind to tell the bitch to just stay put."

"Might be you can use her to find out what he's up to, hey?" said Johns.

"Might be, hell," Paul said. "She'll be back, sure as hell, but she wouldn't never turn table on that brother of her'n. She thinks he's the big wheel cannonball, the little shit."

"Well I don't like it," said Johns. "Maybe it's her that got the sonofabitch a sniffin round in the first place. How about that?"

"I don't like it neither," said Paul. "Dammit, that's what I'm talking about, we got a problem. But it aint him that's a going to fuck things up. It's Trapper. I'll handle Leela iffen she thinks she can help her brother be a news reporter, get involved with the bad guys in the county. I'll kick her around the mountain and that'll take care of that. No. They's two problems: the stranger, one. Who in hell is he and what's he lookin for that he'd go to the newsman and the newsman'd run him straight out to Trapper's place? Huh?" He ran his hand across his forehead. "And it's Trapper, the other. He's got a wild hair going to give that stranger something to find, and then we're all of us in the pig shit."

"Maybe you could go over to the paper, demand to get your rights, get your wife back, kindly. Put a scare in them two and find out what's this other feller up to from out of town. How'd that be?"

"Not yet," said Paul. "I tell you we got to take care of Trapper, first. This other feller, he don't even know we're up here, yet. All he knows is Trapper and the gal, and if we can shut Trapper out of it then that's all he's a going to know."

"Well, I reckon we'll just have to take care of it," his father said.

"I know that," said Paul. "But just how in hell do we take care of it?"

Johns stood up, stretching himself then dropped to his knees, bending and dragging the huge bible out from under the table. "Look here," he said. The bible thumped down onto the tabletop and Johns flipped it open at midpoint, looking through the Psalms until he found it.

"Number 143," he said, drawing out a faded news clipping.

"Look a here."

"I know," Pawp," Paul said. "I seen it, fifty million times." He hesitated. "Don't think I aint pleased to look again," he said, placatingly. "I got a right to be proud of this here family, just as you do. And you a part of it, that time."

"Well that's why I'm a showin you," Johns said. "What's did once can be did again, aint that right?"

"And this has been did twice, already, aint it?" Paul said.

The two men laughed.

Paul arose and went to the door. "I'll think on it, and you do too," he said. "Between us, I reckon we can figure up a way to chop that sonofabitch down to size." He started out the door.

"Wait," said his father. "What about Trapper's gal?"

Paul hesitated a moment. "I'll figure her out," he said. "She aint no problem at all, far as I see." He stepped outside and began walking toward his trailer, parked obliquely across the clearing. He began to whistle.

Dicky Hampton was perched on a crate in front of Glen Crary's store, running an orange freeze-pop in and out of his mouth, and listening to Dave McCann tell about the stranger who was in the filling station yesterday, and Sam, asking around about Morelocks and Hamptons.

McCann reached into an overalls pocket and produced a small barlow knife. He snapped it open and reflexively began cleaning his nails. He was a thin man, and grimy from working around machinery, but shaven so cleanly his neck and chin looked rawly naked in the summer morning light.

"What in hell is he doin? Dicky said. "Preachin?" He had a squat, round face, with big, bulging eyes and a furious, meaningless grin produced by a pronounced underbite. His head extended from a short-waisted, blowbellied body. Sitting on the crate, sucking his freeze-pop, he looked, Dave thought, *like a frog on a triscuit tryin to choke hisself with a carrot.*

"Don't know a thing about him," McCann said.

"Shit," Dicky said, dismissively. "'Nother goddamn kook." He took a long suck on the freeze-pop. "We oughter go find him. Bust him up."

"Bust him up," Dave said. He looked at Dicky. *Aint that jest like him? Jest what he'd be like to say about anything or anybody he didn't already know all there was to know about. Bust it up.*

Dicky Hampton had been born a few hundred yards from where he now sat, and his range of experience did not extend much beyond what he could actually see from his crate. He had rarely been beyond the slope rising in his face and shaping the creek, whose course determined which way the two-lane highway would twist and turn as it spilled itself out of the high mountains, down from Needle Gap. He had been over the gap, more than a few times, running odd jobs, and sometimes money, for Paul Morelock, who would go along, sometimes and buy Dicky a beer at Pink's Grill, the old dance hall. Dicky was proud to be what he called an *associament* of Paul Morelock's. Meanwhile, he went up the road every day, as far as Keys's Wreck and Body, where he worked as "general help," hefting sheet metal, shunting cars, and cleaning up.

Once, two young backpackers had stopped at the shop, seeking directions, and Dicky had asked them where they were from. When they answered, "Connecticut," he had asked, "is that up the road or down the road?" This had so tickled Dicky's boss that he had taken to using it as an expression of befuddlement. By now, it had entered the general language of the hollow and folks who hadn't understood someone's explanation of something would say, "Is that up the road or down the road?" without even knowing they were quoting Dicky.

"You want to go on up there?" Dicky asked McCann. "Bust him up?"

The other man looked at him. Out of the scores of brawls Dicky had been involved in, McCann could not remember a single fight he had not lost. Still, when in doubt about how to behave, Dicky generally chose once again to try violence.

"I don't reckon so," said McCann, dryly.

"Shit," said Dicky. He finished the freeze-pop, wiped the stick on his jeans, licked it again meditatively, wiped it again, and tossed it into the parking lot. He reached along his right thigh and un-snapped a leather sheath, from which he drew a long, wicked-looking knife. He picked his teeth methodically with the eight-inch blade, its sharpened edge flickering like an electrical spark. When he finished, he got up slowly, stretched himself, sheathed his knife, and walked away.

"I'm a going up to the shop, see what's going on. You want me, you give a shout, hear?"

Good God, thought McCann, as Dicky walked up around the sharp bend, out of sight. *What in hell would anybody want you for?* He walked into Glen's store, the screen door *fwopping* softly.

Glendora was sitting behind the counter, a round-faced old woman with blue hair in a loose print dress. She was reading a paperback. The bright red cover showed a picture of a muscle-bound man in a gypsy scarf embracing a swooning, busty woman in a dress like a theatre curtain. She turned over the book, setting it splayed out on the Formica counter, and said, "Hidy, David." Her voice was thin, high-pitched, and friendly. "You all right?"

McCann said, "Hidy," and, "Can't complain," to Glen. At the sound of Sam's truck rattling into the parking lot, they both turned to the window to watch. Glen gave a high little laugh. "Here comes the newspaper with that stranger lookin for his maw," she said.

"Stranger?" said McCann. "That'd be the feller Dicky was a fixin to beat up." He laughed and began to fish in his overalls bib. He drew out a bag of Beech-Nut tobacco, pulled it open, sniffed it, stuck thumb and two fingers into the bag, rummaging, and pulled out a loose bundle of the scrap. As he began tucking it up, he said. "Lookin for his ma?"

"That's what Sammy says," said Glendora. "I aint talked to

the feller yet. Sam says he's a nice enough man, comes from Roalton and is a big guitar maker, somethin nother. Says his mamma was a Morelock who give him up for adoption. Now he's lookin for her."

"She's the right kind of Morelock, he may not be wantin to find her too damn soon," McCann said. "But I reckon a boy's best friend is his mother, like the song says."

The door swung and *fwopped* again and Sam entered, followed by Jim and Leela.

"You brought the whole team this time," Glen said, turning and walking from behind the counter toward the coffee machine on the wall.

"You all want a cup?" she said. "Help yourselves to a doughnut. There in the case."

"Thank you, Glen," said Sam, reaching, "Howdy Davey," he said to McCann.

"Hidy," McCann answered, looking Jim over.

"Glen, Davey, this here's Jim. You all know my sister, Leela, I believe."

"Hidy," McCann said, shaking Jim's hand and nodding pleasantly to Leela. Glen smiled, carrying three paper cups toward them. "You want some, Davey?" she said.

"No'm," McCann said. He looked at Jim, again. "I believe I saw you yesterday down to the gas station."

Jim colored, and said, "I think I made something of a fool out of myself. I didn't mean to barge in there like that," he said, awkwardly.

"Oh that was probably Paul Morelock was being ugly at you down there. What'd he say, 'You better watch out,' something like that." McCann smiled.

"No. Wait," McCann said. "That weren't Paul. He weren't there yesterday. It was one of the other fellers, Orrel, maybe. But it sure could've been Paul Morelock. He's kindly a bit of..." He looked aside at Leela and stopped himself. "A bit of a kidder."

"Yeah boy," said Sam. "Paul Morelock's a real joker."

Jim looked at Leela, who shook her head to silence his question and said, "Never mind."

"So you missed the last of the Shaleen Morelocks," Glen said. "And you just missed the last of the Shaleen Hamptons. Dicky just went on up the road."

"He's fixin to beat you all up," said McCann.

Jim looked alarmed. McCann smiled. "Don't worry about Dicky. Aint too many folks he aint tried to beat up. I don't believe he's succeeded with any a one of them. He's just one of them fellers that likes to fight, you know? Likes gettin hit hisself, I'd say. It don't matter to him if he can't win a damn fight, because I believe he takes a right smart of satisfaction about gettin his own ass whooped."

"He's Tom Hampton's boy," said Glen. "Most of them Hamptons is out of this country, but Tom stayed on, in town here, after the Morelocks run the family outen the mountain. Couple of Hamptons got killed over yonder by the sheriff, and Tom moved into town then. Uncle and cousin to Tom was killed, I believe. Far as I know, that sheriff is still in the prison for that."

"Not back in the feud," said Sam, surprised. "That's too long ago,"

"No, not back then. But a good while ago. Let's see…must be forty year ago. Dicky, he's Tom Morelock's boy, and he's about the last of them you'll see around this part of the country. Dicky, he aint any too bright. Rest of the Hamptons, they was quick. But they's all gone, now, all we got is Dicky. So I reckon we all kindly take care of him, give him a freeze-pop now and again, try and keep him out of fights."

"He fights for fun?" said Jim. "And loses? For fun?"

"Now I ain't a foolin," said McCann. "He thinks that's a hell of a good time. Hand me a cup, Glen, if you don't mind." She passed a paper cup to McCann, who let the amber tobacco juice quietly, decorously, out of his mouth.

"You all have a set," Glen said, pulling rope-bottomed chairs from against the wall. They sat, Sam and Leela looking expectantly at McCann.

"Worse thing is, he has him a tendency you might say of kindly gettin other fellers mixed in with his own squabbles, you know? Fellers that might not think it was all that much fun to get their nose broke." McCann used his cup again. "He jest always manages to get more trouble started up than could be settled down by jest kickin Dicky's ass. So it kindly naturally will slop over onto whoever jest happens to be kindly standin there at the time. Dicky don't have too many friends, just as you might figure."

"But you don't have to be his friend," Sam said, dropping into his country boy accent. "To get snarled up in his fence wire, so to speak, and find out here's some feller you never seen before, or never done nothing to, who is fixin to take out one or two of your teeth on account of somethin Dicky'd jest done."

"Aint that the truth?" said McCann.

"They was one night up to the Lighthouse, up on the East mountain," Sam said, "When he'd done got snarled up with a feller—a stranger, kindly, from up to Morgan's Knob—about who was drinkin somebody else's beer and how'd you like I take you outside and drag your sad ass up and down the parkin lot? And after they'd shoved each other around a while, and somebody sad somethin—made fun of them both or what have you—well, this feller, he gets real mad and says he's a going to go back home, and he says, 'You get some of yall's out there because I'm bringin back a cartload of mine, and we'll be back here and we'll bust every one of you all's asses.' And out the door he goes, madder'n Pawpaw at the weddin."

Jim watched Sam, wondering at this smooth transition into mountain language—McCann's language—wondering if this was a mark of Sam's authenticity or his fraudulence. He looked at Leela, who winked and looked back at Sam.

"That got Dicky excited, I'll bet," said McCann.

"Oh boy," said Sam. "'Jesus Christ,' Dicky says, and them big blue eyes gets to blazin. 'Jee-zus Christ,' he says, 'They's goin to be one hell of a fight.' And he looks all around at the rest of us, kindly.

"Now, they weren't too much choice in the matter. That old boy had done went to fetch his buddies and when they got here they weren't too damn likely to be persnickety about which one of us they was wroppin the towel bar around. As long as he was one of us that'd been in the place when they got here, they might jest as well crack his head open, get him outen the way.

"So we was pretty much enlisted into the fight whether we liked it or didn't. And anyways, if anybody had tried to leave, I believe Dicky would have jumped on his back and bit him in the head, he was that excited about the big fight that was a goin to be happenin tonight, all on account of him. He couldn't hardly hold hisself still. And marchin around and gatherin us up to head us out into the parkin lot. And he keeps on sayin, 'Jesus Christ, aint there a goin to be one hell of a fight?'"

"Sound like Dicky to me," said McCann.

"So we all of us went on out onto the gravel," Sam said. "Some of the young fellers was hollerin about 'we'll kick their ass,' and wavin their arms around like they was tougher than Mawmaw's coffee. And the rest of us, the older ones, we kindly shuffled on out there, none too happy about any of it, but out there, going along with the program. You know. And all of us, we kindly got into a half circle, with Dicky out front of us, in the middle, like he was the damn band leader. And he kept turnin around and grinnin at us with that slungover jaw of his. That big ole moon face. And them big eyes of his, I swear they was afire, he was so goddamn excited.

"He shakes out his beer bottle and throws it over his shoulder, and says, 'Run in, get me a fresh one, Hershel.' Jumpy as all hell. Well, Hershel, he's just as glad to get out of there, even if it's only to fetch back a beer for the band leader. Because if he's lucky, well he'll be in there under the sink time them fellers pulls up and the fightin begins. So off Hershel scoots. And leaves us all out there a waitin."

Sam paused and looked around. Glen took the opportunity to

hand around a plate of doughnuts she'd put together while Sam was telling the story. Again, Jim wondered at the transformation of Sam from dry ironist to mountain storyteller. Again he looked at Leela and again she slipped him a wink. *She loves it,* Jim thought, and decided he did, too.

"So, anyhow," Sam said, munching a doughnut. "We're all just standin there out in the parkin lot, behind Dicky, and we're shiftin around on our legs and tryin not to see if the other feller looks scared or nothin like it. And some of them gets to nudgin their toe around in the gravel and watchin it like it was the most important thing in the world, to crunch their boots around in the stones. And Dickie a jumpin around sayin, 'Jeezus Christ, Jeeeeezus Christ,' just as excited as can be.

"And pretty soon, here comes Hershel back, and he's got him a whole box full of long-necked beers, and they's kindly a sigh goes up from all of us, and the line up breaks apart, all of us headin to grab one of them beers out of the box, all at the same time and crack one open. And it took us a mite to get straightened back out and back into line and all. I recall noticin how the night was beginnin to get a chill. Damp.

"Well, Dicky, he's jerkin up and down like he's got the epizoodick, like he can't hardly stand it, and tryin to tuck each feller back in the line. And he's talkin fast, now, sayin, 'Boys that's right, boys. Git lined up now, because they's fixin to be one hell of a fight, time them goddamn fellers shows up. Them goddamn boys'll wish to hell they'd never come back into this here part of the county, I'll tell you the damn truth.' And then he'd stop and tip up that beer for a minute, like he was pouring it down a pipe, and before he'd even got stopped pouring it, he'd start in to sayin, 'One hell of a damn fight,' so the beer'd run out of the corners of his mouth and down onto his shirt front.

"So we stood there and drank our own beers, and by and by somebody says, 'Hershel, run in fetch us out some of that beef jerky.' So off he goes again, and the same old thing: presently he comes back out with a whole cartload of that stuff and more beers, too, and we break up and gets us some and then we kindly saunter back into line again, drinkin on our beers and gnawin that beef jerky. Standin and nudgin our toes into the gravel."

Sam picked up the plate of doughnuts and offered it around, grabbing another himself.

"It was getting damn chilly out there by now and that beef jerky, now that stuff is right salty, you know, get you thirsty, and in the cold air it's so goddamn tough it's like tryin to gnaw on a Farmall tire. And you could see the circle was beginning to sag and startin to get loose around the seams, coming apart like a Bob Hall suit, you might say. And finally, somebody mumbles, 'Aint a goin to be no goddamn fight.'

"And that's all it took. All at once, we're all saying, 'They aint comin back,' and 'the hell with this,' and 'it's too goddamn cold to be standin out here in a goddamn lot,' and 'let's get us inside.'

"All of a sudden you could see Dicky kindly de-flate. He's been so durn puffed up and enthused about the big fight that you could see when the air went out of him he looked like he'd shriveled. I thought for a minute he was going to cry. And somebody says again, 'Hell, them boys aint comin back here. They aint no fight.'

"But you could see Dicky was workin at pullin hisself back together, liftin his shoulders up and tuckin up his head so he wouldn't look so goddamn out of air, so to speak. And he looks around at all of us, like he's tryin to see can he get us fired up again, like a kid will do when everybody's tired of bouncin the ball against the barn and he don't want them all to leave.

"'Well, damn it,' he says. 'They aint a comin back, is they, the sonsofabitch?' And he throws us that goddamn grin of his'n, like maybe everthing is going to be just fine, after all. 'I got a idea,' he says, all cheered up. 'Why'nt let's just draw straws and whoop each other's ass?'"

Sam bit into his doughnut and looked at all of them. McCann laughed, lightly and repeated, "Whoop each other's ass. Don't that beat all?"

"Nobody seemed too interested," Sam said. "So fellers grabbed another beer out of the box and started driftin back in to the bar. And I reckon that got Dicky right mad, and back in the fightin mood. Anyways, he was standing there a clenchin them little fists of his'n and kindly breathin fast, like he can't get all the air out in time, and watching everybody walk away. And then he hollers, 'Godammit! Godammit! Them dirty sonsofabitch!' like that. So Hershel and me, we turned back to see what in hell is Dicky up to now.

"And damned if he didn't march up to Hershel and snatch the full bottle of beer outen his hand just that quick. Them big blue eyes wild, you know, like 'look out, captain.' So Hershel and me, we both jumped back away from him, and he standing there like he's about to blow something, and a holding that full bottle of Hershel's beer. Dicky aint much fun to look at when's he's fixin to fight somebody, but I'll tell you what, he's even worse lookin when they aint nobody around to take him up on the fightin.

"So now Dicky's bent over a mite, with that beer bottle in one hand and just breathing hard, like he's fixin to go off, and lookin wild, and back we jump, and Hershel starts to say, 'Now take her easy, now.' When I be damned if Dicky don't take that beer bottle and swing her up and crack himself square on the middle of his own goddamn forehead. Like a feller will say, 'I forgot the dern keys,' and will smack himself in the brow, kindly. Only this time it's with the goddamn bottle of beer going KEY-RACSH. And they busted, the beer bottle and Dicky both, and down they both go onto the parkin lot, all that busted glass and old Dicky just like somebody had throwed them out the back of the truck. And lay stiller than the night, both Dicky and his bust forehead and them pieces of bottle, jest a layin there, blood, and glass.

"Well I looked over to Hershel, and he looked over to me. And Hershel, he kindly shrugs and says, 'I reckon he's jest a tryin to cheer hisself up.'"

Sam laughed and wiped his hands on his pants. He got up and put the plate back on the counter.

McCann gave his light chuckle, and said, "Cheer hisself up," laughing. "I believe that's got to be the first time Dicky ever went home on a Saturday night without he'd found somebody to whoop his ass first."

"That's jus what Hershel said," Sam told them. But he said, 'That's okay. I reckon Dicky had done took care of it hisself, that once."

Later, after McCann had gone on, they asked Glen about the Morelock family.

"They aint dezactly the kind to talk much about family," said Glen. She came from around the counter and drew out a chair. They sat by the coke cooler, in a half circle. "You all grab up a drink anytime you want," said Glen.

"Like I told you, we're lookin for Allie—or maybe Allison—Morelock," Sam said. "We know that's Jim's momma's name because we got it on a paper. The adoption paper."

"Well, they ain't no Allison Morelock I ever heard of. They was a Ethlyn, and a Eleanor, and I think maybe a Opal. Way back. The Morelocks in the feud was all boys. Cuddy Morelock and his boys."

"But no Allison?" said Jim. "She'd be about the same age as Johns. She could be his sister, even."

"I don't believe he had a sister," Glen said.

"Lucky guy," said Sam. Leela hushed him.

"Johns's wife's name was Ruthie. Paul's mother. I knew her a bit. She'd come down here now and again. I liked her. She's dead these ten years or so. Paul, he's got a younger brother, has a funny name. Let me think…I don't know what become of him."

"Do you know if there was another branch of the family up on Shaleen?"

"No. They's Morelocks all over this country, but Cuddy's was the family up on Shaleen. Cuddy was meaner'n a boar hog, they say. And his boys, too. They run the Hamptons clean outen the country. Most of them. They was one come back and lived up there, on some Hampton land down to the creek mouth, somewheres. But he got killed."

"They killed him, too?" said Leela.

"No. He got shot by the sheriff. Wait. That boy of Johns. His name is spelt P-I-E-R-O-T. Can you imagine?"

"French, of all things," said Jim. "Pronounced 'Pee-row'?"

"No. It's 'Pye-rot.' Pye-rot Morelock."

"Jesus," Sam said. "Pye-rot."

"Just like Chasteen and Shaleen, isn't it?" Leela said. "You can't tell from the spelling what the name is, rightly."

"Spellin, round here, kindly comes after the name is already made," said Glen. "Or maybe it's the tother way round. They calls it what they wants, irregardless of the way somebody once spelt it. I don't know. One or the other."

"So we're stumped," said Sam. "We got the whole damn family accounted for, but we aint got the momma anywhere among them."

"Well," said Leela. "Maybe that makes sense."

"How's that?" said Sam.

"She run off, didn't she? Something made her run from Shaleen Prong all the way down to Roalton. If she was running off, maybe she didn't want to be found. I couldn't blame her."

"You know what you're a talkin about, there, don't you?" said Sam.

"But how do you run away and take your whole history with you?" said Jim. "You can't do that. She couldn't go back in time and erase her own existence when she decided it was time to get away. That doesn't make sense."

"Well, I don't know," said Leela. "We've got a big dark piece of empty where Allison Morelock ought to be."

SIX

The next morning, Jim awoke to a silent house and tiptoed upstairs, past both closed bedrooms to use the bathroom. He showered, and, when he was finished, came down the hall past Leela's open door and down the stairs, to find Leela in exactly the same spot where she'd been when he awoke yesterday: sitting at the table in the loosely belted terrycloth robe, again working out figures on a sheet of paper, the clean dip of skin above her collarbone, the shadowed body beneath.

He stood still on the second stair, looking down at her, feeling a slight flush of shame because he knew he was looking to see more of her from above, from this angle, and wondering *Does she know what I'm doing? Or what she's doing? Does she know the allure of that four inches of skin?* 'Imperfectly beheld,' he thought, wondering, *where is that from?* Then, remembering, *Dickinson.* 'A charm invests the face.' *Something like that.*

And then she'll pull the gap closer, like she did yesterday, knowing, too, that this will make the secret even more enticing more than if she'd thrown off the robe entirely. 'The wearer dare not lift the veil...'

She looked up at him and smiled, pulling the robe closed.

"Morning," she said. She waved at the paper, the scrawl of arithmetic. "I have no idea what I'm doing," she said, as if answering his earlier thought. "Want some coffee?"

"Sure," he said. He came the rest of the way down the stairs, reproving himself for the peeking. *Maybe all women are better than all men. Maybe the old 'purity of women' thing is really true, because we can't even say hello without noticing the gap in the robe, the shadow under the blouse, when we know damned well they have far more on their minds than what we might look like under our clothes.*

He crossed the room toward the desk and felt her watching him. *Or maybe not.*

"Don't know what you're doing?" he said. "With the budget?"

She poured the coffee and handed a cup across to him along with another momentary vee-ing of the robe.

"Yes," she said. "How do you begin to figure out whether you can afford something when you never knew how much it cost?" She smiled. "Being on your own, I mean."

"Freedom?" he said. "Independence? How much that will cost? Good God, if you ever figure that out, I hope you'll let us all know."

They both sat, sipping the chromatically bitter coffee. At length, Leela set her cup down and sighed. She looked at Jim and smiled ruefully.

"Do you sometimes wonder how in the world you ever got to be who or where you are?" she asked, quietly.

"No," he said. "That's my problem. I just discovered exactly how I got to be who I was: I was adopted by a rich man. And, after that, I was never anyone but the son he made me into." He paused. "But I think I see your point. And, frankly, only knowing you for two days, I've got to say I wonder how in hell you got married to a tough old grasper like Paul Morelock."

"Why in the world would that young girl marry a man like him?" she said. "A young girl just walkin around town and next thing you know she's married to a man everyone's afraid of? Who beats her and bullies everybody else?"

"It seems like a question," he said.

"I know it," she said. "That's what I mean. How do you come to find out you've done anything at all for any reason? That's the hard part, isn't it? How did we come to be sittin here and me telling you—a man I don't even know—that I can't figure out any of this?" She smiled again. "I don't exactly go around talking to folks about it. So why you? Why am I a talkin to you?"

"I'm glad enough you are," he said. He set his cup down too hard, as if to back away from the sensitivity of the conversation. "So okay," he said, in a lighter tone of voice. "So how come you married the tough, grasping son of a bitch?"

"That's what I'm tellin you," she said. "I'm the last one to know why. Aint that the usual way? Sure, I reckon I was lookin for adventure, I know that. I was nineteen, and I felt like I had to get someplace that wasn't home nor school. And you know youngsters, they don't have the sense God gave them, especially about somethin as important as who you're supposed to get married to. And there's a plenty of nineteen-year-old girls that'll think they found a daring, reckless, experienced knight when what they got is a mean old eye gouger. That's about the oldest story in the world, aint it?"

"That's why Eve went for that apple, isn't it?" Jim said. "Because she wasn't supposed to—and she was probably created a full-blown teenager, just to make sure the story would go the way it did."

"You're startin to sound like Sam," she said.

He laughed and tried to mimic the tone. "And partly because that Satan feller seemed slick and daring, kindly. When what he was was a snake. Aint it?"

"That's right I guess," she said. "I guess so." She sighed. "And I was good-enough lookin and graceful enough, I suppose, and I was..." she stopped. "Well, never mind."

"Was what?"

"I don't think I know you *that* well," she said.

"Okay," he said. "I catch your drift." He dared a response. "'Randy'? Is that the word?

She blushed and smiled. "I said never mind." She sipped her coffee.

"And so I thought I was getting what I wanted," she continued. "When there's one thing I didn't know then: it's Paul Morelock who's the one gets what he wants."

"I'm beginning to realize that."

"Anyways, next I knowed, we was man and wife, livin over on the mountain. Just like that.

"Those first years I was more scared of him than anything else, at least after the shine wore off him. And that come off quick enough. He weren't no knight in shining armor. Not by a long shot. I guess I found that out right off the bat. That is, right after he knew he'd got what he was after." Her voice trailed off, and they sat in silence, awhile.

"There was his father, too, and he's a bad one. He's tough too, and a little strange, like he's twisted, somehow, like he's proud of having gotten away with whatever it was he done that was bad enough to make him proud of it in the first place. That make any sense? They're both like that, proud to be bad. And, of course, I hadn't known nothing much about those goings on, none of that. Or just enough to think Paul was a sexy outlaw." She laughed, wanly. "God what a kid can be drawn to. Until I got there and saw too much of everything all at the same time. You can't believe what I didn't know when I decided to marry that man. How in the world...?

"And I was scared of them both and then Paul took to hitting me now and again. He'd black my eye and then he'd be so sorry and swear he'd never do it again."

"Another old story, isn't it?" Jim said.

"Yes, it is. Old as mud," she said. "But the strange thing, you know, is I think it got a little bit better after that, because now at least I had the bruises, you know, on my own body, something he couldn't have, something that was mine in the middle of all that fightin and badness." She touched the bruise on her eye.

"I guess that sounds pretty weird," she said.

"I don't know," he said. "Maybe not."

They sat in long silence, looking at one another. Jim felt good, comfortable being with this woman, who had vouchsafed him so much of her past, in spite of what he had sensed was her deep sense of privacy. *Or is it shame?* But he knew he didn't find her the least bit shameful, didn't even, he realized, think of her as a victim. She seemed to him too thoughtful for either, probing, the way she did, her own history, choices, mistakes, or whatever they were. *She's certainly not "in denial."* Maybe the opposite. Maybe she's too aware.

After a time, he said, "You know what you said about the bruises? About feeling they were yours, and so it made things better, somehow."

"Yeah," she said. "Kind of sick, I know."

"No," he said. "Listen. It reminds me of something, something that happened when I was a kid. Something that makes me think I understand what you're saying. And maybe it has something to do with me, too. You know, this family thing, this search."

"Yes," she said in a voice that was neither an assertion nor a question.

"There was a man who lived in my neighborhood. When I was a kid. Everyone called him 'the artist.'"

"The artist?"

"He was real painter, you know? Quite a good one, it turns out. But I didn't know anything about that, then. I mean, I was a kid. I didn't know what he did. Just everyone called him that. To a kid, it was more like a flavor: 'the artist,' like you might say, 'the madman,' or 'the amputee.' Or 'the saint.' It was evocative. So I held him in a certain awe, even though I knew absolutely nothing about what it meant—the *artist*. And he was old, you know. An older man."

"Not all that old, really?" Leela said.

"Old to us, to us kids," Jim said. "And he lived by himself and that made him older. Even more sense of atmosphere around him, you know? That solitary quality that a kid can't understand, know anything about. Kids don't know what solitary means, do they?"

"No. Kids are always running in packs," she said. "Or bossin one another around. I was a bossy kid, can you imagine?"

"Or kids are—some part of them, anyway—still parts of their parents?" he said. "Kids can't understand solitude because they're always connected to those folks. Don't you think? Not even disconnected enough to be really 'me,' or 'myself,' yet. Are they?"

"That's right," she said.

"Anyway, there he was," Jim continued. "The artist. Well, I guess his wife had died a little before I was born. And there he was, in a big old gray house with yellow shutters. Lots of trees around it. Evergreens, like hemlocks or something. They had that quiet darkness about them, you know? Like it was stiller under those trees than anywhere else in the world. And then the big empty house, in the middle of it.

"He had a daughter, and you'd see her there, once in a while. I was still young enough that this didn't make sense to me, either. Because she was a grown woman. She seemed old, too, to me— as old as he was. So she couldn't be 'a daughter,' you know, not like any regular daughter. Because a daughter would be a kid, living with her parents. Not an older woman, all grown up, like him. That didn't make any sense at all. And so she just became 'the daughter,' the same way he was 'the artist.' You know?"

"I think I know. It's funny, isn't it?" Leela said. "She was probably thirty, or something, and that was enough. She's thirty, he's fifty-five, that'd put them about the same age for an eight-year-old, wouldn't it? Older'n tar."

"Yes," Jim said. "And they would argue. She'd be on a visit, and you'd go by that house, and they'd be sitting outside on wood chairs, around a little garden table, all surrounded by those dark, somber trees. And they'd be angry and talking at each other, as if the words were stones, missiles of some kind. They would argue, rocking back and forth in those chairs—I can see them now—as though they were dodging the words, then leaning forward and throwing some back."

"Scary."

"Yes. Strange and frightening. I think of them and that's how I see them: out there under those damn trees, turning and rolling in their seats, ducking each other's shouts, and hurling more anger out, back and forth, swaying and bobbing. God. It was awful."

"I wonder why they were so angry," Leela said. "Or why would she come to visit him and just yell at him." She mused a moment. "Well, I guess there's people who'll do that," she said. "Families, especially. Here comes Aunt Ruth for a visit and all she wants to do is argue with Uncle Claude about how many chickens they had back home. You know? You think about it, it aint really so uncommon, is it?"

"Well, now, she stopped coming," Jim said. "And, of course, I didn't think anything about it until I heard someone—one of my parents, no doubt—say she had killed herself."

"My goodness."

"Yes. She had hanged herself. People will talk about something like that in front of a kid, you know, without even thinking twice. They'd never tell you that Aunt Ruth screwed the milkman—sorry—anything like that. But 'the daughter hanged herself,' they'll just give you that, right between the eyes."

"It frightened you," she said.

"I don't know. I can't recall. I don't think it was fright. Shock, I guess. Yes. I was shocked."

"Stood up."

"That's how you would say it, isn't it? I think it made the whole anomalous thing seem even more outlandish. I mean, 'daughters' didn't die, much less kill themselves, you know? So now he wasn't just 'the artist,' or even 'the artist who lives alone.' He was 'the artist whose daughter had killed herself,' like you'd say, 'the madman who thought he was Isaiah,' or 'the amputee who was wounded in the war.' Something like that."

"Yes." Leela was watching Jim, as though she were seeing the story in his eyes, rather than listening, hearing him say it.

"But that's not the thing I wanted to tell you about," he said. "Because I learned this much later. I couldn't have learned it at the time, even if someone had talked about it. They probably did, in fact, because it was my mother who told me about it later, after the artist died. After it was all done and he had squeezed himself to death, in a manner of speaking."

"What? What did you say?"

"Wait," he said. "You have to hear this part first. You see, she had killed herself, but she had done it, arranged it, to be a tableau, exactly like a painting he had done. Several years before, he'd painted a woman sitting, nude, by a table. A glass of wine on the table next to the figure, an open bottle. Small vase of flowers."

"This is the painting?" she asked.

"That's right. And the daughter took a hotel room and brought in a bottle of wine and the flowers—set it all up. She poured out a glass of wine, took off all her clothes, and swallowed the pills. And then she must have arranged herself in the chair, just right. Just like her father's painting."

"She killed herself to look like the painting?"

"Right down to the same kind of flowers."

"Good Lord."

They sat in silence a moment. Leela was still watching Jim's eyes, still with that attitude of looking at the story rather than hearing it.

"So the wife was dead, and the daughter had killed herself, that way, and now the artist started to close up the house," Jim said. "It was a big old house, and you'd come by one day and the shutters would be closed on one of the upstairs windows. And it turns out he had closed up that room. Sealed it shut. And then, a month later, maybe, you'd see another set of shutters closed. And it meant he'd closed off another room. You see?"

"Wait a minute," Leela said. "How did you know he'd closed them? I mean, the rooms themselves?"

"They found them that way. Wait, and I'll tell you."

"Found them?"

"So it went on that way," he continued, as though she hadn't spoken. "Every now and again, you'd see the shutters locked up, and he'd have closed another one. So gradually, every month or so, he'd shrink up his living space. You see? So, eventually, he just had a bedroom and the parlor and the kitchen, say. Then, a month later, just the bedroom and the kitchen."

"And then he died, I bet."

"He died. They found him in a front hall closet—the coat closet. He had covered himself in blotches of paint, and, he, too, had overdosed on pills. And they found they had to pry open the doors into the rooms, one at a time. He had nailed them shut. And each room had been painted."

"Painted?"

"Painted, in swirls of gummy, dark colors—browns and purples and blues—like some terrible bruise. I saw it myself: everybody went to look. And not only the walls. Ceilings, furniture, floors, everything, in this clotted contusion of color. Everything."

"So he had spent the month, each time, painting it," she said. "And when he finished a room, he nailed it up? And painted himself into a corner, I guess. I'm sorry. I'm not tryin to joke around."

"Well, why not?" he asked her. "What else was it but a joke? I mean, what was the point of all that? Jesus Christ."

"Sometimes, maybe, there's a kind of sadness—or maybe it's outrage—so deep you can only color it and close it up," she said.

"I don't understand that," he said.

"No. Who would?" she said. "Maybe that's the reason he had to do it. Isn't it?"

Jim shook his head.

"Isn't it?" she said.

***

Lindee awoke early, feeling achy and out of sorts. It was typical for her to sleep late, and she didn't feel right. She slid across to snuggle into Trapper and found an empty bed. This jerked her awake and she sat up straight, feeling her heart begin to race. Where was he? She had fully expected that he would return during the night, slip into bed without awakening her, and be here this morning.

She calmed herself thinking, *Paul said he was busy.* Then she remembered that Paul had thrown her around yesterday—which explained her aches—and had forced from her the story of Trapper's freelance operation.

"My God," she said, really frightened, now. Maybe Paul had gone straight from this bed to find Trapper. And maybe hurt him. She looked at her arm and saw the bruised finger marks, ran her hand across her scalp, feeling the burn where Paul had yanked her hair.

"Mommy," came the small voice from the hallway.

"You get yourself some OJ," she said. "Mommie's busy." Caroline began to whimper, but, oddly, Lindee didn't feel anger, didn't feel that insistent urge to hit the girl. Instead, she called her daughter into the room and hugged her, smothering the little girl's naked body in her bare breasts. "I'll get you some breakfast, honey," she said. "In just a minute."

Lindee got up and grabbed the baggy shirt hanging from her dresser knob, throwing it on. "Where in the hell is Trapper?" she said.

"Is Trapper gone?" came Caroline's small, worried voice.

Lindee turned and looked at her daughter, feeling an overwhelming sadness.

"Honey," she said, "I don't know."

She took a deep breath, trying to calm herself, then remembered suddenly that she could call him, get him on his cell phone, maybe, and find out where he was. She threw herself across the bed, grabbing the phone, then hesitating as she wondered, *What if he don't answer?* Still, she resolutely pushed the button.

He answered on the third ring, sounding strange, saying something like *Mello*.

"You okay, Trap?" she said, relieved at least to hear his voice.

"I'm beat up a mite," he said. It sounded more like *meat up a mite*. "A whole mite," he added.

"Beat up?" she said. "Who beat you up?"

"Who in hell you think?" he managed to say.

"Paul?" she said.

"That'd be the man," he said. "He kindly sucker punched me with a beer bottle. Left me swimmin in the sawdust."

She relaxed, because he sounded like the old Trapper, even if he was hurt. He didn't sound scared, didn't sound defeated, the way he had sometimes become recently. She hadn't been able to understand this sudden weakness. Trapper had always been a tough, independent man, who never let too much bother him because he'd carried himself with that confidence that he could manage most anything. But recently, since he'd worked for Paul Morelock, he'd become timid, jumpy, even kind of whiny. Not like the Trapper who had picked her and Caroline up out of the Roalton bar and made them into a family, set her to dreaming of a real place.

"Did he catch up with you last night?" she said, feeling guilty about giving in to Paul's violence, telling him what Trapper was up to.

"Last night?" Trapper said. "Hell no, not last night. If he'd done this last night I'd still be down dead, a bleedin into the pillow. No, hon. He cracked me day before. Over here at Pink's. I been here ever since."

So Paul had already assaulted Trapper when he was screwing her in this bed. Already knew what was going on when he'd yanked her by the hair hard enough to make her confess something he didn't even need to hear.

"The sonofabitch," she said. "The dirty sonofabitch."

"Best not let him hear you call him that," said Trapper. "He'll take a swipe at you, too."

"He already done that," she said. "The sonofabitch."

"Jesus," Trapper said. "Honey, we oughten't to have got ourselves into this without knowin what we was doing." He sighed loudly. "But I tell you what," he said. "I'm tired of kissin that feller's ass, tired of kneelin down to him ever time he decides it's time to strut some. I'm a going to get him."

"Wait, Trapper," she said. "Hold on." She liked this return of bravado on his part, felt maybe the beating had been what he needed, had brought out the toughness that had somehow gone into hiding around Paul Morelock. But Trapper didn't know what else was going on, and he needed to.

"They's some men been snoopin around down here. That newspaper feller, Sam Lofton. And another one. A stranger. Didn't like what he saw, here, I reckon. I think they might be tryin to find out about the dealin, too. I think we need to be a mite careful."

There was a long pause on the line.

"You still there?" she said.

"Yeah," he said. "I'm just thinkin. Maybe we could use that newspaper feller, fill him in on Paul Morelock. Maybe get some money out of it. That'd show the dirty bastard."

"Be careful, now, Trapper," she said, worried again. "Don't get off on a crazy rail."

"That'd show the sonofabitch," Trapper said.

"I can't quite figure the accent out," Jim said. "You and Sam, you have such soft, almost gentle sounds. And then some others, they sound harsh, mean. It's like there's two different accents."

"Snakes and bears," she said. "Thin and mean or soft and round."

"Yeah. That's it. Like when you say my name, it sounds kind of like *Jam*. And then, when somebody else..."

"A snake."

"Yeas. When a snake says it, it sounds like *Jee-yem*. More like a sneer."

"Like a snake," she said. "Snakes and bears."

"You already know this."

"Of course I know it." She touched his arm. "Why in the world wouldn't I know it? Born and bred in this holler?" When she took her hand away, he felt the afterglow. He realized he wanted her to touch him again. "Trouble is, it don't always work."

"How's that?"

"I thought I was marryin' a bear. Everybody else in the damn family talked like a snake, called me *Leeyel*. And he said *Leelar*. Like a bear."

"A snake in bear's clothing?" he said.

"I reckon," she said, sadly.

"That's the trouble with character traits, you know that?" he said. "Once someone finds out you believe in him: the eyes are the windows of the soul, or whatever. Once a snake gets hold of that information, he knows just exactly how to make you believe in him. A snake in bear's clothing. Like once a liar learns that people believe a firm handshake means forthrightness and honesty, he's going to develop a firm handshake. Eye contact, that sort of thing. Some honest people may not always make eye contact, but a con man is sure to, once he knows you rely on it to judge honesty. Right?"

She didn't reply, and, when he felt her shoulder make a slight shudder, he turned and realized she'd been crying, silent tears running down her cheeks, slowly, like the last rain on a leaf. He felt a flush of regret and guilt, knowing he'd talked on, right through her pain, like a careless boy tearing the leaf from the branch, shredding its slick skin.

"I'm sorry, Leela. Jesus. I didn't mean to make you unhappy. Jesus."

She turned her face toward him, the curve of her cheek bruised and wet, like fallen fruit—a peach dropped into the dew.

This time he touched her. He reached up and brushed back her dark hair, then brought his fingertips to the hurt skin, smoothing away tears, the gentlest of touches, like kissing a child, trying to make it better.

"How do people get into these situations?" Jim asked, later. "You know, regular people, like you and me. You know." Leela was looking at him, her eyes narrowed.

"Regular people?" she said. "Is there some difference? I mean do you think there's some kinds of people who just naturally ought to be in these, these things? And then there's people like you and me who oughten't, but who got mixed in, somehow, and so here we are, too? With them other people?"

"That's not what I mean," he said. "You know that."

"I don't know it," she said. "No. I don't. Because I think it is what you mean. I think it's the way you folks all mean it. That there may be some people down here that are regular, as you call them, but most, most belong here, belong in bein poor and gettin hurt, beatin each other up. That is what you mean."

They stared at each other, silent. She was angry, but, he realized, she'd spoken out at him for the first time, shown something she wouldn't show most people. And so he felt oddly warmed, comforted by her accusation because she had at least felt close enough to accuse him. *Anger, too, means letting down some sort of barrier, doesn't it?* So the indictment stung him, but the fact of it warmed him, somehow.

"Look," he said, "you may be right. There may be some sort of conditioning that makes me lump people into groups—the ones I don't know are not the 'regular' ones, I guess. And I know you, and so it doesn't seem you should be one of those folks that's involved in this, this sort of marriage, where you get beaten up all the time. You see?"

"Nobody belongs where I am," she said.

"And yet you keep going back."

"Kept." She leaned forward and tapped his knee with her small hand. "I aint going back."

"Are you certain of that?" he said. The day was waning, the room growing dim as the sun brushed over the mountain wall to the west. *I was right about that. Daylight doesn't last long down in this hollow. Where, up on the hilltops, it's broad sunshine for hours, yet.*

"I don't know," she said. She looked down at her hands. "I want to tell you about something. Maybe something that has to do with this. Why I've got involved in an abusive relationship, like they say. Why it feels like such a trap, but it feels like I can't change it, like it's where I'm supposed to be."

He got up and reached for the light switch.

"No," she said. "Leave it be." He sat, this time, on the couch, next to her. He felt her take a deep breath, hold it, then release a sigh.

"When I was a girl," she said, "my daddy was everything to me. He made me feel as if the whole world was nothing but a big gift to me, you know? As though he had arranged it all and made sure it would be just right for me. He was like Sam, funny and easygoing, and he never seemed to take anything seriously. But that didn't make me feel silly or foolish, you know? It was more like he was so sure everything was going to be right that he could just be easy about it all. And that made me feel easy, too." She paused a moment. He looked at her profile, the strong forehead, the longish nose, the soft bright eyes, a circle of intelligence floating in the senseless depth of the indigo bruise. She turned and met his glance for a moment, then looked away, back into her own time.

"My daddy used to take us with him to the dump. You know, to take the trash to the dump site. It wasn't a real dump: there wasn't anything like that around here, then. Nothing with a fence, and rules and all that. We didn't have that. We just had a bend up the road, where didn't anybody live, where everybody had just decided we was going to throw our trash.

"We loved going up there with Daddy, to throw that stuff over the hill. We loved watchin it drop over the side and roll down over everything. And Daddy'd always say, 'Keep your eyes peeled for a bear. Them bears'll come right up here to munch them some nice sweet garbage.' And we'd giggle and squirm. And one day we went up, just me and Daddy, for some reason. None of my brothers and sisters, just us two. And Daddy grabs me by the shoulder and he kindly hisses, 'Looky there, Leelie! Looky yonder!' And down the holler, away down the slope, there's an ole black bear, sure enough, a nosin around the pile, and swayin back and forth, the way they'll do. I was so excited, I thought I was going to cry. And I remember hugging onto Daddy, my little fist squeezing at his shirt, and leaning across him to see out the truck window and watching that shamblin ole bear. And every time that critter'd make a step, Daddy'd say, 'Look now! Looky now!' And I think I believed that my daddy had arranged all that just for me. Like he'd called that bear up and said, 'Get on up to the dump, so I can fetch Leelie up to look at you.'"

"And?" Jim prodded, after a long moment.

"And then it all went away. Just like that." She snapped her fingers weakly and looked at him, smiling wanly. "Kaboom."

"What happened?" he said.

"He died, for one," she said. She paused and knitted her fingers, wrestling with them. "But that wasn't all of it. Because he had a friend, a man, a feller in the church that everybody said was just a wonderful feller, and *so good with kids*, they'd say. And Daddy, he sent me down to the church to be in a bible group with some kids, and this man." She looked at her hands, as though the wrestling fingers weren't her own, as though she'd just now noticed them, there in her lap, and now she was going to study them.

"He molested you," said Jim.

She nodded. "For a good long time."

He reached tentatively, a little awkwardly, toward her, resting his hand on her back, running a small circle on the soft cotton shirt, trying to comfort. "I'm sorry," he said.

"It's such a typical story," she said, "It's almost like a dirty joke. The Sunday school man who's so good with kids. And then it turns out he's just wantin to get on em. So no wonder he's so good with em; he's dyin to be around them so he can put his hand…" She shook her head.

"So it sounds just stupid when you say it out loud," she said. "But, you see, the terrible thing wasn't so much this man and his big hands, or his wet lips."

"Bad enough," said Jim.

"Bad enough, sure," she said. "But the worst was really that Daddy had been wrong, you see? And I found out just like that. Kaboom. The world wasn't so warm and easy and kind, after all, was it? And Daddy's own friend, as though, this time it wasn't that he'd called up to set up something nice for me, you know? This time it was horror. And I couldn't understand it. The treachery, you know? I couldn't bear it. And then he went and died and I couldn't even ask him, accuse him, tell him he was wrong about the world. And about me."

"I'm sorry," he said, again. "I'm sorry you felt so betrayed."

She laughed. "Felt? I *was* betrayed. And so I spent my life trying to find out which father I had, the wonderful man who made me feel so important and safe, the man who offered me this warm, kind world, or the other one: the man who sent me to the church, where his friend did those things to me. And the fact that I'd believed in the first Daddy made the thing even more terrible. Because, you see, I had no protection, no way to mistrust anybody. And then Daddy was gone, so I couldn't never figure out which was which. And I couldn't go back to him and say, *What happened? Why did everything just go so wrong?* It was like I'd had my pocket picked or been a part of some con-man operation. Do you understand?"

"Oh yes," he said. "I think I do. Because my Daddy did something like that to me. Only I didn't know it until I'd already turned out the way I am. And here I am looking for a mother who never existed, and, I suppose, for a little boy who never was, either."

"I'm sorry, too," she said.

So she was right, he realized. It was the typical story: the abused child becoming entrapped in abuse relationships. The wounded girl finding a man who would control her, wound her again because that might give her another opportunity to figure out the thing. Or because she felt she deserved this sort of thing—wasn't that a part of it, too? *If my Dad sent me to this man for abuse it must be because I failed him, somehow, must be that this is what is supposed to happen to me.* Was that a part of it? He thought so. But he wondered why it felt so familiar to him, who had never been molested, never felt those big hands controlling him, taking something from him. Nothing like that. *Only the betrayal. And I wasn't even around for that.*

They huddled at the table as if they'd been caught in a downpour, their shoulders hunched, heads down, sitting shoulder to shoulder, musing.

After lunch, they sat in the office with Sam while he pasted up the week's issue.

"Obits and lost dogs," he said, bending over the big spread of paper, moving Xerox copies of stories around, arranging and rearranging. "You know, if this was a real newspaper, we'd be doing this on the computer. I got the god damn computer. What I don't have is the real paper." He made another switch and stood back, looking at the page. "Obits and lost dogs. No wonder I drink too much."

"So what do we have so far on Jim's momma?" said Leela. "Can you talk while you paste?"

"Honey, I could feed the monkey and let him do this," Sam said. "Sure."

"So where are we?"

"Well, we think he's a Morelock from up on Shaleen. That would make him a close relation to your loving husband, god help him. And we know they's two Morelocks up there: your husband Paul, and his daddy, Johns Morelock. And Johns is the son of Jessum Morelock who was son to old Cuddy. I got that much from Glen. But she never heard of no Allie Morelock. So we got missing folks up on the creek, somewheres. There's a missing link, somewheres."

"Wait. That's not the only Morelocks up thataway," said Leela.

"What?" said Sam. "You know of some others?"

They were interrupted by a soft knock on the door.

"Who in the world?" said Sam.

"I'll get it," Leela said.

She opened the door to Lindee Macleen. The two women stood, silently facing each other, for a long moment. They were a study in contrasts, the slack, heavy-breasted Lindee and the thin, delicately-framed Leela, the younger one looking used and weary, while Leela looked taut and youthful. But the two shared one salient feature: each had bruises on her face. Though neither knew it, the bruises in both cases had been made by the hands of Paul Morelock.

"Is the newspaper man here? Sam Lofton?" Lindee asked.

"Come on in," said Leela, stepping back to afford entrance to the younger woman.

"Well I be damned," said Sam, when Lindee entered the room. "The motel redecorator, aint it?"

"I'm Lindee Macleen." Her voice was hesitant, obviously nervous.

"Did you drop a hammer on your face?" Sam said. He looked toward Leela. "From the looks of it, sis, you might be suited to the motel refurbishin business, your own self."

"Shut up, Sam," said Leela.

"Can I speak to you about something?" Lindee said.

"Shoot," said Sam.

"I'd rather talk to you in private," she said. "It's kindly a private matter."

"That's all right," said Leela. "Come on, Jim. Let's us go for a walk."

It was a bright day, and they walked slowly down what Leela called "East Drag," one of two main streets. The other was the "West Drag," she explained.

"I walked down the West Drag the other day," said Jim. "It was a pleasant enough walk I suppose. But, toward the end, I guess it got to be a drag."

Leela smiled at the feeble witticism.

"Funny thing," said Jim. "The sunshine makes these mountains look even darker, doesn't it?"

"They're always dark," Leela said. "On overcast days, they look like big empty spots, like huge caves. And when it's sunny, they seem to bulge outward, like a dark storm front coming up. See?"

"Yes. I see," Jim said. "You learn that in old instruments, the inlay and what they call the purfling. Ornamentation. If you want to make something appear really dark, you frame it in brightness. And the other way around. Sometimes I feel like these mountains are the perfect setting out of which I ought to have come. Like I'm suited to this place. Then, other times, it feels like the most foreign thing in the world, like I could never so much as get close to this place. As if I'm trying to walk through a wall."

"Well, maybe that's the way it is," Leela said. "For everybody. Because there's times, at least for me, when I feel perfectly comfortable with who I am. Inside, you know? And then I'll wake up sometimes and wonder, *who is this girl*? And I couldn't be more of a stranger if I spoke Lithuanian to myself. So maybe it ain't the mountains at all. Maybe it's just you."

"Still," Jim said. "The mountains sure provide the appropriate backdrop for that kind of thinking, don't they?"

"I reckon," she said.

They walked along in silence, passing a drug store and a small brick office building. Leela took his arm. "Let's cross to the sunny side," she said, and they trotted across the street, together. He felt the small swell of her breast against his arm. *She doesn't seem foreign to me, at all. Not at all.* He found it difficult to believe that this woman lived away up in the deep mountains among a brawling, violent family, moonshiners and fighters.

"What do you know about Paul Morelock's family?" Jim said.

"Not a lot," Leela said. "His father lives up there with us. He calls his father 'Pawp.'"

"You were saying they weren't the only ones up there."

"No. There's somebody named 'Pawper,' or 'PawPawper.' I've never met him, but Paul or his father, they go up to see him quite a bit. And someone they usually call 'the woman.' She's up there, too."

"Allie?" Jim asked eagerly. "Or Allison? Maybe?"

"No," Leela said, thoughtfully. "No. It's Evelyn, I think. Something like that. I think I remember because I had had an aunt named Evelyn. Anyway, it aint Allie. But they talk about taking pills up to her. And Paul's brother. Pierot. He's up there a lot."

"Go up?" said Jim.

"That's what they say. They'll say, 'Let's go up to Pawper's.' That's all I know. They never let me go."

"Up?" said Jim, again. Then he checked himself. "I guess that doesn't mean anything, does it? I've said that, too: 'I'm going up to the store.'"

"It means something around here," said Leela. "Round here, the two cardinal points are 'up' and 'down.' If they're 'going up' to see Pawper, you can be sure they're going up."

"You mean further up in the mountains?"

"That's what I mean," said Leela.

"Do you know anything about Hamptons and Morelocks? The feud? Know if these fellows are directly related to those

Morelocks?"

"Oh," Leela said, "Sure. They're from the same Morelocks. Sure."

Later that evening, they sat with Sam in the office. He wouldn't tell them about the young woman's visit, citing "professional discretion," and winking. Then Leela repeated what she'd told Jim, about the other Morelock man, "Pawper," up on the mountain. And the woman. Sam perked up at this, but Jim shook his head.

"No. It's not Allison Morelock. Her name is Evelyn, Leela says."

Sam laughed dryly. "Well that was easy enough to find out. I reckon I should've asked little sister instead of snoopin around in the official records. Saves time to have a sister married to one of them bastards."

"Sam," Leela complained.

"Sorry, sis."

"Anyway, I think it's Evelyn. Something like that," Leela said. "You think maybe she could be a sister of Allison? She might know something, anyway."

"How do you know they're from the Shaleen Creek Morelocks?" said Jim.

"Paul's father talks about the feud, sometimes as if it was goin on today. He's mighty proud of something he did himself."

"Couldn't be in the feud," said Sam. "That was back in the twenties, before Johns Morelock was even a bad idea."

"Well, I don't know," said Leela. "All I know is the old man—Paul's father—he talks when he's drunk about having finished off the damn Hamptons and nobody'll ever know how. He and his Pawp."

"Wait," said Jim, "I thought he was Pawp."

"They both are," said Leela. "He's Paul's Pawp, but he's got a Pawp, too. Right?"

"Pawper," said Jim. "Pawper, or Pawpawper, that's got to be

Paul's grandfather, Johns's Pawp. So Johns is Paul's Pawp and granddaddy is Johns's Pawp. Granddaddy would be Jessum Morelock, according to Glen. Right?"

"Christ, I need a drink," said Sam.

"So, listen," said Jim. "If they're Shaleen Morelocks, and Grandpa is alive, and they go up to see him…"

"Maybe they're going to Shaleen Prong?" said Leela.

They looked at each other. Sam was behind the desk, pouring stumpblower from the big jug into a smaller pint jar.

"Okay," Sam said. "Let's you and me go up to Shaleen."

"I've got a apartment appointment," said Leela, sadly. "I wish I could go."

Jim touched her shoulder. "Me too," he said.

"We'll bring you a arrowhead," said Sam, heading for the door.

SEVEN

They left at dawn the next day, pulling out of town and onto a narrow, two-lane blacktop that rose through the ring of mountains to the south. Again Jim watched as the foliage changed seasons—*time travel*, he had called it—the leaves gradually turning into bright washes of autumn color as they neared the gap at the first ridge. They descended briefly into a hollow, then rose again, twisting around the flank of the big mountain. They turned again and dropped precipitously into a broader cove where big streams fell off the mountainside into a broiling, rocky river, as the truck turned again, following the contour, dipping into the hollows carved out by each stream, then bulging outward, vertiginously, across the rounded flank of the mountain, then back in again, into a dark, humid ravine. At the fifth of these stream beds, Sam pulled the truck off the road. Jim had no firm idea how long they'd been driving. Though he felt it had been an hour or so, it had probably been less. The curves and swooping dips had seemed to stretch out the time until it had become unknowable, like a long, passionate scolding in a language you didn't understand.

"Shaleen Crick," Sam said, pointing to the waterfall plunging off the rock ledge. "They's a track runs up here somewheres. The bottom leg of that letter E. Let's us get out and have a look."

Jim felt the cool air wafting from the falls and saw the deep green pool where the water landed, sending up a turbling swell of white bubbles. The noise from the fall pulsed, as though he were alternately pressing his ears closed and open, the way he would sometimes do when he was a child, listening to the air rush and halt, rush and halt.

"Looks like a nice swimming hole," he shouted at Sam, as they worked their way down the slope from the road, toward the jumbling water.

"You want to freeze the fambly jewels, you might like it," Sam yelled back. "That water's colder than Jesus's pecker. Though I reckon kids will jump into any water they can find, sometime or another. Not me, buddy."

Once they'd reached stream level, by the pool, the sound seemed to muffle itself, and the light to fade, so they walked in strange, quiet shadows. They skirted below the pool and found a row of rocks across which they wavered and stepped, crossing the stream where it narrowed and caught into the transverse current of the falling river. Across, they scrambled up rocky banks and stood facing a narrow, grassy space, about ten feet across and running in switches up the steep, humped hill. Parallel muddy lines, tire ruts, ran a foot or so in from each side, announcing that this was, indeed, a roadway, or at least a way.

"There she is," said Sam. "Somebody's been up here, anyways. Them ruts is fresh enough." He glanced around at the dark woods. "So they's got to be a bridge, or a ford. Maybe we can follow this track all the way up to the prong. Specially if somebody's already done it a few times. Let's follow this back to the road, and we'll get the truck and give her a try, what you say?"

Fifteen minutes later, they were turning the truck to face an exiguous wooden bridge that leaned shakily on five or ten props, as it spanned the rocks and crashing water just below the confluence of Shaleen Creek.

"I've got to lock the hubs," said Sam, opening his door.

"You sure that bridge will hold us?" Jim said.

"Held them," said Sam stepping down and moving forward to the wheels. He bent to the hubs, raising his voice against the distance and the spill of water. "Whoever they was, they been across here more than a few times, to judge by them ruts. Held them, it ought to hold us, right?"

Jim didn't answer. Ahead, the track seemed to disappear into undergrowth of locust and sassafras. He knew it would rise very steeply, and presumed it would enter into real woodland, oak and shag bark, all of it dark and steep, a landscape he didn't know. He felt at once drawn and repelled by the depth and the furious growth, the grape vine and maple already turning toward high autumn, as though the landscape, the mountain, the cold, impetuous water, were flowing into his own deepest core, a place he longed to find and feared to see. *Am I going up here to confront myself? Or to find the place where I'm forbidden: the place that abandoned me, so that it can never embrace me again, because I'm not the one it produced, because I have come to be another? Grown up without the embrace, or the place. On my own.*

"What did you say?" asked Sam, climbing back into his seat. He didn't wait for an answer, shifting the small lever into "4-WHEEL-LO" and setting the truck onto the bridge at a slow roll.

The bridge groaned and seemed to settle as the truck snailed across, Jim peering out on the water rushing below, while Sam leaned forward, gripping the wheel, as though this were a race car speeding toward the sharp corner of a high-banked asphalt, and not a dilapidated truck, crawling no faster than a man would, across a propped and rigged plank-mended bridge, toward the deep, dark red ruts that disappeared up the far slope, like parallel scars, blooded and raw, rising into an oblivion of rock and vegetation.

"Jesus," Jim breathed.

"We're fixin to get up into the woods, now," said Sam. "This here, this is just the suburbs, kindly. A half hour and, boys, we'll be up on the mountain, right sure. Up with the buzzards and the bears, kindly." He turned and winked.

Ten minutes further, at a huge granite outcrop, the track switched back and rose diagonally above itself into a forest of black balsams, the pebbly trunks standing at even intervals, each tree ringed on its trunk with strange parallel bands, no undergrowth beneath, but only a thick bed of needles, lying on the haunch of the mountain like the coarse hair of some animal, swathed in steamy haze, as if the ground were warm and breathing. The regularity of the trees, spaced in rows, each reaching naked, circled trunks to the high, darkneedled canopy, was as unnerving as the chaos of undergrowth they'd emerged from.

"These are Plotts, they call them," said Sam. "You run into spreads like these all over this side of the county. This here's a plantation, put in by some timber company after the federals bought out the land. After it had gone to seed when the earlier clear cuts—like the Hampton and Morelock timber—played out. This is all federal land. So the new timber companies ripped out every damned thing around here and replanted in softwood, after they'd bought into the paper mills. Pulpwood. They'd cut it and pulp it right on the spot. Then they decided it weren't even worth the trouble to cut. Let it all go back to the government. These big old dark pines just kindly grew on up on their own. They wasn't supposed to: they ringed em to make em spread and branch—so they could bring in a chipper and turn em all into teeny little pieces—but once they walked away from their own paper-tree farm, I reckon the balsams just grew up the way they was a going to."

"Eerie," said Jim.

"I went out to write a story on a burned-out farm, a long time back. The tobacco still standin in the field, and the house three-quarter burned and still falling into itself. You know? And five years later, I was back up that way for somethin else. And they's still tobaccy out in that field, but the farm, well, they aint a sign of it. No folks, no house, no barn. Just rows of tobacco, all lined out like they had been. But too big. Great big yaller leaves, the size of a man. Overgrowed, somehow. Because it'd been let go. Like these balsams."

"Abandoned." Jim said.

"I reckon. Government bought the land and gave it to the companies to plant trees on. Nowadays, they're doin it all over again, giving away timber. You think a forest ranger is a feller that nurtures the trees, don't you? Like a good parent? But you know what he does? He gives em away. Figure that out. But these here balsams I reckon are too far back up the hills for anyone to take the bother to cut them out again. Just as well."

The truck crested a rise and moved beyond the balsams, leveling and rejoining the stream, now brushing its way through dense thickets of laurel and rhododendron, the branches screeching and whining on the truck's windows, nothing in sight but more thicket.

"Not far, now, I'd say," Sam said. "We ought to open out pretty soon. Let's see that map."

He let go of the wheel, allowing the truck to wallow along, still rising, steered by the vegetation that had closed in tight, now, shoving against the cab, crashing like hard rain, so that they had to close the windows, the steering wheel jerking and stuttering, back and forth. Sam opened out the map and traced his finger along the hyphenated track, up into the huge green that meant Forest Service property, and on into a section where the contours widened. "See here?" he said. "This broad spot—we're just coming into it—this here is the wide place in the mountain, where you might could put up a sawmill, maybe a few houses. Let's hope it aint all scrubbers like this. They's got to be an old narrow-gauge track, or at least a sledge track in here somewheres, too, to drag the finished lumber out. Likely it's part of the road, now. The trail."

Jim thought of the tire ruts they'd followed into the mountain. "I'm not sure I'm any too happy about meeting anyone up here," he said. He peered vainly out the window, seeing nothing but the tangles and leaves of laurel, inches away.

"Likely if they's anyone here, they'll be a heap less eager to meet you than you them," Sam said, resuming his grip on the yawing steering wheel. "Besides, I aint worried. If anybody tries to go after me, all I got to do is push you out the door for bait and head this truck the hell down the mountain." He looked across at Jim. "Just kiddin, cousin," he said.

"That's reassuring," said Jim. He was silent a moment and the truck screeched and screed blindly along, through the thicket. The lack of viewpoint made it seem as though the men, the vehicle, were standing still, as though the bushes were moving, being drawn by, scraping their way along the sides of the static truck. He couldn't have said how long they'd been riding since Sam had turned the hubs. It seemed like days, or only moments; he couldn't have said. He thought again of the tire ruts.

"Have you got a gun?" Jim asked.

"What in hell you want with a gun?" said Sam. "You want me to put you outen your misery?"

"I just thought I'd ask," said Jim, feeling a flush of anger at Sam's ironic jesting. "I just thought it might be nice to have a gun with us, up here. I'd guess whoever made those tracks has one. And if we were to run into anybody up here, I just thought my expert mountain guide might have had the sense to bring along some protection."

Sam stopped the truck. When the branches ceased screaming, the silence settled in like deep snow. A fly buzzed somewhere in the cab. Sam turned toward Jim, the seat cushion moaning slightly.

"You think you could shoot a man?" he said, holding Jim's gaze. The fly buzzed raggedly, again. "You think you'd even know how to point a god damn gun?"

"I didn't mean me." Jim's eyes broke away from the stare, looking toward the laurel.

"I reckon you didn't," said Sam, warming. "No, I reckon

not. Because, you know what? Because you don't belong up here. Hell, I don't belong up this far, and I grew up on the base of this goddamn mountain. But you? You?" He shook his head. Now he was angry, too, his face flushed, too. "What are you doing up here, anyway? What do you think you're going to find except what you already know—we already know—that you don't belong here? That this place aint any part of you, nor you it? That you got no business poking around up here, where all there is for you is the sure-fire certainty that you aint anything like it, here, and all you want is for someone who is, or at least is closer to it, to bring up a gun so you might not get shot by the folks you're so eager to find out is your kin? Is that it?"

"You don't understand," Jim said, weakly, still looking out at the glossy, dark green leaves closed-in all around the truck. *Like pack ice. And we've sailed into this arctic, up this cove, until the ice has closed us in and left us all alone in the bubble of this cab, like those half-crazed explorers, huddled in their wooden ship, wondering when the ice will break through the beams, into the cabin, and close them in, forever.*

"You're god damned right I don't understand," Sam said. He revved the engine, the rumbling noise sounding warm and satisfying to both men. The tension seemed to drain off into the surrounding thicket.

"Anyways," Sam said. "Of course I've got a gun. I'm just not crazy enough to let you know where it is." He grabbed Jim by the arm, drawing his attention, and when Jim turned to look at him, Sam gave him a quick wink. "Let's go," he said, screeching the truck further into the enclosing thicket.

Fifteen or so minutes later, the track turned sharply, skewed uphill, and lurched out of the laurel, like a prow breaking the surface of a sea, onto the curving shell of a broad meadow, fringed at its near end by the thick tangles, and at its far end, giving onto an expansive view of the bulking mountain, rising above, fringed, too, with light blue sky and clouds.

Jim opened his window. From some distance came a wheezy,

pulsing sound, half familiar.

"What in hell's that noise?" said Sam.

The tire ruts they'd been following now spread out and separated in arched, parallel pairs, disappearing onto the pale, thin grass, twisting out of sight around big clumps of high-bush blueberries.

"Well, now, she appears to go ever which way," Sam said. He stopped the truck, again. "Let's see. Give me that map."

"Wait," said Jim. "The picture. The photo shows their sawmill tucked into the edge of the mountain. It must be—"

"Yessir," Sam interrupted. "Down to the far end, over the swell and down a bit, into the rise. Good. Where the hell is the creek? Must be runnin' alongside this rise, but the prong, it would come in up ahead, somewheres." He drove straight ahead, out into the clearing, up the slow grassy curve. "Well, who cares? The mill has to have been over this rise and, like you say—"

"Wait," Jim said again, as the truck turned around a copse of high berry and began to speed up. He turned and looked out the back window, toward a markless snarl of undergrowth. "You sure we can find the track again, to get back?"

"What's that?" Sam said, slowing the truck to its walking pace.

"The track," said Jim. "The way out of here. It's blocked out by this thicket. We need to mark it or something, so we can find our way out of this meadow."

Sam stopped the truck and looked back. "You're right," he said. "Jesus. From here, it just looks like a wall of leaves, don't it? Well, I'll go back, tie a bandannar at the opening." He opened the door and hopped out, reaching into his back pocket, pulling out a red handkerchief.

"Don't shoot nobody while I'm gone," he said, heading back down the slow curve of the meadow, disappearing around the copse, toward the fringe of thick tangle.

Jim turned and watched Sam a moment, out the back window,

then straightened and scanned the view ahead. Above, the mountain pushed its uneven knob, black against the bright sky, the fleece of cloud. *Fleece. To fleece: swindle. I wonder why.*

He settled himself, staring vaguely at sky, clouds, knob, feeling the tension of the day relax, feeling himself easing, drifting, *out of the pack ice. Fleece of clouds. Swindle of clouds.*

He was startled suddenly from daydreams by a sharp, metallic knocking at the driver's window, where a tanned, narrow-eyed face peered in at him, tapping the glass with the blue barrels of a shotgun.

The man marched Jim, the shotgun pointed lazily forward, along the rising curve of the meadow, the same way Sam had begun to head the truck. Neither man spoke, the gun jerking in hurry-along gestures every now and again, Jim trying to take care not to stumble on the rocks and sedges they walked through, wondering *where in the hell is Sam?*

When they crested the brow of the meadow, Jim faced the steep knob, the cleared land narrowing into a bowl shape, like a natural amphitheater, toward which the weathered man gestured him. As they walked jerk-legged down the grade, Jim began to make out lumpy metallic shapes scattered around. He saw, as they passed, several galvanized tin tubs, large ones, the grasses growing through jagged holes in their bottoms. They passed a strange wooden structure, like a bookshelf, caved in and leaning crazily into a granite outcrop.

They reached the bottom of the slope where the land leveled into the shallow curve of the bowl. There Jim saw wood, lots of it, piles of rotted sawn planks, mossed and turning to earth, grown through with sedges and briar. They passed a thicket of twisted barrel staves, rusted metal hoops, until, as they entered the rounded scoop of the hollow set into the rising mountain's flank, he could see bigger forms: a long, iron-bound span like a trestle, set onto the ground and running along the bottom, toward the mountain. At the far end of this trestle, a wreck of rusted metal, levers sticking wildly upward, like alien figures, their knobbed heads burled with rust. He saw the flywheel, then the blade, an enormous curve with fangs like shark's teeth, the entire circle cracked in the middle and canted crazily to one side, off its track. They passed a mass of copper tubing, greened with age, and another galvanized tub, this one huge, with high sides, covered at the top, a stovepipe thrusting through the cone shape, and two narrow pipes angling out of the tub's sides.

He saw, too, in the bare ground around the old sawmill, that the tire tracks had reappeared, coalescing into a single track running by the old blade, and further down the hollow, where a large steam boiler chuffed. There the tracks separated again, one set of parallel ruts turning broadly in front of the pulsing engine, the only piece of the old mill still operating, it seemed. *That's what it was. The sound of a locomotive.* From the engine, the track headed to the right, into a narrow cove. The other set of tire tracks ran straight to the left of the old engine, to a muddy turn out in front of a haphazard cabin, more like a lean-to or awning, made of logs and planks, its doorway seeming to open directly into the side of the looming mountain, which rose almost perpendicularly from the ground at the rear of the engine. There was no sign of a vehicle, though it was clear there had been one up here a number of times, either stopping at the strange, dugout cabin, or moving off to whatever was up the hollow to the right.

Somebody does live here, Jim thought, *sure enough,* thinking, then, *where in the hell is Sam?* He realized he was at the sawmill, or the former sawmill, near what must be the confluence of the streams, Shaleen Prong flowing into the main creek. He tried to picture the space on the map, tried to orient himself, but it was no use, beyond confirming what he already knew: the curving meadow, the steep wall of mountain, beyond the bowl-shaped sawmill, where, on one side or another must be the actual juncture of waters. But he couldn't tell where, couldn't hear any flowing and dashing of water, either. And then he realized that his ears were roaring, had been roaring, from his own blood, the fear and effort, the exertion of marching across this place, to the prodding gesture of a gun barrel. So if there were any stream water rushing around here, he'd never have been able to hear it, anyway, for all the chuffing of the engine, and the surge and crash inside himself. And he thought again of the old, Boschean visions of hell, the *devil's ingines*. And he heard Sam's voice, earlier, saying, "You think you could shoot a man?" and, "You think you'd even know how to point a god damn gun?" And, later, saying, "You don't belong here. Don't belong here."

"Fetch you a place to set," the man with the gun finally spoke. Jim turned toward him. He was younger than Jim—perhaps thirty, perhaps not quite—dressed in shaggy overalls, the bottoms of the legs smeared, stained, with mud and sedges. The man spat a mouthful of amber juice onto the toe of one huge, steel-colored leather brogan, rubbing the splashed gob meditatively with the sole of the other boot.

"I don't mean any trouble," Jim said. "I just came up here to see if I could find my folks." He was wondering why he would say such a thing to this man, when the gun barrel was thrust hard into his belly and he gasped, doubling and dropping onto a slab of broad granite.

"I said set," said the man. "Lest I have to shoot you."

They sat silent, Jim on a steel rail leaned across two round chunks of granite, the other man on a piece of discarded machinery, a large cogwheel on one end of the flat, square surface of flaking metal. Somewhere in the distance a bird sounded two sharp notes. The man spat. Jim suddenly realized who this man was: the brother of Paul Morelock, the one with the name they'd all laughed at over at Glen's...what was it? Yes: Pierot, *Pye-rot* Morelock, sitting here on the mountain holding a gun on Jim.

Some minutes later, Jim spoke. He listened to the quaver in his own voice, recognizing the sound of uncertainty, a modulating undertone of indefinite suspense, like a foreigner must feel arriving in a new country, or trying to communicate—trying to place an order at a restaurant—for the first time. He was surprised that he wasn't more scared.

"What are you going to do with me?" he said. "You can't very well just keep me sitting here the rest of the day, can you?"

The man leaned forward and spat. He laid the shotgun across his lap and scratched desultorily at his left ear.

"I don't mean any trouble," said Jim. "I was just up here looking around," thinking *Where the hell is Sam? Where is Sam?*

"Lookin round," the man repeated. "Whut you lookin round after?"

Jim said nothing. He watched the man pick the shotgun off his lap and point it again, the barrels aimed at Jim's chest. *Surely he's not going to shoot me*, he thought, again surprised at his own lack of fear, as though, strange as this all was, it was something he'd imagined, expected, ever since Sam had pulled off the main road and headed up the steep grade, as though this man, the gun, the threat, this strange captivity were, in fact, what he'd been *lookin round after* all along.

"Hey?" the man said pushing the barrels at Jim.

"I wasn't snooping after anybody," Jim said, raising his hands, again, thinking, again, *Jesus Christ, he's not going to shoot me, is he?* "I didn't come up here to get anyone in trouble, if it's that." He remembered Sam's talk about *croaching*. "I don't care if you're living up here. It's none of my business."

"Pawper!" the man shouted, so loudly that Jim jerked, reflexively. The gun barrels jabbed toward him again. "Pawper!" the man shouted, again, calling.

Again, they sat in silence, though this time Jim kept his hands up. After a few moments the man rose and gestured with the gun for Jim to get up. He herded Jim into the end of the hollow, following the tracks toward the lean-to, and shouting, "Pawper!" every few steps.

As they approached the sloping cabin, Jim could see that it

wasn't standing in front of the mountain but had actually been dug into the rising slope, the lean-to front only an awning of sorts, projecting from a log wall, with a door and two windows framed in clumsy sawn timbers and set into the mountainside.

"Pawper, goddammit," the man called, motioning Jim aside and kicking the wood door open. They entered a dark space smelling harshly, a disagreeable odor he had known, somewhere, before. But, like the locomotive sound, he couldn't place the smell.

As his eyes began to darken to the room, he saw, first, a plank table on which a red kerosene lantern burned dully through a smoked globe. The light through the window on his left showed a wall hung with two cast-iron skillets. Next to these, a long pale item of clothing—overalls or a dress—hung from a nail. A figure, a person, was standing behind the table, hands outstretched toward him.

He gradually made out the face of a middle-aged woman, drawn and weathered. The eyes were widening in astonishment or fear and she was lifting one hand, pointing at him. She stepped backward, as though she'd been shoved, amazed eyes still widening, hand still pointing at Jim. "Who's that?" she said, quavering. "Who's that?"

"Pawper! Goddammit," the man shouted again. "Got me a feller here was pokin around, Pawper." In the darkness at the back of the room stood a very old man, stooped over, wearing a long, white nightshirt, one sleeve pinned up to cover an amputee's stump. He limped forward, until, standing beside the woman, he arched himself, raising his face upward to peer at Jim.

A moment later he, too, raised one hand, pointing. He appeared to be very frightened.

"God almighty!" he screeched. "God almighty! God almighty!" He dropped forward, catching his hands on the tabletop. "Great God almighty!" he shrieked.

The woman stood, silent, still pointing, while the old man slid to the floor, his face in his hands, weeping, crying, "O Lord, O Lord, O Lord," to nobody, his voice rising into a keening wail.

PART TWO

JESSUM

The deep, still river of her heart hoarded its images, ever reflecting them in the racing current, letting them sink deeper into memory than most of us can. Real innocence can do nothing that is trivial, and when it is allied to generosity of heart, the combination makes it the most vulnerable of qualities under heaven.
—Lawrence Durrell

ONE

For some time, he'd already been living that half-drowned existence so common to very old people. The details of daytime, the material items of food, clothing, the woman, herself, who picked up the dishes and brought him his whiskey, the eating and drinking, itself, and the fumbling labor of unbuttoning to relieve himself all these had already begun to recede from reality, like irrelevant intrusions, stones dropped into the bowl of the spring, or dirt churned up by the slim paw of some animal, so he would have to wait for the moiling cloudiness to settle out—the meal eaten, the plates drawn away—until the water was still again, and he could see through to the bottom, where the real things were, clear and distant and cold.

As it is with all people nearing their end, the retreat of his consciousness seemed to circle back upon the early past, so that the older he became, the more immediate became those times of youth, until, finally, at the end, perhaps, he would disappear peacefully into his own beginnings, back through time itself, and return directly to the long-ago nothing that was already there before he had been born out of it.

He was ninety-eight years old on that day when the stranger walked into the dark, earth-smelling place—half hut, half cave— where he spent his time, peering through the chinks between the daily disturbances that the ghostly, silent woman brought to him and fetched away, tending to him. He didn't remember when this phase of his life had begun. He thought the woman was much younger than she actually was, thought she was a young bride, or a neighbor girl, when, in fact, she would not see fifty again. But he was ninety-eight and already living most of his real life in a confused struggle to wrest himself away from the cloudy present and toward the lucid, settled past. And then he heard the name called, *Pawper! Pawper!* And when Pierot brought the stranger through the door, the clear, cool past suddenly welled forth, flooding Jessum, drowning him in an insistent present.

The old man, Jessum Morelock, had looked up and seen the man—though he didn't know it was a man—and suddenly the day, the hut, the woman, were no longer the frame of his easy, bemused age. He saw the stranger and suddenly there was no distance, no need to peer into the spring at the lost times beaming up through the still bowl of water. Because suddenly it was all cold water, and he was at the bottom, surrounded, trying to breathe, facing the thing, itself: the last time he had ever seen that face.

He had been born on that mountain, near the prong, and he'd spent so much of his childhood at the mill itself that the huff of the steam engine and the sharp smell of cut wood (he could tell what kind of log they were cutting by the smell: clean and sweet walnut, damp and soft pine, acrid and stomach-churning maple), and the high, terrible scream of the big blade, all were as much a part of his life as the round of chores, tending to tobacco plants, pulling the plump green worms off the leaves, dashing the fat, writhing shapes to the ground. Then they'd stopped farming, except some chickens and hogs, and just ran the mill, and it was mules and oxen, turning the stubborn handle of the big red corn grinder, making feed. Shortly after he began to walk, he was driving the teams. He knew mules better than he knew other children, though he played at odd times with Lon Hampton. He couldn't have said when he found the time for play: *boyhood,* as a region of his lifetime, simply disappeared behind the mountain of work. But he did remember the fun of cane squeezing times, in the meadow at the shoulder of Timb's ridge: the ox plodding a circle, turning the rollers as the men fed-through the brittle, splintery stalks. He remembered the smell of the cooking juice, sweet and dark, like blood: the deep odor that you felt at the roof of your mouth. And he remembered how the kids would play together and sneak pieces of cane to gnaw until lips and tongues bled. And how they'd grab up a few of the longer trimmings and would heat the ends in the big fire, then strike them on the ground—how they'd CRACK, loud as a gunshot—and the older folk would jump and the women would put hands to hearts and say, "Heavenly days!" while the men muttered curses to one another, "Goddamn kids."

He was a quiet boy, a little "backwards," they'd say, meaning "bashful," not "slow," and this quality made for stark contrast in a family full of loud, brawling older brothers. He liked to be on his own, working with the animals, or, better, off in the corn lots stripping and bundling fodder. He'd challenge himself to see how dexterous he could become, stripping the stalks and hanging the shucks, and later, tying the bundles. He'd gotten so he could throw a bundle into the air and tie the next one while that first one was fluttering down to land in his arms atop the new bundle.

He showed that trick to Lon Hampton, at one of those rare times when Jessum wasn't working all day. He'd been walking along the lane and had met little Lonnie coming along toward their own corn lot, on his way to make fodder. Lonnie said he hated bundling fodder, so Jessum shyly offered to come along, saying he didn't mind and he'd like to help.

He remembered always the tan strips of fodder hung over the cornstalks, the wind rustling and sweeping the long ribbons of "made shucks" into curved, waving forms like bird's wings. And he heard himself tell little Lonnie Hampton that they were wings, that "you tuck a bundle of fodder up against your chest and you could fly."

Lonnie, who was about three years younger than Jessum, did not, at first, believe this, saying, "You're crazy."

"No," Jess said, watching the wind-curved made lines rustle and crash in the sunlight, like whole flocks of wings. "You could. Just let the air catch them things and it'd take you clean off the mountain, fly you wherever you want to go. Roalton, iffen you'd want to, even."

Lonnie's eyes opened a little wider, then narrowed.

"You're crazy," he said. "You aint just backward; you're right crazy."

"I'll show you," Jessum said, warming to the idea, beginning, in fact, to believe that it sounded quite plausible.

So he showed Lonnie his trick, gathering the first four shucks and tying them into a bundle, then taking up four more, ready to tie them off, too.

"Now you watch," he said. "And I'll throw this here bundle up in the air. And it'll kindly hover up. It'll stay up in the air long enough I can tie the second bundle." And he did his trick.

Lonnie's eyes opened up for good that time. He was impressed. "Lord," he said. "Let's see that again. Make her do her again."

So Jessum did it again, telling Lonnie, "Keep a eye how that fodder will kindly float up there, like it's a hangin on a string, whilst I'm a tyin off a whole bundle of fodder down below." And he did it again, and said, "There. You see? Them things can fly."

"I want to make one fly, too," Lonnie said, excited, and gathered up four lines, tying them. He got the next four strips and tossed the bundle into the air, getting ready to go to work on his next bundle, when the first came down on his head.

"It didn't work," he said, accusingly. He looked at the bundle. "Maybe this un aint fledged."

"You didn't launch her right," said Jessum. "You got to know just how to launch her, just like you got to know how to sling a stone to get it a skippin on the crick. Watch." And he did his trick again, this time taking exaggerated care about tossing the bundle into the air, before quickly tying off his next bundle and letting the first drop lightly into his hands.

"I'll be damned," said Lonnie.

Later that week, Jessum was at the supper board, eating, as usual, in silence, his solitude enveloped by the noise of his older brothers laughing and pushing and fighting over the ham. Tonight, they were roaring at each other about haints, and how they weren't a scared of no haints, day or night. At a lull in all the scuffling, his mother had said, "Katie Hampton says she believes her little boy Lonnie been visited by a haint. And that he broke his leg yesterday, all on account of the haint."

And Jessum had felt a rush of hot guilt, feeling—knowing, somehow—that he'd been to blame. He looked down into his plate of ham and beans, stirring it around.

"She said he'd stuck a bundle of fodder under either arm and jumped outen the barn loft on the creek side. Broke his leg." The brothers roared. Jessum looked downward.

"Lucky he didn't kill hisself," said Jessum's father.

"She says it had to have been a haint told him to do that, because she might see how a boy could tell hisself to jump outen the loft, but he'd never decide on his own to tuck a couple bundles of mule feed up under his arms before he done it, would he? So she believed it's got to been a haint that had told the little boy to jump outen the barn and feed the devil some fodder."

"Damn lucky he didn't kill hisself," Jessum's father said again.

"Preacher's going up there today to cast them spirits out," said his mother. "Then they'll get the broke leg attended to."

A few years later, Jessum's family stopped sawing wood and went to making whiskey, full-time. He'd gotten big enough to guard the still, holding a heavy, blued double-barrel shotgun and trying to stay awake, while the big pot cooked the beer and the worm ran streams of clear liquid into jars, turning, Pawp said, hog feed into money. They'd made whiskey all along, of course, but not on this scale. Not enough to replace the sawmill itself as the family business. It had been an extra source of some cash money, like the walnuts and ginseng. "Make do," money, Pawp had said.

He couldn't have told you when the feud began any more than he could tell you how he'd learned to *gee* and *haw* the teams. He remembered "feudin," and could even remember a time before, when Hamptons and Morelocks were just neighbors, even working together, some of them at his Pawp's mill. But how it started, he didn't know. There was no event, no moment, that he could recall as the *beginning*. It was more like a change in the landscape, like a slide or a big windrow that altered the whole look and feel of the mountainside. Or a change in the air, itself, a thickening. And then he was a Morelock and they were Hamptons and we wanted to kill them.

And then came Laura. He had been into town with his brothers, that day, when she became something more than just Laura. He'd known her, of course, all his life, when they'd been among the smaller kids at the canings or music-makins. And then she'd become a Hampton and he a Morelock, and so he hadn't seen much of her at all, except at the brush arbor meetings, sometimes, and then later, when they'd raised the new white clapboard church where the brush arbor had been, when the folks had agreed they wouldn't fight each other on a Sunday. And then, while he was still a little boy, he might say "hidy" to her or her brothers. But she hadn't been anything at all, since he wasn't yet anything, either, neither of them aware even of their own bodies, much less the other.

And then, several years later, he'd made that trip into town. He'd been into town with the brothers before, of course, but this time they'd come fully armed and had made him drive the wagon while they squatted in the back among the sacks of walnuts, and whispered in sharp hisses and shushes.

Jessum had always liked getting up walnuts, out in the big woods, scrambling along the slopes, knocking nuts to the ground and stepping on them and whacking them with hickory sticks to clear off the black, greasy rinds. The whole family would crack nuts every night for a week, talking and telling tales in the dim lamplight, the stories told in fits and starts because you couldn't talk and hold a walnut just right to hit it on the top, or it would slip and you'd have a mess and a bruised thumb, likely.

But this time the nut cracking was tense, the talk was anxious and strained, *likely they won't even be in at the same time...*or *don't let them get a hop on you, boys.* So that now, driving the team down the long slope to the mountain and then on the broader way, he felt none of the usual glee over a trip to town, instead felt exposed and foolish, sitting alone on the plank seat with the whispers behind him, and now and then the knock of a metal gun barrel against the grained boards of the wagon bed.

It always surprised Jessum when the woods opened up and they were in town, the two white sheds on either side of the rail tracks, and then the big, long tobacco warehouse, the ramshackle seasonal café next door. This time, his brother, Vernon, rose up behind him, whispering, and he felt himself jump from the sudden fright.

"Jesus, baby brother," Vernon had said. "Settle down now. Aint nothin a going to happen to you. You jest drive her on in nice and easy and take a turn over to Snide's. Then you set the team and get the hell outen there. You get on over to Crary's, you hear? And stay around there until somebody comes and gets you. You hear?"

Vernon dropped back into the bed and began grabbing and whispering to each brother in turn, making plans, as the wagon moved slowly down the main drag, toward the new courthouse. Just as they entered the square, Jessum *hawed* to the mules and they turned out the narrow lane leading to Snide's stable. He knew Snide's, of course, knew that his brothers often traded whiskey there. He recognized Snide, himself, standing out front of the big double stable doors, a lean figure, a cousin, with a narrow, pointed beard, who was always arching his back, hands on hips, and saying, "I be goddamned." There was whiskey in the back of the wagon today—Jessum knew that, too—though they hadn't brought it to trade. He'd smelled it all the way into town as the brothers passed the clay dimmie back and forth. Now, as Jessum pulled the team up and kneed the brake, Vernon leaned across and slung the jug over to Snide, while the others jumped down, guns in their hands, and ran through the small door—the "man door" Snide called it—into the stable.

Snide took the jug and held it to his ear. "I be goddamn if you can't hear the frogs on the bank of the pond," he said. "The water's gone on down the crick, most of it, aint it, Vernon?" He drew the grapevine plug out of the jar with his teeth.

Vernon gave the boy a sharp look. "Scoot, now. Crary's," he said, as he flung an arm around Snide's shoulder. They lowered their heads, speaking, and nodding.

Jessum jumped down the far side of the wagon, unhitched and reversed the mules in the traces—he could have done this in his sleep—then ran off, further down the lane, away from the square to where it turned left, toward Crary's store.

He remembered this part, always like a story someone else would tell, the images and figures floating up in his mind the way he'd imagine Jack meeting the giant, or Old Paw-Pawper, fighting and building the trail toward Kentucky with Daniel Boone, before he left out and settled here, on the prong. Those past stories had blurred into myth, so that the giant and his own ancestors had become too large to fit anything like a landscape or a time and had become, instead, the atmosphere itself, through which he walked, puny and powerless. But he would remember this part similarly, because, later, the feud had become a part of the mythology, almost instantly growing and transforming into something it never had been, at the time, something huge and determinate, that had actually begun when he, the angular boy, not quite thirteen, not quite yet a young man, ran through Crary's flopping screen door, smack into Laura Hampton, knocking her down.

She had come up, crying, and slapped him hard, right across the face, and he'd *youched*, and complained, "What you a hittin on me for? I didn't mean to knock into you, Laura." And he'd seen she was sorry, right off the bat, and she'd stopped crying and said, "O Lord, I didn't mean it, neither, Jess. You knocked me down and I naturally thought you was feudin or something."

Brady Crary had come up quick, like she always did, and said, "You kids just don't get started, now. I had enough of this with your dern folks, I don't need to mind you two carryin on, neither." And they'd both assured her that they hadn't meant no harm to each other and that they were both just staying out of the way of the older brothers, like they'd been told.

"They sent you here, too, I reckon," he'd said to Laura and she had nodded her head.

"They's up to somethin," Laura said. "They got out at different places, all up and down the square, and then Hab, he sent me a runnin for Brady's. He told me stay put and he'd fetch me."

"Me too," said Jessum, watching her eyes. She had great big eyes, rounded outward, under heavy lids, Indian eyes, because they glistened and looked almost sad, except hers were a deep blue. But even the blue was dark, like a late sky. He thought her eyes were beautiful, and when she looked at him, he felt a deep pull, inside, like the feeling way down when you swing out on the rope over the swim hole and drop and something pushes up inside. And as she turned and walked back into the store, saying, "Let's us find a play-purty," he watched her move, feeling, perhaps for the first time, that aching grace, the recognition, like seeing something entirely new through some window in his mind, that her cool, barely curved flank might be everything in the world, if he could only touch it. Or maybe not: they were just reaching thirteen, so desire was only just beginning to peek through the blinds of childhood. Maybe he was still too young to feel that much of beautiful, useless hope, and only found her "nice," the way he'd find the shade and the cool air by a big spring "nice."

Still, there it was, the turning movement, and it was suddenly different from the way he'd watched her—or anyone else—before. And he would always wonder at how that single motion of her girl's body had made him forget the other thing: the whispers and the whiskey in the wagon, the knock of steel against wood, the fear.

And then the first gunshot sounded, too sudden, and too loud, as though it had gone off just outside the door. They both jerked around, staring, as the fusillade roared—three shots, then several, then one—echoing into silence. A voice shouting. Then, further away, two more shots. Then more dreadful silence.

Laura had thrown her arms around him, breathing into his neck, beginning to cry. "O Jess, what in the world?" And he felt her breath, and the damp of her cheek and he must have been in love with her, he thought later, the moment she had pressed against him and breathed like that, full and warm against the hollow of his neck. *My God*, he would think, later. *O my God*.

Brady had tried to hustle them both to the rear of the store, but they had refused, standing, stiff, in the middle of the floor, looking toward the door, listening to the silence.

A moment later the screak and clatter of a wagon sounded outside and they heard sharp cries and curses, anger and pain, mixed. Hab Hampton, a big man, with the same large, deep eyes, lunged through the door, flustered and hurried.

"Let's git, Laura," he said, reaching for her. Jessum remembered squeezing her, as though preparing to resist the pull of the other man's hand, then feeling the futility, the weakness of his youth against this much adult strength, this much anger and hurry. He let go and stood, desolate and foolish, while Hab tried to pick her up, literally trying to carry her out of the room.

And she had saved him. She had kicked and flailed, shouting, "Wait. Wait." And then, when Hab slowed, saying, "What about Jess?" And then, in a voice he hoped he would always remember,

"You can't just leave him." And, "I aint going without Jess."

So, even with the cries and curses still ringing out front, Hab had stopped long enough to recognize him, see him for the boy he was, just a kid, and so an obligation to any adult, anywhere in these mountains. He had to be protected, even if this kid was a Morelock. And Hab had drawn a breath and let out a deep sigh.

"Well," he said. "Your folks is gone off a runnin. So I reckon you'd best to kindly come along with us."

Jessum was scared. He faced them, hearing the noises from the street, still hearing the too-loud gunshots, thinking of the knocking of gun metal against wagon wood, his brother saying *don't leave until I send for you.*

"I don't know," he said. "I might ought to go to Snide's.

Hab laughed grimly. "Your cousin Snide aint fit to take company tonight, I guess. You come on with us.

"Don't worry," Laura said. "It'll be all right." She reached up and touched his cheek, the first time in his life a girl had touched him that way, almost like a mother comforting a child, but something else, too. And so it would be that touch, too, that he would remember all his life. "Don't worry," she said, again. "I always liked you, Jess, and I don't believe in none of this business."

"Let's git," said Hab, sharply, and Jessum followed Laura, feeling lost and bewildered, out the door.

They made Jessum drive the wagon. They were all breathing hard, scared, and he realized they were afraid his brothers would ambush them on their way up the mountain. So they wanted him up front and visible, saying, "If his folks is a laying for us, they might can see him at the reins and might let us pass on, lest they shoot him, or we shoot him, one." They had hung a coal oil lantern on the stanchion post next to Jessum and he could feel himself shy at its heat, afraid the jouncing of the wagon would swing the hot globe too close and burn him.

Glay Hampton had been shot in the thigh with a solid round that had struck bone, and he lay, screaming, in the back of the wagon, as they worked their way out the side lanes, getting out of town. At one point, Hab had shouted to Laura, "Baby sis, get back here with some water," and she had ducked down into the bed for several minutes, and returned, pale and shaking, a smear of brown blood across her cheek. She had squeezed his arm.

The wounded man continued to scream with every jolt of the wagon bed, and Jessum prayed with each turn of the wheel that he would miss a rut, or a rock, and it seemed he always hit them, feeling the blood and the splintered bone with every sway of the creaking wagon. Later, when he rolled the wagon over a large root, the bed had come down with a hard jolt and Glay had gone silent. Hab shouted again for Laura to fetch some water, and she had looked at Jess, the deep eyes forlorn, and disappeared into the darkness behind. Then a hand had come up and grasped his shoulder, hard, and a man's voice, smelling of white liquor, had said, "You jounce this wagon again, Morelock, I'll cut your throat." Then Hab's sharp call, "Orville, leave that boy alone and get down here."

The wagon rolled through the deep hollow, climbing the mountain, the laurel branches hanging in bundles from either side of the road, showing blackly against the night sky, the mountain slope a surge of complete darkness. Laura reappeared, though he could barely see her, now, a pale shadow that moved against him, her face a wan glow, her eyes deep pools in the dim light from the swinging lantern. In the black well of the wagon bed, the man began to whimper, then groan, then scream, again.

Jessum relaxed, letting the reins droop, clucking the animals. He knew these mules would know their own way home, up and around the dark mountain.

The Hampton place was just like his own, a big log kitchen, set on a rise above the stream, with four chink and daub houses notched into clearings on the side of the mountain. Only a practiced eye could have seen that this family was a step poorer than Jessums: the tools were more often hand-hewn, the blankets picked-wool felt, the kitchen floor unplanked, the hard-packed earth, the puncheon benches. The only exception to the homemade furnishings was a big, walnut-framed mirror, hung on the wall. Next to it, a row of nails held overalls and shirts. He saw all this, and the feel was the same as his own place: a big family, rangy men and tough women, and a ramble of kids all around. He expected they would feed him first, almost the moment he walked in, and ask after his comfort, though he was unsure about how they would want him to sit to table.

And then he saw that no one would sit to table, because they carried the wounded brother—Glay—into the room and laid him out flat on the broad hewn oak table, holding lamps up and leaning toward the man's leg, looking at the dark wound, while Glay, exhausted from the wagon ride, moaned and stirred.

"You kids fetch some waddin," Hab said. "Mam, cook some water. Vernon, clear these little'uns outen here and bring us the knife. And boys, let's grab this leg and hold him down." The brothers all bent over the man, their shoulders taut.

Jessum stayed near Laura, following her lead. She went to a corner and opened a crude box, pulling from it small, raveled pieces of thin, homespun rag, handing it out to Jess, who bunched it against his chest. As they came back toward the crowd at the table, Jessum had a glimpse of the wounded man's face, gray and glistening in the lamp light, the lips twisted into an odd shape, like worms of gray clay, pushed together and smeared to one side. The man looked straight at Jessum, those same deep blue eyes, bulging, hurt.

"Leg's broke," said Orville, holding the knife and bending over the table. "No tellin where the ball mayt be. We caint just cut him and hope," he said, looking up at Hab, both faces amber in the lamp light.

"We caint do much else," said Hab, taking the knife from his brother. "You want to just let him lay here and holler, let that leg turn black and kill him?"

"What you fixin to do, saw down til you hit somepin?" said the younger man. "Whyn't you just shoot him again, put him outen his misery? I'd a heap rather you shot him and me both than watch you roust into that leg." The two men faced each other, now, intent, staring, two brothers. The father was dead long ago, Jessum knew, killed in an accident up on the mountain, pulled under a log by one of the big cables, as big around as your forearm. Now, Jessum could feel the will of each brother, like a ray, pushing outward, striking the other, tense, seeking the father's role, brother and brother, neither knowing even what he wanted, hoped for, both of them desperate, while the hurt man, another brother, lay moaning, glistening with sweat, his gray lips twisted like they'd been pushed by a thumb.

"You boys fetch aside." The stern, gray-haired woman moved into the lamplight, and the brothers gave back. So Jessum knew immediately who was really in charge, who the authority had devolved upon, if it had ever been elsewhere even when the father was alive. "Where's that waddin?" she said, answering her own question by grabbing into the bundle at Jessum's chest, the thin, snaky fingers closing and pulling. She held a long, thin, hooked implement, like a large needle, raising it into the lamplight and then down toward the wounded leg. "Hold him, boys," she said.

The men bent and grasped, and the entire group surged, horribly, while the woman pushed hard with the thick needle, packing wadding around the wound with her left hand, pushing again, relentless, hard and deep, with the steel implement, while the room screamed and rocked, pitched, and then fell back, silent.

The woman turned from the table, sighed once, then said, "I reckon you all could use a bite. I reckon we'll have to eat on the ground. Somebody get Glay a sup of whisky." She handed the blood-soaked wadding down to Laura. "Get rid of them things, and let me get this blood washed off me and get this boy a mite to eat."

TWO

On Sunday, they'd taken him to church with them, in the same wagon he'd driven back from town, and he'd watched his maw and pawp ride up in their two-wheeled buggy, followed by the brothers in the wagon. The Hamptons had stood him straight next to their wagon and pushed him gently toward the buggy. He walked across the intervening space, both families watching him as though he might somehow disappear or ignite, until he reached his folks, and then he'd gone home.

But not before he'd spent that one night, walking around the Hampton place with Laura, helping her do her work, letting her show him the glade, where the spring had washed through, glittering with quartz, her favorite spot on the whole place.

"The path here leads right on up over the knob and across the prong, down to your country," she told him. "It forks off over on your side, one of em goin on down to the sawmill, and the other directly to your home place." He was surprised to hear about this: he'd never had much time to poke around over the knob. The hunting was better down the other way, along Bald Ridge. "They's a nice swim hole up yonder, too," she said. "That nobody never goes to. You know where?" And he said no, he didn't, but for a moment he imagined her swimming, the lithe body turning in slick water.

And they agreed that they'd try to use the back way and see each other now and again.

* * *

Glay's leg healed up, though he would walk crooked-over and limping for the rest of his life. The law got involved because the shooting had been right in town, but neither side would declare against the other, each family saying it had all been an "accident." The sheriff was a distant cousin to the Morelocks, anyway, and not inclined to push matters much. He warned each family sternly to keep the gunplay out of town, and that was that.

Meanwhile, the moonshine business was becoming big business, and Jessum's Pawp and older brothers began building two big stills, both fired by the steam engine from the sawmill, both dug into the mountainside behind the old works. Jessum was made to stand guard, and it was at this point that he informed his Pawp of the back trail running from Morelocks' works to Hamptons', hoping he'd be posted to guard that way in the evenings.

And he was sent up there. He would finish charging the boiler and would check the mash in the late afternoon, then would head up the steep slope behind the engine, through the sassafras and locust and into the big trees, the hickory and oak. As the trail neared the top of the big knob, it would straighten and climb, the path itself deepening, from the rainwater that washed down its length, so that at times he would walk between shoulder-high banks of clay and rock. At the brim of the crest, the trees gave way to sedges pushed up around big chunks of granite and thickets of laurel. His lookout post was on the very top of the knob, where he could see down the trail in both directions.

But he never stayed there long. As soon as the sun began to flirt with the western line of ridges, he would move cautiously down the pathway on the Hampton side of the knob, picking his way, crouched low, stopping every few yards to look around, making sure he wasn't seen.

At the bottom, before the trail spread out into the Hampton clearing, he ducked into a stand of small pines and crawled to a big block of granite that was fractured in a strange, stairstep formation, as if it had been deliberately cut by giants. Scrambling and reaching, drawing himself upward, he would climb to the top step, where he could peer over the side at the out buildings and the big chink-and-daub house. And he would sit there, waiting to see Laura.

He probably couldn't have said why he did this, each night, why he was hoping to catch her alone and talk with her. But he had thought of her, steadily, in the two years since the night he'd spent here. He'd remembered her, that night at Crary's store, when she'd said, "I aint going without Jessie." And so, he wanted to see her, and hear her voice. He was a quiet, timid sort, not like his big, boisterous brothers, who drank hard, fought hard, and talked about women as if they, too, were a part of the drinking and eye-gouging. Jessum had never been a fighter and had never had a girl. So Laura's frightened embrace that night, when the gunshots began, her hot breath in the curve of his neck, stood clearly and powerfully in his mind because there were no other events to rank beside this. And, though he was completely inexperienced, he wasn't ignorant. He'd grown up around his brothers, heard their talk, had seen animals in their mating and birthing, had felt the insistent cycle of the seasons, drawn by the incipient pull of spring, and had a country boy's instinctive sense of male and fe-male, body and earth, the sexual urge at the base of everything. And he would have assumed without even wondering about it that she, too, had the same essential knowledge, the same deep associ-ation with land, sex, and being, a sense he believed, somehow, his own brothers—and the Hampton boys, too, for that matter—had lost, or betrayed.

Because he was still a quiet, sensitive boy who could sit on the rounded granite at the top of the knob, staying still enough to watch a bobcat pick its hunched way across the trail, not twenty yards down. He thought Laura must have this same sensibility, this feeling for silence, too, because, up here, silence was a form of contact, and if you waited and watched long enough, you could see the mountains breathe.

But he knew his brothers had never experienced anything of this sort, knew they'd frightened away this entire world of bobcats and mountain with their hollering and their knives, the quick slashing fights they liked, so that, even after the fight was over, they could disturb the quiet night for hours with all the brash bragging and posturing about a thing so pointless and futile.

So now he waited and watched the Hampton house, leaning against the cold granite step, feeling the shadows begin to deepen, the coming night. He had seen her more than a few times but hadn't dared to call out to her. She would be carrying water from the spring, or tossing out scraps to the chickens, and he would look hard, trying to remember the turn of her body, the feel of her breath on his neck. Once, someone had called her and she had answered back, "Yessum," and he had taken the sound of her voice back down the mountain with him that night, and had dropped off to sleep still trying to hear the tone, the timbre of that one word, "yessum."

Then, one night, she came out the kitchen door and turned, walking directly toward the rock, carrying a big tin bucket, her shoulders sloped, hips braced against the weight. He held his breath as she kept coming, unbelievably, right toward him and then, even better, around the flank of the big rock, out of sight of the house. She rounded the mass of granite and stood below him, at the very spot where he'd climbed up, and, while his heart hammered—he was afraid to startle her, afraid she'd holler, but he knew he had to talk to her—she set the heavy bucket down and arched her back, stretching herself, her body taut and her head tipped back, a sleek pale shape in the deepening shadows, looking at the top of the rock.

So he simply slid slowly down a step and whispered her name, very softly, hoping she would catch the slightest wafting of sound and would respond, not even sure she'd heard, with more of curiosity than fear. And it worked.

"Is somebody there?" she said, almost in a whisper, tilting her head to see.

"It's me, Laura," he said. "Jessum."

"Jessum!" She laughed, and he thought, *thank God*. "Good lord," she said, quietly, and then, "Hush. Don't let the folks hear you."

"What you got in the bucket?" he said.

"Clabbered milk," she said. She reached down and took the bale, tipping the bucket, letting milk flow into the depression at the base of the rock. He watched the cotton dress tauten against her back, the soft nubs of her spine. "I dump it out here where the chickens won't get to it." He smelled the sharp, pinching odor of the sour milk as she bent further, lifting the bottom of the pail to empty it, the quiet incurve of her waist, the light curve of breast. She looked up at him.

"What're you doin up on the rock?"

"Waitin for you," he said.

So they arranged it. She told her brothers she'd seen someone up on the trail, and they'd come out looking, finding his prints all the way to the rock, and Hab had said, "That aint no good." And Orville had said, "Hell, brother, they aint enough of us'uns to watch ever damn track up and down the mountain." And they had stood in silence, trying to think, their toes nudging the twigs and pebbles at the base of the rock. And Laura said, "I could set up nights on the knob. They got to go over the knob to get down here, no matter what. I could set up, and you all wouldn't have to waste no manpower, kindly."

"You aint going up there toward Morelocks alone, baby sister," Hab said.

"Why not?" Laura said. "I could take up a cedar whistle and let you know was somebody comin, and then kindly tuck back into the laurel whenever they did come over the top. And you know they aint a Morelock in the world would hurt me iffen they did find me. They may be after you all but they aint a going to do nothin to a little girl."

"You aint dezactly a little girl, no more, baby sis," said Hab.

"She's right, though, Hab," said Orville. "Most they'd do is tell her to scoot, try'n scare her a mite. They surely wouldn't hurt her."

"You don't think so?" Hab said. "Morelocks? I reckon they might like to hurt a young gal startin to get growed, them boys."

Laura reddened. "They aint never going to see me, to know if I'm growed or not," she said.

"And we surely don't have men folks enough to cover everything," said Orville.

Hab scrubbed the stones around for a moment.

"All right," he said. "We'll give her a try. Sister, you get your chores done fast and we'll let the kids get the washin done and get themselves off to bed, and you get on up there where you can see over the other side. But don't you stay up there for no Morelocks to come over the top. You see sign of them you get the hell on down here. Don't use the whistle nor do any hidin in the brush unlessens you can't get out of there no other way, you hear."

Vernon said, "You aint a going to get scared of haints, baby girl?"

"I aint so little," Laura flounced. "Didn't you just hear Hab say so?"

So it began. Every evening during that late summer, Jessum and Laura would meet at the top of the knob. They told each other they really were guards, and had to keep watch, lest one or the other group of brothers planned mischief, and they decided they were doing a good thing, together, to help avoid what she called "more hurtin and wretchedness." Since each had to watch for invasions by the other's family, they decided they could fend off all possible raids by helping each other out. He told her how Paw-Pawper Anse had said they used to talk to the Rebel pickets this way, during the war, since about two-thirds of the folks up here had people in the Union army and the other third in the

Confederates. Well, they all knew somebody's cousin or other, and couldn't see sense in shooting somebody who was just standing guard against any big battle, especially since that was what they were doing, themselves. So, he told her, they ought to do the same.

At first, they sat together on a rounded granite boulder flecked with quartz, just off the trail, where they could see both ways. Down the side toward the Morelocks', the trail wound in a narrow, eroded ditch for thirty yards or so, then dropped out of sight. In the other direction, the knob humped upward over a large stone outcrop, so he would watch for her to appear over the round of the rock, first her dark hair, then those deep, rounded eyes, then the slight form, walking toward him, her chin pointed upward a bit as if she were trying to see over the curve of the knob. And she would see him and smile, and hurry forward, in that striding, deliberate way she had, and sit next to him, saying, "Howdy, Jess boy."

Mostly, at first, they talked. She told him about her family and growing up on that side of the knob, and, as he thought, her life had been much the same as his. Still, they shared the talking, even when the other knew precisely what was coming, because it was comfortable hearing the quiet sound of their voices, as the evening turned to gloom and the darkness welled up from below, leaving them in the black shadows of forest and laurel bush, her face a pale lozenge, her eyes darker even than the surrounding mountainside, though he could see them glisten, too, in the night air.

She took him to the secret swim hole on one of the first nights. He had wondered what it would be like, swimming with this girl. When he was little, they'd all gone into the creek naked, splashing and shouting. But that had been a long time ago in a big hole on the main creek. This was a pool up on the prong, surrounded by heavy laurel, the water itself bordered by deep ferns and moss hidden in a small cove off the Hampton side of the knob. And now it was only the two of them, no longer kids, and he felt a thrill of anxiety and desire as he followed her off the trail, into the hollow, where he could hear the water falling off the brink of rock, down into the fern-framed pool.

"The water's colder'n all misery," she said when they got to the edge of the pool. The air itself was chilled, even at this height of the summer, the hollow dank and smelling of cool earth. Without saying anything else, Laura unbuckled her overalls and let them fall to her ankles. Beneath them, she wore a thin cotton shift, with "pant-legged" bottoms. He closed his eyes when he saw the sharp points of her nipples, dark beneath the fabric, pushing out from her small breasts. He felt completely stricken.

He would wonder later what she had been thinking at that moment, whether she was trying to dissolve or to increase the intensity of the moment, as she said, "I reckon I'd best leave this shift on," and then said, "Come on, Jess, get outen them overhauls and let's swim." She had reached out and unbuckled one of his straps, saying, again, "Come on."

So they swam, she in her shift and he in his underdrawers, and once they had let themselves into the pool, all the awkwardness and suspense disappeared in the sheer frigidity of the water.

"I told you it was cold," she said, when he came up spluttering.

"It's so cold, it don't feel wet," he said. It felt like an immersion in an element thinner and sharper than water. His toes and knees ached with a deep, blood-chilled throb, and his lips, eyelids and brow felt swollen and tender. But he was happy, here in the dark pool with Laura Hampton.

When they got out of the water Jessum no longer felt fearful or anxious. The cold of the spring pool had somehow transformed his connection with this girl, so that he felt an easy naturalness. He knew the water had turned his own thin clothing to transparency, knew she could see the small bend of his sex, and he saw her flesh showing through the sticking wet of the cotton—saw the puckered nipples, the shadow of her navel, the dark whorl of hair below her curved belly—and he felt only a sudden rightness, an elated sense of release. So when she stripped off the shift to wring it out, and he followed suit, he felt only a new notion of intimacy, friendship, with this young woman, Laura. He knew that the tension, the pain of desire and uncertainty, would return soon enough. But, for now, he felt a pure, easy grace standing by her side, naked and innocent, in the cool depth of the hollow.

So the summer went on. They didn't go swimming again, perhaps because they both knew they were moving beyond this, into a deeper contact, where the anxiety and suspense had to be given its place. So they sat on the curved rock at the top of the knob, talking, and waiting.

At other times, they would sit silent, listening to the night sounds on the mountain, the sharp snap of a nighthawk's call, or the chuff of a bobcat, or a thousand small sounds that had no identity but were only the mountain at night. And they would watch the pale moonglow touch the granite, like a dappled wash. He would feel her small shoulder against his, and sometimes she would lean into him just slightly, so that he could feel the press of her arm and the warmth coming from her slim body.

He kissed her one night when the wind had come up, booming across the slopes, rumbling into the hollows and bellowing into their faces, here at the top. They had to bellow, themselves, in order to talk, and they sat very close, his shoulder tucked in front of hers, their legs crossed, Indian style, his thigh tucked beneath hers. And he found himself turning and reaching across to her far shoulder, turning her toward him, and drawing her mouth to his, feeling the cool of her lips giving way, softening, and the damp warmth inside. She broke the kiss, and leaned back, a moment, saying, "Jessum." Just that, "Jessum," so he didn't know whether she was upset, or angry, or surprised. Or pleased. And then she was back, and this time she did it, the lips opening further, this time, giving him her breath, bringing her hand up to rub along his chest, so that he thought he might faint, or cry out, or begin to weep.

* * *

So it began. They would meet, now and find a place back in the laurels, where they would kiss and embrace. She let him touch her, and then, one day, she touched him, opening the side buttons on his overalls and snaking her hand down his belly, the cool fingers spreading out, then closing around him and caressing until he spurted, the hot fluid falling across his belly and her hand.

She told him her family had it all set that she would marry Billy James, but she swore she would never let it happen, that she would run away first. But when he told her he loved her, she only leaned forward and kissed him, saying nothing. He would lie awake at night furious with desire, remembering her body, her soft breasts beneath the rough fabric of her shirt, her mouth against his neck, and he would turn his face into the rumpled tick, breathing the hot, musty smell of the feathers and murmuring, "I love you, I love you," pushing himself against the rough canvas of the tick, seething with the knowledge that she had not said it to him.

Still they met, up on the crest of the knob each night, and still they kissed and touched. But she would not let him undress her, would not bare herself to him, the way she had so easily down at the spring pool. It had all changed. And it was as though they were both waiting, though they couldn't have said what it was they waited for: some sign, or movement, an event, or a word spoken that would release her to say, "I love you," to him. And he knew that until she did say this, the touching and caressing would go no further. And still, each night, he fumed and raged, mouthing love and longing into the musty feather tick, saying, "I love you, I love you" to the hot darkness of his own breath.

And then, one day, she wasn't there.

He had waited, sitting in the late shade of the laurel, anticipating her form appearing over the curve of the final rise to the crown of the knob, seeing her, the straight dark hair, the big, deep eyes, the way she walked with that hurried grace, the turn of her flank, that he had first seen years before at Crary's, when the very strangeness of the female's body had first entered his mind, become an image that forevermore, for all its remote inaccessibility, would be inscribed within himself, as potent to wrench and shake him as chills or fever. And now, the evening drew on and the view over the brow of the crest deepened and blackened, so that he wouldn't have been able to see her had she in fact appeared, rising over the swell of outcrop. And still he imagined he saw her, the deep eyes, but now he saw her in an agony of loss, indecision, and fear. Something had happened.

He waited for her each day that week, more desperate each evening, as he became increasingly to expect that she wasn't coming, as Tuesday became Wednesday, and he sat on the rounded rock by the entrance to the laurel thicket, until, by Thursday he knew that he wasn't even waiting for her, at all; he was waiting, instead for her non-appearance, for the moment when he would rise in the dark and turn back down the trail *on our side of the mountain* and head back home. And so he sat, tasting the first acrid beads of bitterness that rolled and dropped over a shelf to accumulate in some well deep inside, where he would sip them for the rest of his life.

Because he knew, by Thursday, that she'd been caught, that her brothers had somehow found her out and had forbidden her to come here, to meet this Morelock boy. Perhaps he'd known it all along, known it even in the silence that always followed his vow, all the times he'd spoken *I love you* to a kiss that came too quickly, so he knew now the kiss had been a defense, the way a feint in battle can be a way of protecting the main force, the real thing. Perhaps, on this Thursday—there was a light rain falling, and he sat still, feeling the wet slowly working its way through his shirt and his overalls, that had actually felt warmer and heavier when the rain first began to work into the thick cotton, now turning cold and wet, *soaked through*, and the skin itself puckering and shivering—

perhaps he believed now that she'd known all along, that she'd withheld the ultimate vow, the ultimate baring of flesh and self, because she'd known that this day, this slow rain, was coming, and that the entire summer of talk and touch, the sweet bruise of flesh against flesh, had all been make believe, as ephemeral as those mythical giants. Because, even at sixteen, the female is so much older and wiser than the male, generation after generation of woman taking man into herself, where he loses himself into the dark, wet center, and then she loses him, watching him go off to destroy other men, driven, somehow, by the very passion that had brought him—whimpering like a child—into her, all because he didn't even know what it was he needed so much, that she could give him, offering herself, if he only could understand. So that now, by sixteen, every young woman already knew—was born knowing—that love is loss, life is loss, love is only the tingle on the skin after the warm, wet glisten has already evaporated and gone.

So he knew, by Thursday, that she wasn't coming, that she had been turned aside by her brothers, that she had probably acquiesced, since he now believed she had always surrounded herself in that fatalism, the expectation of the end of this impossible thing that he had insisted was the truth, when she had known all along it was no more than the glow of moonlight on stone.

Still, he waited, through Friday and Saturday, because he wanted to see for himself, and he knew he would see, on Sunday, at church. *If they let her even go to church*, he thought, and then the waiting became an agony, again, because now he had to wonder if she would be there at all, for him to see, test, whether in fact she had become a Hampton again, and he a Morelock, once more tasting the beads of bitterness that had already accumulated into a deep layer, somewhere inside, where he could actually feel their weight, and he realized that he felt older and that *age* was really nothing but the fall of those beads, the growing heaviness at the bottom of nowhere.

* * *

But she had been there. He saw her the moment the wagon pulled into the clearing, at the base of the mountain, where the stark white church stood, almost exactly the same distance from each homestead, the rutted tracks diverging diagonally up each side of the big creek, splitting and disappearing around east and west slopes of the humped, balsam-clad knob, and descended, each Sunday, by each family, in creaking gray wagons, their beds curved and worn, looking more like molded clay than wood, each family tying up at opposite sides of the plain clapboard church house, stacking shotguns and pistols into the wagon bed, tugging frocks and coats into place and entering, decorously, silently, into the one place and one time where, by mutual consent, they set aside violence and strife, prayed for grace and sang about *that peaceful shore.*

She was there, in a cream muslin dress, her arm held by an older brother, who directed her, pulled her along, in fact, into the church, while she tried feebly to draw away. She looked at him once, the big blue eyes, dark as a well, while her brother was marching her up the steps of the church. But her gaze told him nothing; there was no look of affection, or pleading, or of comfort, or even of pain. There were only the dark eyes, large, rounded, bulging a little, looking at him steadily as the older brother pulled her through the door.

And now, though he still lay awake at night, burning and aching, it was no longer *I love you,* no longer the memory of her lips and hands, but only those eyes, expressionless and forbidding, and now he turned his face to the tick, smelling the thick residue and sweat of his own body, and pushing his mouth into the feathers, muttered *Hamptons, Hamptons, Hamptons,* hating them, because he knew it was Hamptons who had dragged her away, and so, now they had made him, forced him to be, a Morelock. And, being a Morelock, he hated them.

Hated them, but feared them as well, because they had been

able to do it, to take her away from him as easily as telling her she couldn't see him. So he felt like a furious child who had not gotten his way and has come to realize that he is too small and powerless to enforce anything he wills, because the larger stronger folks will simply take it away from him, subvert his will by the simple expedient of ignoring him. So he hated them, and feared them, and felt shamed by them.

Besides, he began to see it was true: the cascade of bitterness, the growing weight at the bottom of his soul, was nothing but age, and perhaps, now, he had simply come into his heritage. Perhaps this was only the way it always was, had been with his brothers, and this was just another version of youthful love that turns somehow into murder because young love is always only a preparation for age and regret.

Still, he wasn't ready. He still felt the quiet timidity that had always marked him as different from his brothers, and so, all those nights when he lay, sweating and cursing *Hamptons Hamptons*, he railed, too, against himself, wondering *how can I strike and wound, as I should, when I am so afraid?*

So it was with profoundly mixed feelings that he received his father's order to join them in the ambush. It was a month after that Sunday, and he had heard his father and brothers talking, sensed the tone of conspiracy in their voices, knew they were planning something. The liquor running had become a larger and larger business, so that now they had brought Snide into the operation. No longer an active hostler, though he kept up the semblance of a business, Snide now drove a canvas-covered flat-bed truck that would meet the wagons at the head of the hollow and load a few hundred jars at a time. And now up at the mill, they would adulterate some of the whiskey with creosote, some with lye and turpentine, so they could call it by different names: scotch and rye, and sell it for higher prices, because city folks wanted red liquor.

The Hamptons had been trying to do the same thing on a much smaller scale, running a wagonload of white liquor into

Glade, where they sold it to a dentist—he was a nephew of the mayor's—who peddled it out of the back of his office.

And it was time, Jessum's father, Cuddy Morelock, said, to "stop that leak," and to let the Hamptons know "who runs the liquor bidnits around these parts."

So Pawp took Jessum aside and handed him the short-barreled, single-shot carbine so old its stock was worn into a spoon shape, but perfectly clean and greased, perfectly deadly. And said, "It's time you help protect this here fambly," and, later, "We'll get them sonsofabitches and finish it once and for all."

And he was frightened. Eager enough, because he still lay awake, watching her eyes and hating the Hamptons for taking her from him. But to fight? To stand up and fire a rifle and be fired upon? He didn't know. He had no way of knowing how he would do, who had only a little over a month ago lain in the soft sedges beneath the laurel and felt her mouth move beneath his, heard the intake of her breath when he touched her, spreading his hands to frame the slope of her breasts and her belly. And now these same hands were curled around the carbine, eager and frightened.

When he lifted the rifle, hefting its weight, he realized with something of shock that he felt the same dropping pulse, deep inside—like swinging out over water—that he had felt when he first looked at her.

There was a plan, though he had not been allowed to discuss the details—he was still only sixteen, after all, and when he asked, he was told, "Jest do what you're told, baby brother, and everything'll go jest as smooth as water." So he only knew it had been some kind of setup: the Hamptons called in for a meeting, a "palaver," his father had called it, to discuss their share of the liquor business. A cease fire of sorts had been called, and, in a cordial and inviting manner, the Morelocks had intimated that they wanted to patch up old wounds, for the mutual benefit of both families. They hadn't expected to be trusted, entirely, of course, had, in fact, told the Hamptons they could bring their own weapons, just to show that there was no "funny stuff afoot." But, they said, "they aint no use squabblin over somethin can make us all rich, so come on over and let's kindly talk it out."

But, of course, there was ambush afoot.

"They aint going to fall for it," Kinnie said. "They'll never believe it enough to come prancing in there and wait to get blowed up."

"Did I say they'd fall for it?" Cuddy snarled. "Hell, of course they aint going to fall for it. What in hell you think?" He spat. "But they'll think we'd fall for it, or I don't know Hamptons. So they'll try and set us up at our own ambush. Like they done back in town." He laughed, a harsh cackle. "So we're a going to just set up the settin up. We'll get there before dawn and watch them come in and make their plans. Kill us a few of them."

THREE

On that Saturday morning in mid-autumn Jessum Morelock slung his rifle and dropped to his knees, pushing through the opening between two locust trees. The air was thin and bright, cool, though the sunshine itself was warm, and, inside the scrub and thicket, the late insects were working on the waning blackberry hips, the leaf debris beneath the evergreen laurel. The creek was only now just beginning to lose its "Indian surge," and Jessum could hear the slapping water behind him as he worked his way into the dense undergrowth. Immediately, he was surrounded by tangled, spider-webbed brush, thorned and alive with gnats, buzzing flies, briars. He was so constantly beset by snags, nettles, or insects that it seemed the thicket was crawling through him, rather than the other way around. He shrugged his carbine from his shoulders and used it to poke ahead, trying to wedge enough space to move toward the clearing at the mill. Behind him he could still hear the turbling creek as he worked his way through the hot, sweating, insect-thrumming brushwood, the red-and-yellow autumn foliage.

He felt a swell of fear wash over him, as though he were passing through a curtain of hot water, and for that moment forgot the lesser irritations of briar and nettle. *What in hell am I doing here?* He felt a countercurrent of shame. *Just didn't know how to say no, did you?* Because Pawp had told him, last night, had said,

"You're big enough to rut around the mountain, stickin your dick into them Hampton gals, you're big enough to have a shot at the sonsofabitches."

He stopped crawling for a moment, letting the emotion move over him. Then a sweat bee plunged at his arm and the sharp, cold sting made him jerk and fall forward as though he'd been shot.

"Jesus Christ," he breathed, rubbing his forearm and feeling the clammy sting shudder through his body. He had let go of his rifle and was lying outstretched in the deep redolence of leaf mould, his temples pulsing, hot, beneath the thin slick of cooling sweat. His ears were cold and he pushed one back against his burning skull, a small pool of relief. He felt the anxiety edge away, felt the drop into relative calm. Okay.

"Y'all in?" came a shout from his right. "Y'all in?" again. It was Vernon. *The chief of this here operation,* the young man told himself. *Iffen that's what he wants to call it, a operation. And what in the hell am I doing here?*

Cuddy had put Vernon in charge, and the oldest son had gathered Jessum and the others up the night before, and told them the plan, to get into the mill at daybreak and wait on the Hamptons to come in. "Get em all into the holler, like shoats in a pen, let em have it once and for all."

And I couldn't even find me a plain "no" to say. What in hell am I doin here?

"Y'all in?" Vernon called, a third time.

"Gimme minute," Jessum called to the tangle. "It's thicker'n a boar hog in here."

"Well get movin, little brother," came Vern's high, thin voice. "Aint going to be long now."

Jessum willed indifference to the nettles and stickers, the tremendous racket he felt he was making, and shoved his way bodily through the thicket until he spotted flickers of light through the brake. He smelled the pale trace of woodsmoke, the damped-down mill engine.

"I'm about there," he shouted. Using his carbine barrel, he forced open a cross of branches and looked out upon the flat ground, dappled here and there with autumn flowers. The piles of logs and timber, the big, slumbering engine. The flash of the old blade, the long, straight path of the sawtruck. The two big stills.

"I'm to it," he called. "I can see the truck."

"You still out of sight?" Vernon asked.

Still on hands and knees, Jessum haunched backward a foot or two, letting the crossed branches fall into place, covering. He reached forward and broke off a few smaller twigs and leaves, opening a slight view hole. He could see the blade. Propping himself on elbows, he hoisted the rifle and aimed, drawing a clear bead and sweeping boards, truck, and stills against the carbine's closely filed front sight.

"I'm good," he shouted. He settled his weight and again, suddenly, felt the fear splash over him, everything made ironically more ominous by the pale fall sedges in the mill ground, beyond. He wrung his hands around the carbine and began to feel real panic crowding his consciousness. "Goddammit," he said, aloud, fighting with his own mind, trying to negotiate with his own consciousness, to find something like peace, or at least easiness. "Goddammit."

"All righty," said Vernon's voice, cracking slightly. It seemed to come from behind Jessum now. "All righty. Let's all of us be pert goddamn quiet because they's going to be along in a mite. Now don't get flustered and shoot the first one of them boys. Wait on the whole goddamn lot. Just set still and don't shoot at nobody til I lets off the first round. Then y'all pitch in and let's nail the bastards."

Jessum had heard no one but Vernon and himself, though he knew his brothers were out here, across the way. And Kinnie, down at the end of the meadow, all of them set to lay down what Vernon called a "crossin fire."

The thought scared him again, and he felt perspiration pop from his forehead and hands. He tasted a dry, metallic acridity and his tongue felt slow and thick. He turned onto his side and reached for a small silver flask from his pocket. Vernon had given him the bottle last night, saying, "This here might help you keep your gunsights polished." It gleamed dully in the brushdark air. He watched his hands tremble as they unscrewed the thin cap. He tipped and swallowed two vigorous mouthfuls, feeling the liquid slide and burn into his stomach. He coughed and shuddered from the hot alcohol. *What in the hell am I doing here?*

He screwed the flask closed and set it on the ground near his hip, then drew out his cartridge box and set it below the view port he'd cleared. He let out a deep sigh and lay still, propped on elbows, feeling the liquor begin to set in.

Around the tangled perimeter of the meadow the five lay in wait, Jessum feeling intensely unready. He felt a victim of some oppressive power, and, again, felt a stab of regret at the thought of Laura. It was only four or five weeks ago they'd been together, out here on the mountain, her mouth to his, his hand on her soft breast. And now, here he was, forced to exact his family's revenge for his own deed.

And he didn't even know if he could. If he even knew how. He'd shot plenty of rabbit and deer. But to draw down on a man. To do it from cover, just to shoot a man, unawares. The others had been into town, had fought hard men with their fists, or with clubs, even, striking fast at the face, aiming to hurt a man as badly and as quickly as possible. The brothers could do it, bragged about it, about how they could thumb a man's eye out of the socket.

Kinnie, stationed at the south, the open end of the mill ground, carried a ten-gauge pump-action shotgun that Vernon had said, "Ought to hit somethin another." He had winked and said, "Don't none of you'uns get scared and run off south, down the meadow toward Kin, or he'll let fly with that ten-gauge, turn y'all into a pie safe." He had guffawed thinly.

***

Jessum had been lying still, waiting for what seemed a long enough time. *Maybe they aint a going to show up.* He turned his head and surveyed his small patch of thicket. *Like a coon in a canebrake.*

The brush shook and crashed, and a man dove into the narrow gap, nearly landing on Jessum, who jerked sharply, looking wildly backward.

The man rolled to his side and grinned.

"Sweet Jesus God," said Jessum. He wiped his hand gingerly across his brow, as though checking for blood, or testing a bruise.

"Couldn't draw down a goddamn thing over there," said Vernon. "Couldn't see around the planer-trimmer, rightly. So I figured I'd come on over here, keep you some company, baby brother. You got a good line?" he said, nudging the foliage aside with his rifle barrel. He drew the rifle back and licked its front sight. "We'll have us a shootin contest." His laugh sounded like a little boy's.

"You'd best not to come divin in here on a feller like that," said Jessum, hearing the quaver in his own voice. "Jesus Christ. You're a sight lucky I didn't shoot you." He wiped his brow again, with that same tentative motion.

"Would've shot you first, baby brother," Vernon grinned. "Your eyes was whiter than the holy ghost at midnight." He giggled, the little boy's laugh. "And your mouth was dropped open like you'uns was tryin to swaller a punkin."

He acts like this here is a play-party. What's he think this is?

"Yessir," Vern said. "We'll have us a shootin contest."

"I'm a hopin this aint no contest," said Jessum. "I'm a hoping we get one good shot at the bunch of them and knock them down. Go on home."

"Best make sure they stays down before you hitches up the damn sled."

They lay still.

"Maybe they aint a comin," Jessum whispered, after a few minutes.

"Hush. They'll be here directly."

They lay still, again. Waiting.

Some time later—Jessum couldn't have said how long—four figures entered the meadow. Their appearance seemed so sudden, Jessum and Vernon recoiled reflexively, then tensed forward.

Jessum could see the Hamptons talking as they moved to the center of the ground and turned, facing the way they had come.

Vernon nudged him and slid him a sly wink.

The Hamptons turned as a slim figure ran into the meadow, shouting something in a high-pitched voice.

Suddenly Jessum's eyes widened. His head jerked up and around, looking fixedly at his brother.

"Goddammit, Vernon, that's the girl," he hissed, his whisper scared and desperate.

"Hush," Vernon said.

"It's Laura, goddammit," Jessum said again.

"Shut it," whispered Vern. "You want me to rap you with this here gun barrel? I don't give a damn who it is, baby boy. What in hell do them Hamptons think, they can hide behind a gal?"

In the clearing, the men and the young woman were talking animatedly. Jessum saw the man shake his fist at the girl, threatening her. He could hear the sound of the man's voice, raised, round with anger. The girl turned and strutted away from the man, confronting another brother, who pushed her roughly aside.

"She's trying to stop them," he said.

"Hush," Vernon hissed.

Jessum wrung his sweating hands around the stock of his rifle. He wanted this all finished and found himself imagining it had already happened. He pictured himself at home, drawing off his brogans, or later, lying in the laurel with Laura, telling her it had been a mistake, and how it was a good thing nobody'd fired on them boys. Or as though it hadn't happened at all, even the waiting, and he was sitting at table with his brothers, eating dried beans and corn bread, talking. He wished he was at home. Anywhere.

He watched a shiny black insect laboring across the mould. It carried a filmy piece of debris, a wing from some dead fly, waving and turning as the animal finicked across broken leaves and rotted seed.

Silently, Vernon picked up a small stone and crushed the insect. He slid Jessum another wink, and mouthed a silent message: *Buck up, baby brother.*

A moment later, Vernon tensed and brought up his rifle. Two more men had entered the clearing.

Oh my God. Oh my God. I don't know what to do, what am I going to do? Jessum raised his rifle, shaking.

One of the newcomers gave the young woman a hug and said something to the other man. Jessum set his rifle down, reached back, and wiped his hands along his flank. He picked up the gun again and pointed it, just as the girl turned again and strode angrily, straight toward Jessum.

A moment later, the view was obliterated by the roar of Vernon's rifle.

Hab Hampton would never be able to explain how he'd seemed to know. Instinct of some kind, he supposed, or maybe, without actually hearing it, he'd reacted to the rolling click of a single-shot carbine being cocked, off behind, to his left, just beyond his sister's angry, flouncing form. Whatever it was, Hab was moving even before Vern Morelock's first shot was fired, diving for cover, behind a barked oak log. He shouted at Laura "Git, Laur! Git outen here!" at the same instant that he saw the muzzle flash from the thicket.

Hab fired one shot directly at the place before he leapt and side-stepped and rolled toward his sister, while shots rang out from the slopes. He heard the *whang* of a bullet striking a piece of machinery, as he dropped behind the partial cover of a rusted fly-wheel, and swung his weapon, looking for movement. He saw a flash and fired again, shouting, "Get down, Laur, goddammit, get down."

Jessum heard the bullet strike Vernon. It made a sound like a booted foot thumping into a mudhole: a heavy, resonant plunge, followed by a deep, sucking yawn. He felt the thick spatter on his right arm and turned to see Vernon throw both hands to his face and emit a loud sound, more bellow than scream. Small fountains of blood were spurting between the Vern's fingers, and then, as he pressed with his hands, came a great gush, as though he'd twisted a sodden rag.

Still making the noise, Vernon rose a little way, then fell over onto his back, his hands still wringing blood from his face. He was quiet for a moment, and then he made smaller sounds. He appeared to be trying to speak through the curtain of his bloodied hands.

Jessum leaned toward his brother, hesitantly, staring, then reached and pulled at the forearms, easing the dripping hands away.

From the eyes upward, the face was intact and had an expression not so much of horror as amused surprise. But downward, the shattered bridge of a nose was all that remained. What Jessum saw wasn't his brother, at all, but a gelatinous mass of flesh, flecked with bone and tooth. From where the mouth should have been, large pink bubbles rose and broke, scattering a fine spray of blood, then falling back, dripping off a stark white band of tendon, into the ruined maw. A guttering sound continued to come from somewhere inside.

The impending clouds of panic that had threatened Jessum's consciousness all day now broke over him, obliterating Vern, mill ground, gunfire, beneath a squall of terror. With a high shout, he leapt up, tearing at the vines and brush, yanking and thrashing out of the narrow nest, while, below him, Vernon's body began convulsing.

Jessum was standing, still flailing and grabbing at branch and vine, when his panic exploded outward. He raised his carbine, fired one wild shot, and turned to run, just as the bullet—like an enormous hammer—shattered his right arm. He spun and fell on his brother's lifeless body.

When he came to, he was lying on the wide front porch, at the home place. He heard the shouting through the dimmed gauze of shock and confusion: the terrible wound in his arm, the taste of dried bile, like bitter sap.

"Goddammit, who in the hell shot that gal?" his Pawp shouted at them all.

They stood, tense and anxious, in a ragged line in front of the porch, their heads lowered, each mumbling denials: "I didn't fire nowhere near the gal," or "I wouldn't shoot no gal," and then Claude raised his head and came back at his father, as though the old man had been at fault.

"Well, goddammit, why in hell'd they bring a dern girl along for?" he shouted. "You tell me that."

"Because they's a going to be hell to pay, that's why." Pawp's voice had raised even louder and he shook his fist.

"They kilt Vernon," Frank whined and began to moan, keening.

"They kilt Vernon," Pawp shouted. "And blowed Jess's arm half off," his voice rising. "Goddammit, and you shot a goddamn gal." He turned toward Jessum, who lay flat out along the porch, on his blood soaked tick—the same feather tick into which he had poured his nightly sobs of love and desire, and then, later, of hatred and loss. Now he turned his head, watching them, though they all seemed indistinct, wavering, as though he were looking at them through glass. He felt nothing but a strange pounding, a hot flame, where they'd twisted up the tourniquet, just below his shoulder, and a huge weight pressing somewhere further down his left arm, which felt enormous, larger than himself, larger than the whole clearing, even. Monstrous.

"Let's get this boy took care of," said Pawp, teeth clenched. "Where's Kinnie with that doc? That arm's going to have to come off."

Kinnie hollered from down the lane a few minutes later and appeared around the blackberry thicket leading Doctor Grimley, who rode a saddled jenny, his black leather satchel tied over the pommel.

"What in hell is going on up here?" Grimley said to no one in particular, as he slung a leg over and slid off the mule, staggering a bit, then straightening himself and brushing his black coat with over-scrupulous care. Beneath the frock coat he wore a filthy, collarless shirt, with worn striped trousers and button shoes of cracked patent leather. He had a three-day stubble of beard, and his breath had the rank-sweet reek of ether.

"You got Hamptons down into town, a hollerin murder, sayin you all done kilt their young gal, Laura," he said, stepping up to the porch.

"She's dead?" Pawp said. He spit. "Godammit," he said, turning to stare wild anger up and down the line of brothers. He looked back at the doctor and said, "We got dead up this aways, too." He paused a moment, scratching his head, then whimpered, "They kilt my boy Vernon."

"Well, I don't know what, Mister Cuddy," said the doctor, "but I wouldn't go down the mountain anytime soon, iffen you don't want a rope thrown round your neck. Them boys has got the whole town riled up."

Kinnie pointed and said in a high, thin voice, "Dammit, Doc, we got a young'un shot up, too. And Hamptons shot that gal themselves, trying to dry-gulch we'uns." He looked around at the others, inviting assent. "Aint that so?" The brothers began nodding.

"I reckon that's right," said Pawp. "Them sonsofbitches wanted so bad to get the drop on us, they done shot that poor girl of their own and this boy of mine, both."

"Well, I don't know what, mister Cuddy," the doctor said again, showing his palms. "I'm jest sayin I'd stay up from town until the law gets things settled. Folks'd be like to grab you all up before you could tell one side of the story or the other. I reckon the law'll be up thisaway tonight or tomorrow. I aint going back down, myself, before they get here, I'll tell you that. I like to got shot jest because I kindly agreed to come up here to treat one of you all. Or because I'm a side kin to you Morelocks might have been enough to set them all at me. No sir. I'm stayin put til the law come and kindly helps me back down. It's jest luck that your boy and I got out when we did."

"Well, let the bastards come," said Pawp. "We'll tell them boys the truth, if nobody else will. And it aint nothin like them lyin Hamptons'd say. Why else'd they run into town as fast as they could, except to kindly get their story told first? Well?"

"Well, I don't know what," Grimley said a third time. "Let's us have a look at this boy of your'n."

Jessum saw the doctor's grizzled face looming over him, smelled the sickly sweet breath. The others gathered round, watching the doctor as he knelt down and peered at Jessum's wound. When Grimley pushed a finger under the tourniquet, testing its tautness, Jessum didn't feel the pain so much as he saw it: a blinding flash exploding, white, then red. He screamed and kicked each leg once, his heels thudding hollowly on the porch boards. Then he lay still, sweating hard, his breath coming in long, ragged gasps. The door opened and his mother came onto the porch, drawn by the screams, wringing her hands in her apron, saying, "Lord help."

"Get a blanket to cover this boy, Mamma," said the doctor. "And you boys hold him good. I'm a'going to have to cut loose what's left of this shirt sleeve, and he aint going to like it too much. Somebody fetch my satchel."

This time he tasted the pain, coppery at first, and then sour, acid, like the hot smell of maple being cut, rising up from his stomach. He thought he would be sick, then he was whirling, falling back down a long, curved slide, spinning yellow and green and grainy.

When he came back to consciousness, someone was wiping his forehead with a wet cloth. He heard the doctor's speaking, sharp and loud, too clearly, as though it was the voice that was probing at the wound.

"Hell fire, what'd they shoot this boy with, a cannon?"

"It's pert bad, aint it?" said Pawp.

"Bad enough," said Grimley. "He's got a plenty clumps of dirt and shirt and God knows what else blown clean down into the bone. What's left of the bone." The doctor coughed and the boy smelled the sickly ether again. "We're a going to have to take this arm off. And we best do it quick as we can, or he'll poison-up."

"Well, I done figured as much," said Pawp. "It's a dreadful thing, I reckon, but we might's well get her done and get her over with."

The doctor pulled a dirty blue handkerchief and wiped his brow. "We got a mite of a problem," he said, his eyes flicking here and there, like a ring snake. He looked round at the father, and the brothers, then down at Jessum. "I come out of that town so quick. I aint got no bone saw on me. Nothin like it."

Jessum had listened emotionlessly to it all, until now. It had just been something to listen to, while he lay out here on the porch, head turned, watching them, their foreshortened figures as inconsequential as a stand of trees, the sound of their voices distinct and meaningless, like wind through the boughs. But when Grimley said those two words, *bone saw*, Jessum began to tremble violently. The wet cloth brushed his forehead again and he felt a hand smoothing his hair. His mother's hand. He tried to say something to her, to tell her he was afraid—because she might protect him from these men, from all this—but his mouth was too dry, and no sound would come. His mind began to shudder in time with his body, his heavy boots thumping the floorboards, like a dancer's.

The men stood around him, not speaking. The shuddering stopped for a moment, and he heard the grate of a guinea hen, from somewhere off behind the house. He began to shake again, feeling his thighs jerk, hearing the clatter of his feet.

"We got to do somethin," he heard Pawp say, at last. "Can we get him down the hill, into town?"

"He wouldn't live the trip," said Grimley. "I don't believe. And I done told you, anyways, aint none of us likely to live too long if we go down there before this gets cleared up. They's a dead gal layin down there, with a big ole hole in the side of her head. They'd be up here fixin to hang you right now, if they thought they wouldn't get shot themselves, for their trouble."

"I told you, them Hamptons shot their own kid and our'n both," said Kinnie.

Jessum's mother took her hand from his forehead. "You men hush," she said, "And let's get this boy of mine took care of, however you all are going to do it."

They stood silent, again. At last, Pawp said, "What do we need to do, Doc?"

"I don't got a bone saw," said the doctor querulously, like a spoiled child missing a toy. "And that boy'll poison-up iffen we don't get that arm off," he said hopelessly.

"Hell, we got a plenty saws," said Claude. "We got two-man saws and limbing saws and hand saws, what in hell kind of saw you need?"

"You all don't understand," said Grimley, still whining like a child. "It's got to be a quick, fine saw, take the bone off fast and clean. That's all that'll work. You don't take it off quick, the shock, it'll kill him."

"They's the small cross-cut trimmer, up to the mill." Kinnie said. "On the steam belt. It's still runnin and it's sharp as hell. It'd take that arm off quicker'n a snakebite."

They stared at Kinnie.

"Are you clabbered?" said Pawp. "You want to run this boy through the goddamn planer? What in hell's the matter with you? Whyn't just shoot him as he lies here, you won't have to pick him up to kill him."

"Goddamn it, Pawp, he's right," said Claude. "Doc says quick, can you think of ought quicker than to run him through the trimmer?"

They stood again, looking at Doctor Grimley. He mopped his brow, fast and nervous, and tucked the handkerchief into his coat pocket.

"Get some whiskey in this boy," he said.

From there on, he remembered it in snatched scenes, like snapshots, not even from his own perspective, remembered it as though he were one of the men, or the guinea hen—that far off—watching, outside the scene, impassive, seeing himself thrash and scream, his brothers holding him while the doctor tried to fill him with white liquor, that he choked on, spewing it, and his mother said, "Come on, son, take as much as you can. It'll help." So he drank it, his stomach curling back, flinching, but holding the liquor. He saw them pass the jar, three times around, steeling themselves. Saw Pawp look them over and say, "Let's get her did."

And then he saw another scene: they were preparing him, his body wrapped tight in the blanket and bound with bale wire. He saw the blasted arm tied at wrist and shoulder to a flat narrow board, a cut-down tobacco-grading board, hand and forearm looking fine, normal—the fingers curved slightly upward, as though holding an apple, or cupping water—while, above the elbow, the blasted wound gaped, framed by the tourniquet. His mother held the board out from his body until Pawp made Kinnie take it from her, made her go away, and he saw her standing, a handkerchief pressed to her mouth as they carried him to the wagon and slid him onto the bed, Kinnie stepping up to steady the arm, and saw himself scream when the grading board hit the iron post-brace. Saw them gee up the mules for the ride to the mill.

He remembered the whine of the saw blade, and the one scene he was to recall directly: the sunlight flashing into his eyes from the waving red-and-gold treetops, the bright, bluewhite patch of sky overhead, the hard, flat surface of the board sled beneath him.

But he was far off again when the blade took the arm, and he saw the mangled length of flesh leaping away, the worn, marked board jerking out of Kinnie's grasp, flipping and spinning, away, showering specks of blood and flesh, the wrist still tied to the whirling board, the perfect fingers still curled upward.

And then he remembered nothing for a long while, so they had to tell him how they'd taken him back home, still wound up in the blanket, how the doctor said the blade had gone through the bone just fine, but had "gnawed up" the soft tissues, and how, before he got drunk, the doctor had tucked together as much of the ragged flesh as he could and had sewn it over the bone end, saying, "That stump aint going to look any too pretty. But I reckon we got the arm off about as good as could be done. Where's that jug?" Within an hour, the doctor was drunk and was weeping noisily about hurt and dying children and how he'd lost his daughter with diphtheria, and "Lord save me from ever havin to do what we done to that boy today."

FOUR

Shortly after dawn, the sheriff showed up with about eight others, all armed and ready for a fight. By then, the brothers had been up for hours. The two eldest had sat up with Vernon's body and were preparing to bury it first thing, along with Jessum's arm, in the family plot on the hill. But Pawp had stopped them. "Get Vernon in the ground quick, but leave that dead arm in the bucket for a bit. We're a fixin to need it. Now come along," he said.

Cuddy had taken each brother aside and questioned him closely about when he fired, where he fired, who he might have shot, saying, "You tell me dezactly, and no funny bidnits, because we got to know who kilt that gal before the law comes on up here."

He determined, finally, that the killer had to have been either Vernon or Jessum, since the others had fired further down the clearing, hitting two of the Hampton men. So he called the boys together again on the porch, where Jessum lay naked and unconscious, again on the bloodstained feather tick, sweating and trembling, while his mother ran the wet cloth across his brow and crooned to him.

"If Vernon kilt her, we're in good shape, because Vernon, he's gone and they can't do nothin to him. But we need to take care of what if this boy done it," Pawp said. "Kin, fetch me that carbine."

When Kinnie brought the rifle Jessum had carried, Pawp grabbed it and strode off the porch into the clear, saying, "Fetch me a mule," he said. "Fetch me Stephen, he aint worth a goddamn, no more."

They led the old jack mule out on a halter, bringing him up alongside the shed where Pawp waited, carbine in hand.

"Hold him still now," he said. He directed the rifle at the animal's front leg, just below the hock. "Hold him now," he said, and fired.

The mule went sideways, its weight held by the brothers while the foreleg blew up, mushrooming sinew and blood. The animal made no sound, leaning against the brothers, its eye bulging, showing white.

"Jesus, Pawp," Claude shouted. "Jesus."

"Hold on to the damn thing," Pawp yelled. He moved three strides and leveled the rifle at the mule's hind leg. He fired, again, again the blossoming flesh, the animal still making no sound, falling, not back against the brothers this time, but the other way, toward Pawp, who danced out of the way, like a beach walker dodging surf. The brothers stood back, quiet, as the mule began to thrash, still making no sound, its ruined legs flopping like broken sticks.

Pawp turned and began walking away, saying, "You boys dig them slugs outen there and bring them up to the house."

As Pawp strode away, Kinnie ran to him, shouting. "Pawp, dammit, Pawp. At least kill the damn mule. Don't let him just buck around like that."

Pawp turned and looked his son in the eye. "Do what?" he said.

"Put the damn mule outen its pain, at least," Kinnie said. Behind him the animal flubbed, spastic, its head turned back, the great curved neck, eyes wide and white, watching its own body shudder and wrack. "Jesus, Pawp!" Kinnie said, showing his own eye-white.

Pawp raised his chin, looking over Kinnie's shoulder, watching the wracking mule. He took a deep breath, then released it in a long, loud, sigh. "Nevermine that mule," he said. "We aint got no time to waste on a mule."

"At least just kill him," Kinnie said. He turned and looked at the quaking animal. "What in hell's wrong with just killin him?"

Pawp turned and thrust the carbine into his son's hands.

"You kill him, you're so god damned worried about him," he said, and strode off. After a few steps, he stopped and shouted, "Make sure you hit bone. And bring that slug up here along with the other two. We're a going to need one looks a hell of a lot like it hit a boy's arm."

Twenty minutes later, the brothers came back to the porch. Claude held out his hand, three misshapen bullets in his palm.

Pawp peered closely at each slug, then picked one up. "Here," he said. "Somebody take this un."

Claude opened his other hand and Pawp dropped the bullet into the curve of the palm.

"Now listen," Pawp said. "Take that slug and get up that dead arm outen the bucket. Take and shove the bullet in there, right down into the bone, hear? Junior, you wipe down this here carbine. Smear a little mite of oil on it, real light and push your forearm around on it a mite. Just your forearm: don't get no fingers on it. Then run it up to the sawmill and drop it over near to where Hab Hampton was, yesterday. And Claude, take them other two slugs and get rid of them, where nobody'll find them."

Pawp spat. "Then we can show the law how this all transpired, kindly. Get shed of it."

"What in hell is this all about, Pawp?" said Claude.

"You nevermine. I'm just doin' a little fix-em-up. You just make sure you shot at them other Hamptons after they shot at you. Self-defense. Once we hand that bullet to the law, we're in the clear and it's the Hamptons'll be dodgin nooses." He turned away, then stopped. "Get that mule the hell outen here, too. I don't care if you have to feed it to the dogs, I don't want no sign of that mule left."

By the time Jessum came out of his delirium, two days later, it was all over. But they told him about it, gloating over it, saying, "Aint no flies on Pawp, I'll tell you that."

Because the law had come, angry and threatening arrest. Cuddy had met them, unarmed, and shown them Vernon's new grave and the hurt boy, saying, "They got the drop on Vern, the sonofabitches, and when we come runnin, they shot my boy. He weren't even armed, just followin the sound, kindly. My boys, they got a few of them Hamptons after that, sure enough, but you can't hang us for that." In answer to questions about Laura Hampton's death, Pawp said, "We never saw no gal. So she must've been shot before we got there. Must've been one of them first shots we heard, when the dirty egg suckers shot Vernon."

The sheriff, clearly disbelieving, said they'd found a rifled bullet in the girl and he wanted to check their weapons. "I find the rifle that shot her, I'll hang the bastard that owns it."

Pawp rubbed his toe in the ground, saying, "That's a good idea, Sheriff." Then, as if just thinking of it, he said, "Say, you mayt want to gawge around a mite in Jessum's arm, too. We aint buried it yet. Likely they's a ball in that wound somewheres."

It had worked perfectly. The sheriff found a bullet in the arm, just as Pawp had said, and took it away with him. Later that day, his deputy found the carbine up at the mill, and, since Hab Hampton had drawn them a sketch of the ambush, showing where he and his brothers, and Laura, had been standing, they could pinpoint the carbine as having been dropped at around the spot from which Hab had been firing. Hab, eager to avenge Laura's death, had told the full story to the sheriff, even already owning to probably having shot Jessum, himself, "Because that boy jumped up right where the gun shots'd been comin from and so I fired at him and down he goes." And on the same drawing, he showed that Laura and Jessum were both generally in the line of fire from his position. So he had set himself up for Pawp's "fix-em-up," by telling the truth in his eagerness to bring the law down on whoever had killed his sister.

Later that week, the new state laboratory declared the bullet that killed Laura, as well as the one out of Jessum's arm, had probably come from that same carbine, certainly not from any of the other weapons they'd checked, from either Hamptons or Morelocks. Hab had protested, "It aint none of my gun," saying he wouldn't have carried "a squirrel gun older'n your grandpawp," and saying he'd shot Vernon in self-defense, "And if you all will kindly dig around in Vern Morelock, you'll find the slug from my Remington, goddamn it."

But Vernon was in the ground by now, and even the law was afraid to tell the Morelocks to dig him up. Besides, Hab's argument sounded pretty far-fetched, since it still didn't explain how that carbine had gotten to his own spot on what they were calling the "firing ground." Nor did it explain why the sheriff found a bullet from the carbine in Jessum's arm—when Hab had already admitted to shooting Jessum—unless Hab had been firing the carbine. The logical conclusion was that Hab had shot Jessum, Vernon, and, in the heat of battle, had accidentally shot his own little sister. And, the sheriff (and the town) said, "You mayt've shot them Morelocks in self-defense—though they'd dispute you on that—but you sure as hell didn't shoot sister Laura in no self-defense, hey?"

So they gloated when they told him how Pawp had fooled them all and gotten the town to change its allegiance overnight from Hamptons to Morelocks. How Pawp had created the evidence proving Jessum and Laura were victims of the same gun, then switched that gun from Jessum's hand to Hab's. How Pawp had said, "Well, shit. They can try to put it on Jessum all they want, but you tell me how they're a going to say Jessum shot hisself in the arm with his own rifle?"

But all Jessum saw was the figure of Laura running into the scene, trying to stop the fight. And his own panic: the wild shot, the frenzied running, and the bullet tearing into his arm. And he saw himself falling, while Laura lay, already dead, in the meadow.

When Hab's bullet smashed into Jessum's arm that Sunday afternoon, he had still been the timid, quiet young man—so different from his brothers—who had met Laura up on the mountain, vowed his love, learned bitterness and pain. His love had turned to hatred of the Hampton brothers, who'd taken her away from him, but even that hatred was tinged with a kind of fearful unwillingness, the shadow of his earlier temperate diffidence.

But when he awoke, after two days of fevered delirium, to find he'd killed Laura Hampton with that one wild, panicked shot, during what folks were already calling the "Shaleen Creek Affair," he had been utterly changed. The gentleness was gone, along with any margin of sadness or grief. Even the beads of bitterness were coated over with a hard, cold lacquer, so that he no longer felt pain, or even disappointment. When he was up out of bed, he walked in a sort of stupor, responding clearly enough when approached or questioned, but without expression, his speech and gestures—even his walk—devoid of personality.

He was unable or unwilling to accept blame for killing Laura. He was equally incapable of seeing that his father and his own brothers had been the central cause not only of her death, but of Vernon's, not to mention the loss of his own arm. It was, instead, all the Hamptons' doing. And where, before, he had hated them in an agony of loss and bewilderment—because they had forced him, no matter how his own soul was at variance with his brothers, to be a Morelock—the hatred was personal and directed. But now the Hamptons had become something like a determinate, natural principle, as total and invariable as the orbit of the earth, the tides, or the seasons. So there was no frenzy to his hatred, now, because what purpose did it serve him to rail against the sun or the rain? Instead, there was a settled, grim enmity, in which he walked and breathed, ate and slept, a state of being, because now Laura was gone, and there was only the detested notion, *Hamptons*, that had taken her away. And with no one left in the world to understand the quiet boy, to know what it had been, touching her, looking into her big, deep eyes. No: there was nothing left but the cold, impersonal hatred.

Gradually, the extreme enervation faded, and he would speak, and react almost the same as any other person. But always the grim center remained. In this, he eventually came to resemble his father, Cuddy, the narrow glaring eyes looking out from some stark cave of resentment or hostility, not at anyone in particular, but at everyone, everything.

He resumed a round of "normal" life, working in the family liquor operation. As central as "Hamptons" were to his own personality, since the ambush they had ceased to be any sort of rival to the Morelock clan. There were too few of them left, and Hab, having barely escaped prosecution, moved the remainder of the family down the mountain, across to the eastern, the "Carolina," slope, and had shifted his own modest moonshining operation toward Asheville, where Morelocks weren't involved.

A month or so after the shootout, Jessum's brother, Kinnie, had caught Lon Hampton on the lane down the mountain, had wrapped the man in swaths of barbed wire, and shot him. But the act had been witnessed by a farmer, and Kinnie had gone to prison for it.

And from that moment, the feud appeared to have melted away from the life of the county and to have entered into its folklore, the heritage of un-memory, so that the region could forget its own brutishness and recreate itself as inheritors of colorful "mountain ways." Laura and Jessum even took their place in the legend, becoming the obligatory Romeo and Juliet characters mandatory to the mythology of any feud, anywhere.

The government turned most of the area around Shaleen Creek into national forest, though the Morelocks kept their home place, with the long wooden porch where Jessum had lain, wounded. The mill ground gradually became overgrown, abandoned, at least for the time being. Jessum married, rather late, a plain-faced stupid woman who bore him three sons, and who carried on the harsh round of housework, endured his beatings, and died without complaint or comment. Two of the sons left for work on northern factories as soon as they were able. The one remaining boy took in all of his father's bitterness and grim, bridled fury, and turned it into a cocky insouciance as baleful and threatening as a loaded shotgun. And twenty years later, they, too, would decide they weren't finished with the Hamptons.

But now, some seventy-five years after the blow that had taken his arm and severed his last strands of sensitivity, Jessum Morelock looked up at the man—Jim—whom his grandson had ushered through the doorway of his dank, dirt-smelling dugout cabin, and saw those eyes again. And the sight propelled him backward, through the years of grisly death, the harsh decades in which he walked through a world forever and entirely drawn by the orbit of Hamptons, back into the soft times, the nights on the top of the knob, the touch of her hand and the hopeless words—*I love you*—spoken from the last full season he would ever know.

PART THREE

MORELOCK

Out of this same light, out of the central mind,
We make a dwelling in the evening air,
In which being there together is enough.
—Wallace Stevens

ONE

But Jim didn't live in the old man's world, didn't know or feel any of the lifting of the veil, time's shift away from the dark dugout cabin to the old times of love and death. All Jim saw was the ancient, one-armed man, the look of shock on his weathered face; all he heard was the terrible keening cry, "O Lord, O Lord," as the man fell to his knees.

After her first, quavering question, "Who's that?" the woman had stood stock still in the background, not responding at all to the strange cries, playing no part in the scene itself.

Although Jim had been amazed and, for a moment, paralyzed by the old man's outcries, the young man with the shotgun had been the most obviously moved by what had happened, He had leapt to the old man's side, and, letting the gun drop to the floor, had fallen, as well, onto his knees. Grasping the grieving old man's shoulders, the young man cried, "What's it Pawper? What's it? What's he done to you,"

For a moment these two strange figures kneeling and rocking on the dirt floor in the dark, redolent dugout were the single point of resolution to the entire trip up the mountain, the furious thickets of laurel through which Sam and Jim had driven, the bowl of the meadow, the rusting and enfeebled machinery, the sudden captivity, and the march into the back-throat smell of the cave-cabin. And then the woman and the old man, suddenly and pointlessly reacting to Jim's figure coming through the doorway, as though they had seen something they'd been expecting and fearing but that had nevertheless amazed and shocked them, the way people can become inured even to an obsession, or a fear, so that its effect is numbness, a kind of ennui, in the place of the compulsion, the intense emotion. And then the thing appears again, and the shock is all the greater, the shock of recurrence. So Jim had walked through the door and his own presence had triggered the impossible, anticipated thing.

And now Jessum Morelock, embraced by his strange and violent grandson, rocked and cried, and the two swayed back and forth in grotesque embrace, the one keening, "O Lord," the other holding him and nearly blubbering, "What!" What's it, Pawper?"

And then the younger man seemed at once to recall Jim, and, turning, said "What the hell you done to my Pawper?" as he closed his hand, again, around the shotgun.

But Jim had shaken off the initial paralysis caused by the bizarre scene and was already fleeing, dodging out of the doorway and out into the meadow. He could see nothing in the bright sunlight of the meadow, but he heard the chuff of the steam engine as he veered by its bulk. He believed he had gotten away clean, when, at the very moment of thinking this, he tripped on a piece of rusting rail, and fell headlong.

"You damn sonofabitch, you stay right there," the young man's voice rang. Holding the gun to his shoulder, at full point, he marched out of the doorway, angrily yanking back both triggers. "I'll kill you, you dern sonofabitch," he cried, striding another pace and stopping to steady his aim. Jim watched him come, the fear swirling and shrieking inside, knowing, *I'm going to die now.*

He'd almost forgotten about Sam, in the strangeness and fury of the past moments. But now he heard the familiar voice, and he thought, *Sam. Sam.*

"Drop the gun or I'll turn you into souse meat." Sam stepped out from behind the engine, his arm extended, pushing a pistol up against Pierot Morelock's temple. The shotgun clattered to earth.

Turning to Jim, Sam said, "You ready to go, cousin?"

The truck was parked up behind the steam engine. They took the shotgun and ordered Pierot back into the dugout, whence Jim could still hear faint wailing.

"Let's not waste no time," said Sam, pulling Jim in the direction of the truck. "Let's just get the hell out of here."

As Sam slung the truck around the panting engine and began to head it onto the curved expanse of the meadow, Jim wiped his brow, shaking his head.

"Jesus," he said. "That was…"

"Shit!" Sam shouted, just before a loud cracking sound, as the truck's rear window spiderwebbed, followed immediately by the noise of the rifle shot. "He's got hisself another gun," Sam said, grimly, as he punched the accelerator.

Jim turned to look. Behind them, the man was running onto the meadow. He stopped, pointed and Jim saw the puff then heard the skewing sound of the twenty-two. Sam lurched at the wheel as the truck slewed into a dip and threatened to wallow. He nudged the shotgun toward Jim.

"Here," Sam said, "Take a shot at the sonofabitch. Slow him down, some."

"What?" Jim said, alarmed. "I don't know how to shoot a gun."

"Pull the goddamn hammers back and shoot the thing."

"What if I hit him?"

Sam gave Jim an incredulous look, just as the tires found purchase and the truck bounded forward.

"Nevermind," he said. "Let's go."

***

When they had entered the laurel thickets, Sam began to tremble. Fifty yards into the tangle, he stopped the truck, leaned out the door and threw up. Finished, he slammed the door and looked at Jim.

"You okay?" Jim said. Sam's face was ashen.

"There's a pint in the glove box" Sam said.

Jim found the pint mason jar filled with evil-looking brown fluid.

"Stumpblower," he said, handing the jar to Sam.

"Stumpblower," Sam said, grimly, unscrewing the lid and taking five big gulps. He wiped his mouth, ran his sleeve around the jar rim, and handed it dourly to Jim.

"Now just what the hell was that all about?" he said.

That night in the office, after a quick supper of frozen pot pies, Jim had told it again, this time for Leela's benefit. He told about the strange, vacant-eyed younger man—Pierot—who had appeared to have no reason to hold Jim at gunpoint beyond the mere fact that he was up there, "snoopin." Told about the march to the dugout, the woman and the ancient man, the woman's single question—*Who's that?*—and the man's startling reaction, the wailing and pleading. And, finally, Sam's nick-of-time appearance, and what Sam insisted on calling "the gunfight" on the way out of the meadow. Jim told Leela about the strange smell in the dugout, that he'd finally placed it: it was the same thing they'd smelled that first day, when they went to the motel.

"Well I know what that is," said Sam. "It's methamphetamine. Smells like somebody took a shit in a can of hairspray."

Leela listened through the entire story in silence, sitting on the couch with Jim. At last, she spoke.

"What in the world do you suppose it means?" she said.

Sam cleared his throat and took a sip of his drink. He had continued to consume stumpblower in steady quantities all the way back and through the evening. Though he didn't appear drunk, he seemed to have lost his shakes and to regard the day as something of an adventure.

"Cousin says he thinks they recognized him," Sam said.

"Recognized you?" Leela asked, raising an eyebrow. She was drinking honeyed tea, as was Jim, though he had accepted the addition of a shot of Jack Daniels, at Sam's insistence.

"I know it's impossible," Jim said. "The man had to be close to a hundred years old, and it's not as though either one of them got a very good look at me before it all started. But what else could it be? What else could explain the reaction?"

"Do you think maybe that was your mother and your grandfather?" said Leela, very quietly. "Maybe you walked right out of nowhere into their memories. That would sure explain the reaction."

"God," Jim said. "I hadn't even thought of it, in all the confusion."

"That's what we went up there for, aint it?" Sam said. "Find your momma? Maybe we did."

Jim sat still for several seconds. Leela squeezed his hand.

"I don't believe it," he said, at last. "Would you recognize someone you'd never seen, at least since he was one year old? And besides, the old man, he wouldn't ever have seen me before, would he? Ever? And his reaction was the strongest. He looked like he'd seen a ghost."

"How old was she?" said Leela, still speaking quietly, thoughtfully.

"She was the right age, I suppose," Jim said. "Hard to tell. She didn't look too good, from what I could tell. Remember, I didn't get but a glimpse. She could have been the man's daughter, too, I suppose. Neither one of them looked like me."

Sam pulled himself up and waved his glass at both of them.

"But we already know about her. That's why we went up there, had to shoot our way out of there, aint it? Leela already told us about her. And her name was 'Evelyn.' Not Allie."

"I'm not sure it was Evelyn," said Leela, hopefully.

"But it wasn't Allison," said Jim.

"No," said Leela. "I'm right sure of that."

Jim held his cup out to Sam. "I think I might take one more little bit of that whisky."

"Surely," said Sam. He got up and walked around the desk, a bit unsteadily. Halfway around, he stopped and swayed, leaning, resting his right hand on the wall, against the big contour map. "Whoa," he said, speaking to himself, "Steady, big fella."

Jim watched him. Suddenly, he felt a deep, dropping sensation, as if he'd been on a high-speed elevator, his stomach dipping reflexively. But this was no elevator. This was Sam's hand on that map.

"Wait," Jim said. He began to stand, then settled back onto the couch, turning to Leela, excitedly. "Wait!"

"You don't want the booze?" Sam said. "Whyn't you tell me?"

"No," Jim said, then said, "Wait," again, and again, "Wait." He squeezed Leela's hand. "How do we know her name was Allie? I mean how do we know that, really?

"Because it's written on the paper," Leela said.

"Sure," Jim said. "But the paper also says she's from Shaleen Prong. And she is," he said, growing more excited. "But it's Chasteen—C-H-A-S-T-E-E-N—isn't it?" He looked at Leela, then at Sam.

"So you're sayin…"

"I'm saying the only reason we know her name was Allie Morelock is that's what's written on the paper. And she didn't write it. The lawyer or somebody did, and they wrote what they heard, just like they did with 'Shaleen.' So we don't know her name is Allie. We only know it sounds like that."

"Sounds like it to a city lawyer, who spelt it that way." said Sam. "Could be most anything, down here. But you'd be hard put to get Evelyn out of Allie. Or vice-versa."

"But I don't know if that's right," said Leela. "I can't remember exactly."

"Emily?" said Sam, still leaning on the map. He made quick motion, half belch, half hiccup. "Elizabeth?"

"No," said Leela.

"Look," said Jim. "Let's sleep on this. It's been too crazy a day. I'm not sure this is really on the right track, anyway. It was just seeing Sam at the map made me think of it. It could yet be her."

"It does make some sense," said Leela.

"Surely does," said Sam. "But I be damned if I'm a goin back up there to ask her."

"Our momma used to go around the house recitin poems," Sam said, next morning after breakfast. "She loved poetry and she came from a time when they had declamation classes and contests and all that. She won the county once and I reckon that set her off. She'd go around declaimin, left and right."

He and Jim were sitting in the office, while Sam worked out the "lay-down" for this week's issue, moving clips of type and advertisements around like a shell game. At times, he would say, "Hell," and come around the desk to shuffle through piles of paper by the wall, where he would come up with another piece and say, "Let's try this one." He seemed to be perfectly able to carry on a conversation while he did this, and Jim had asked him how he'd gotten to be the owner of a weekly paper. Sam had answered by talking about his mother.

"It was pretty bad poetry, I suppose, at least by you all's standards. 'Life's Final Star is Brotherhood,' that sort of thing. She loved 'O Captain, My Captain,' too, used to stalk around the house with a dust mop in her hand, a sayin, 'The prize we sought is won,' and she'd get to 'fallen, cold and dead,' and you could hear her choke up, like she'd just got the bad news that old Abe had got shot. As if she hadn't declaimed the damn thing a hundred times that week.

"So I believe it was Momma who made me decide I wanted to

be a writer, and it was probably my daddy who turned it into being a newspaper man. Because Daddy, he wanted to know everything that was goin on. He wouldn't just hear some story from somebody, but he'd want to know when was this, and how'd that happen and you could see him light up as he got folks to telling him what was up. And I wanted to be able to do that.

"Isn't that funny," said Jim. "Leela didn't say anything about your father's curiosity. In fact, to the contrary."

"How's that?" said Sam. "What did she say?"

"Never mind," he said. "So you decided to be a newsman."

"I did," said Sam. He looked around the room. "I'm not so sure I became one, though, did I? Not much of one."

"Well, maybe part of growing up is realizing you're going to wind up where you are and not where you thought you'd be. Sort of the opposite for me, I guess."

"About the only thing I do that's really anything like a newsman is drink," Sam said. "You know, I've been all over Leela for putting up with that skunk of a husband, living a life so far below what she could be. And look at me." Sam gestured to the office, the piles of papers, his expression taking-in the utter triviality of the venture. "I'm writing lost dog stories and obits, and pasting up ads for the barber shop. It's a hell of a ways from what I'd thought I'd be. A newsman."

"You said Leela was probably afraid of what she didn't know," said Jim. "Any chance that's about you, too?"

"I need a goddamn drink," said Sam. He turned to the cabinet behind the desk. "You want any?"

"No," said Jim. "Thanks."

Sam fetched a bottle and a small glass. As he poured, he looked around the office. He laughed. "Yeah. Maybe that is me. This aint much of a news office, but you got to admit it's comfortable. More like a halfway house than a newspaper office. Like I said, a missing person's bureau and a battered wives' shelter." He tossed back a swallow of the whiskey.

"It could be a rehab center, too, if you want to cut back on that booze," said Jim.

"I'll make a deal with you," Sam said, gesturing with the glass. "I'll go out and get me a real story. Be a real reporter for once. Think maybe I could do that? Huh?"

Jim said nothing. Sam took another drink.

"Hell, I've got a story sitting right in my lap, and it might help Leela get shed of that bastard, too, if it goes anywhere, since he's up to his eyeballs in the damn business."

"You're talking about the drugs?" said Jim.

"Drugs, yes," said Sam. "Lindee and Trapper, at the motel. That's what she wanted to talk about. Didn't want nothing on the record, as they say, but still, wanted to tell me. Methamphet-amine being cooked up here and took down to Roalton in trade for pain pills and crack. Run those up to the coal fields—along with what's left over of the meth—and sell for a dollar a milli-gram. Fifty-milligram pill of oxycontin yieldin fifty bucks. Not bad, when you know you traded for it with ten cents on the dollar meth. And guess who's behind the whole operation."

"How do you know that's what he's doing?" said Jim. "Why would you have to buy meth in Roalton from somebody down here? Why not just make it in Roalton?"

"No connections," Sam said. "No local contacts. Keep the sup-plier out of the seller's neighborhood, always a smart idea. Same as runnin white liquor. And it's a hell of a lot easier to make it down here, just like the liquor, too, where won't nobody smell it and bother you about it. Right?" He waved his glass, a dismissive gesture. "And they've already got a million connections, from all the generations of doin somethin like this. Got the local law in their hip pocket. You couldn't go to the law on them or they'd just come right back at you.

"Still, I don't see how you can know for sure that's what he's doing. Maybe the girl has a grudge against him and is trying to set him up. How are you going to prove it?"

Sam waved the glass again. "He's from a long line of runners. Booze and probably drugs, too, for generations. The local crime family, really. Aint that what you Morelocks are? A kind of mountain man's mafia? Run the other families out of the business, take it all over? Hell, that weren't no colorful mountain feud. That was a gang war, at least on the one side. Why would you be the least bit surprised if it's still going on, one way or the other? And we smelled the meth. Over to Gracie's. And you, up on the mountain. If you're a smellin methamphetamine in a mountain cabin who in hell do you think is runnin that show? The old man? The woman? That moon-faced idiot that caught you, marched you around up there? Hell. It's Paul Morelock and his goddamn 'Pawp,' all the way."

"That doesn't prove anything," Jim said. "You want to be a real newspaperman, you've got to be able to write the truth and back it up it."

"Don't worry about that," said Sam. "I didn't make this up. I got my sources, for once."

That night, while Jim was out getting groceries, Leela stood in front of Sam, her eyes bright, saying "No, Sam," again and again.

"Why, Leela?" Sam said. "Aint it about time one of us was true to something other than moonshine thugs and lost dogs?"

"Because it's dangerous," she said. She pointed to the bruise on her eye. It had lost some of its deep indigo color and was turning into what Sam had said was "a color chart," showing blood red and yellow and green, even bright blue, shading into the ring of deep violet. "You been watchin me when I've come through the door over the past years? Does it look like he's a lot of fun to tangle with?"

"Hell, if my baby sister can…"

"No, Sam," Leela said again. "Leave it alone. Don't get yourself hurt."

"Honey," Sam said, "All my life I've been telling myself I was going to be a reporter and run a newspaper down here that had some matter to it. All my life I been pretendin I was doing that.

But I aint, and you know it. And I know it. Now for once in my goddamn life I'm a going to write something that matters. And I'm going to send it down to Roalton and get it printed there, too. You watch me."

"What's got into you?" Leela said. "Why can't you just stay put? This aint a bad life, is it? Bad enough to lose it?"

"What made you to finally pick up and leave that sonofabitch?" Sam said, his voice rising. "Or are you going back soon, because he's too dangerous to leave? That's it, isn't it? Instead of a romantic outlaw, you got yourself a murderous brute of a bastard. And now you're too scared of him to leave him for good, scared of just how bad he can be? That it."

"I left him, didn't I?" Leela said, eyes blazing. "I left."

"Yes, I reckon you did," said Sam. "And I reckon I'm a going to write this story, too." He set down his glass and headed for the door.

"Where you going?" Leela said.

"Going to work," Sam said.

"You're too drunk to drive anywhere," she said.

"That'll be the day," he said, and shambled out the door.

TWO

"I don't know where he is," Leela told Jim, later that evening. "He's working on a story he says is going to make him into Peter Jennings or something. It's like to get him killed."

"I know," Jim said. "He told me, too." He considered a moment. "I don't know. Maybe it's best to let him do it. He says it's what he always thought he was supposed to do. To be. A newsman."

"Damn it," she said.

"He says he got it from your father. Says your father was always the curious sort."

"I reckon so," said Leela. "I reckon he was."

"And yet he didn't ever find out about the man molesting you. Never dreamed of it?"

Leela sat still. She looked at Jim. "It wasn't his fault, you know. Really. I said he betrayed me, and he did, but not because he didn't know what was going on. No. Besides, maybe he did, down inside, maybe. And he knew if he discovered it, it would be too much. Maybe he was the one betrayed. Or as much as me. Because maybe he believed the world was such a good and protected place, just like I did. Maybe he had a daddy or a mom who taught him that and he'd never had it betrayed so he passed it down to me. Maybe we all of us just learn what our folks tell us, and then try to hang onto it, in spite of anything, until it gets torn or beaten out of us. Maybe. And if he'd found out he'd been settin up his own daughter all along, maybe it would be too much. Maybe it was too much. He died, you know."

"That sounds like you're blaming yourself for being molested. And it's little far-fetched, don't you think? That he knew you'd been betrayed and he knew it was because he'd made you feel so safe that you were so traumatized? And so he died?"

"Listen," Leela said. "Some time back, there was a man up on the north mountain, Keasy Taylor was his name. We all heard about it. He let his big hog get loose somehow, and it got right into his house and ate his baby."

"Jesus Christ," said Jim. "A hog?" He laughed. "Come on."

"You don't believe it. Well, a boar hog will eat anything like that. Babies, pups. It will. Believe it."

"My God," said Jim.

"Yes. That was an awful thing. He come back in from the barn—wasn't gone fifteen minutes—and there's that great old boar a tuggin and tearin at that baby's body, shovin it around like a hog will. Believe me. That sight isn't never going to leave him alone, is it?

"He'd try to get rid of the sight, the feeling. Sam told me about this. Sam, he wrote a story about it, but he decided not to run it."

"I can see why," said Jim.

"Anyway, he said Keasy tried right from the start to get it over and get back to regular life. It wasn't like he wanted to just curl up and quit, like some people. Some people, you know, you get to feel they're comfortable feelin mournful, that they enjoy it, somehow. But not Keasy. He wanted to get shut of it, Sam said. Get the whole thing out of his head and try to live his life.

"And I'd say he did, maybe. He did what he had to, to work it out of himself. Right on the spot, he'd already killed that boar and skinned it and stretched the skin out on the barn door. I don't know. I reckon he wanted to show himself it was over by provin that hog was dead. But every day, Sam says, folks up there would see him standin in front of the barn, just a starin at that hide. And he tryin to get over that and all he can do is stand stock still and look at that thing. And what do you think he was seein?"

"I'm not sure I like this story all that much," said Jim.

"So it got to how it ate on him all the while, you know?" she said. "Went to a doctor down to the city and told him he was 'hainted by that sight,' the hog a snufflin that dead child around. And the doctor told Keasy about how we all go through what he called the stages of grief and how he just had to keep on until all that grief was 'processed.'

"But that did him no good. And five years, five whole years, after that baby died, Keasy got up one morning right around dawn, just a bright morning in September, nothing unusual about that day that anybody could see. But somethin in Keasy said *that's enough*. And he marched himself out to the hog pen and wrenched off the iron latch that held it shut, that Sam believed he figured he'd forgotten to latch five years before. Just wrenched it right out of the plank on that pen gate. And he walked on into the barn and picked up his ax. And took the gate latch and the ax back into the house. Into the room where that baby had been killed. And laid that iron latch out on a towel and spread out his right hand next to it, grabbing it, the way he would to shut it, you know. And he chopped off his thumb and forefinger—the whole third of his hand—with one swing of that ax. And wrapped up the latch and thumb and the finger in the towel. And when they found him he was lyin out next to that little baby's grave site that he'd gotten about half scooped out before he fainted, and his hand all covered with a gluey mud made out of the grave soil and his own blood, so it looked like he was wearing an oven mitt, the sheriff said. And he was fixin to dig up that grave and put that latch and his own fingers in there with that baby.

"You see, he just couldn't get over it."

Jim jumped to his feet. "Why are you telling me this?" he complained. "I don't want to hear this. What kind of place is this, anyway?" Again Leela appeared not to have heard him.

"And I believe my daddy might've known that feeling," she

said, "That deep down feeling that you aint never going to stop asking yourself about it, feeling the drain out of your heart because you just feel so bad about it and there aint a thing for you to do about it and it jest keeps on going. So he left it. He died because he couldn't bear to watch me with it, like he tore his own heart out, the way Keasy Taylor chopped off that hand. You know? And so now I carry it around, too. Like that phantom pain they talk about with folks who have lost a leg can still feel their toes a crampin up something terrible and aint a thing they can do. Because the toes are gone. Only the feeling of them is left behind and it won't leave, no matter what. That's it, you know. All there is to it."

They sat several moments in silence. Jim could feel the story settle around them, the dark horror of it all, perhaps even more terrible to him because it had seemed so incomprehensible, laughable, even. And so the image of the father, grieving beyond endurance, so that he has to gouge from himself the memorial of his grief, or his shame, or crime, whatever he must have felt it was. Perhaps it was all three.

Maybe she's right. Maybe that's what grief is: phantom pain. Because it's just as real as it was when the person was here. But she's gone, and so now you feel the ache in the shadow of that very absence that tells you she's gone. While it feels just like she's standing there, in the next room, about to come around the corner. And that's what makes it hurt so badly. She's gone, but she just won't leave. Phantom pain. That's what grief is.

"I'll be back," said Leela, standing suddenly, and heading for the door.

"Wait. Wait," said Jim again. "Where are you going?"

"Going home," she said. Then she changed her mind. "Going to Paul's. I'll be back."

"Are you crazy?" said Jim, starting toward her.

But she was already out the door.

* * *

When Sam returned, he had a bright look in his eyes, animation in his voice.

"Boys, we got something here," he said. "Got a real story, sure as hell."

"She's gone," Jim said.

Sam was so deep in his own excitement, he didn't mark Jim's words for a moment. He was stopped only by the incongruity of the response. After a second, he said, "What did you say?"

"She's gone. An hour ago."

"Who?"

"Leela. She up and left, all of a sudden, like she'd thought of something, and said she was going back to Paul's."

"I don't believe it," said Sam, heading for the liquor cabinet. "She wouldn't."

"She said she was. I don't know where else she'd go."

Sam settled into the couch, a drink in his hand. He shook his head. "Well, it won't be the first time."

"But she just got up and walked out the door. If she went back home—back to Morelock's—how did she get there?"

"Same way she got here," Sam said. "She walked. Always does. It's about five miles, I reckon." He took a long pull on his drink. "So she went back to the sonofabitch, after all."

"No," Jim said. "Not like that. I think she thought of something, something she could find out there."

"Oh, Jesus," said Sam. "He'll beat the hell out of her. Why in the hell does she have to go up there, stickin her face right in front of that bastard for him to hit? Hey?"

"Seems like you've both decided to stick your necks out, doesn't it?" said Jim.

"Well, okay," said Sam. "I reckon you're right. So I reckon I'll just have to go up there and get her." He began to rise.

"No," said Jim. "I'll go."

"You?" said Sam. "As I recall, you don't even know how to

shoot a gun."

"Nobody's going to shoot anyone," Jim said. "I'll just go up there and give her some support. He won't hit her if I'm standing there, will he?"

"No," said Sam. "I reckon he'll hit you. Then he'll hit her."

"Never mind," Jim said. "I'm going. You stay here, in case she gets into trouble and calls."

Leela stood in the dark woods, faintly hearing the creek rushing somewhere below and behind her, coming down out of the big mountain. She drew a branch aside and looked at the lights in the house up the hill. She had left the road several hundred yards below and picked her way through the briars and undergrowth, having to backtrack twice, climbing the slope rising around and above the back of the house to where she now stood, on a dim trail that switched down from above, descending the big knob to the Morelock place. Leela had come laterally from the road, up the steep slope to intercept this trail directly above the house. She stood in the solitude of the mountain night, hearing the far-off sough of the creek, feeling a light breeze against her face, seeing the single light from the parlor window at the back of the house, below. *My own place,* she thought with an ironic shrug. *I'm fixin to prowl into my own place.* But she realized it had never been hers, especially not the house, where her father-in-law actually lived. But not even the grounds, not even the trailer—Paul's trailer— none of it. It had always been Morelocks who owned everything, controlled everything, grabbed it all up tight in their own brutal hands. Beat you if you tried to be something other than a thing to be owned, run. *Or killed you.* She felt a chill of anxiety as she moved slowly, silently down the trail toward the back of the house.

The trail opened out into a grassy lawn about twenty yards from the house, and, reaching this point, Leela crouched behind the last of the undergrowth, looking across the expanse, trying to calm her breathing, her hammering heart. She wondered a moment, *What am I doing here?* Then she stopped herself, drawing up her will. *It's nice to do something for him*, and then thinking, *And get something back from them.*

She took a long breath. *If I can do it.*

She heard a door slam, a dog's deep bark, and she shrank down into the foliage. A moment later she saw her husband's bulky figure crossing the front driveway toward the trailer. *One down.* She realized this was a chance: the dog was already barking; Paul's back was to her. So she sprang up and ran to the rear wall of the house, bringing herself into a crouch, below the open parlor window, then slowly, silently, rising to look into the room.

Johns was stretched out on the old red couch, watching the television. In front of him was the long low coffee table where Leela saw the big family bible on the lower shelf, the thing she'd come for. She crouched at the window and waited. If he left the room for anything—to go to the bathroom—she would be through the window and have the page, be back out here in a matter of a moment. She waited.

Several minutes later, she heard an engine and then saw the beam of headlights, as the car swung off the road and up the Morelocks' lane. The dog began barking, again.

Johns uncurled himself from the couch and walked toward the front of the house, out into the hallway, out of sight.

Now!

Jim had driven out of town in the deepening dusk, holding Sam's directions in one hand, trying to read and drive, slowing and speeding up as he figured out the next turn, the next stretch of a mile or so. It was the same way they'd come yesterday, but he hadn't been paying much attention. He'd been watching the rising slopes, the turning, swirling scenery, the billows of undergrowth and laurel, the humped granite outcrops, chunks the size of train cars, cracked off and fallen, and had wondered what that must have looked like when it came down.

The mountains began to close in, just as Sam had said, and he saw the turnoff, just before the white rail of the bridge, the big tree with the board sign, MORELOCK. He turned onto the crunching gravel of the drive, climbed a rise and saw the house, the wide, low porch stretching across the entire front, and, to the right, the house trailer, its battered white aluminum siding stained with rust. Around the dwellings sat two big pickup trucks, a panel truck and a large yellow Lincoln.

"There's some money, somewhere," he said aloud, and pulled up next to the panel truck. It looked newly painted, the side painted with the legend, HANDY'S GROCERY DELIVERY in curling script on the side, and, below, in block print, ROALTON. Jim snorted a laugh. "Yeah. Right," he said aloud.

As he opened his car door, he heard the snarl and bark of a dog. "Terrific," he said, and stepped out onto the driveway, walking slowly around the truck toward the trailer, where he didn't believe he'd seen a dog. *May as well go to the dog-free place first.* The barking continued from off to the right as he moved up the concrete block walkway toward the trailer door.

A bright blueish light came on and the door swung open. Jim saw a big man in overalls, carrying a shotgun, literally hopping out of the trailer onto the walkway. He realized this must be Paul, realized he'd never seen the man before, and wondered, anew, at how Leela could have anything to do with a man, or a place, like this.

Jim stopped, while the man straightened and slung the rifle into the crook of an arm, standing easy. "Shut up, Dowser," he shouted, in the direction of the barking. The dog emitted a low growl and ceased. The man turned, his weight shifting to one hip, and looked at Jim, showing a broad face and heavy brow, a thin mouth, and narrow eyes glinting out of deep, pinched sockets. He smiled, without evincing friendliness, and sucked a tooth. He appeared more imposing than menacing, and Jim tried to smile back, saying, "Hello, Mister Morelock."

"Mister Morelock?" the man said. He threw back his big head and laughed loud. "Mister Morelock. Well, well." He switched the rifle around, crooking it into his other arm. "I reckon so," he said. "What can I do you for?"

"Is your wife here?" Jim asked.

"My wife?" the man said.

"Leela. Is she here?"

Paul Morelock frowned. "What you want with my wife?" he said. "My wife aint none of your goddamn bidnits." He glowered at Jim, the fierce, narrow eyes. "Who in the hell are you, any-ways?"

"My name is Jim Thorwait, and I've come to ask you for some information."

"Information," Morelock said. Jim thought he might laugh again. Instead, he narrowed his eyes further. "You're that feller's been pokin around town, aint you?"

"I'm looking..."

"Let me tell you, friend," the man continued, as though he'd not heard. "Folks round here, they don't dezactly take to gettin poked around, iffen you know what I mean. And we aint in the business of handin round information, neither." He sucked his tooth again, and showed the same thin, friendless smile. "Aint nothin here you could want to know, kindly. And iffen you been talkin to my wife, I reckon I'll show her who she ought to be a hangin around. You too, iffen you need to find out."

"I don't mean any trouble," Jim said. "I don't need to know anything particular about your business. I'm just trying to find out about a woman named Allie Morelock, and I thought you might have some information."

"Allie Morelock."

"That's right. I think she may be my mother," Jim said, feeling awkward, having trouble finding the right words.

"Your mother," said the man.

"That is, I think I had a mother named Allie Morelock. I mean, I know her name sounds something like 'Allie.' It could be some other name, though. I mean it could be spelled most any way. We don't know. And I don't know how to find her. You see, I was adopted, and I'm looking for her."

Morelock frowned and stared.

"Adopted," he said. He spat, then shifted his weight and waved an arm toward the house. "Whyn't you go on over to the home place and talk to Pawp?" he said. "I reckon he'd like to know who told you about Allie Morelock."

"Thank you," said Jim, relieved. "Maybe he can help me out."

"You just tell him how you know about Allie Morelock," the man said, the voice turning threatening. "And then you best get on out of here. Clear out of this country, you hear?"

"I'll just talk to him, then," Jim said, turning toward the house.

It was a sprawling frame house, the wide porch sagging a bit. It had once been painted blue, but that now showed a pale, color-less expanse of clapboard. One window had been covered in a large piece of fiber board, another upstairs was broken. As Jim approached, the dog began again, from somewhere in front.

"Will your dog hurt me?" He called. Hearing no answer, he looked back to see that the man had gone. So he turned again and walked toward the house, surrounded by the barking but still seeing no dog.

Again the door opened before he reached it, and again, a man stepped out, an older, grizzled version of the first, the same bulk, the same narrow, cold eyes. Jim assumed he was looking at Johns Morelock, Paul's father. The man was fifty or so, wearing jeans and a gray T-shirt. The rough stubble on his chin looked like bristle, steely gray.

"Mister Morelock," Jim said again. "I'm Jim Thorwait," he said, without stopping to allow a reply. "But I think my real name might be Jim Morelock, and I need to ask you if you know any-thing about a woman—she'd be a middle-aged woman, now, about your age, I'd guess—named Allie Morelock."

The man looked shocked, not so much at the words Jim had spoken, but at the fact of his presence, itself. His thin eyes showed white and his jaw clenched. He walked jerkily forward until he stood close to Jim, then leaned forward, peering. Then he arched back, awed, hands on hips. "I be goddamned," he whispered.

Jim was wondering what next to say, when the man suddenly reached out his arm and grabbed Jim's shirt, incredibly strong, pulling him hard, dragging him forward toward the house, saying "You get inside, sonbitch, goddamn sonbitch," Jim stumbling, trying to stop, being pulled up the stairs and through the front door.

The older man pushed Jim inside and down onto a stained red couch. Then he turned a chair around and sat, straddling, looking closely at Jim.

"Now who in hell are you and what in hell you want?" he said. He still had that amazed look in his eyes, peering out of the weathered, grizzled face, a hard man of fifty years or more. "What you askin round about Allie Morelock for? What you got to do with Allie Morelock?" He raised his voice, shouting: "Hey? Boy?"

"I think she's my mother, is all," Jim said. He was scared, trying to catch his wind, angry, too, the panicky, bewildered anger from being so suddenly manhandled. He found himself looking wildly around, trying to orient himself in this shabby room, smelling of tobacco and sweat. There was a large print framed on the wall in front of him, a garish over-hued painting of a deer, above which a set of antlers hung, and below, a rifle racked by resting across two deer hooves mounted at either end of a narrow, varnished pine plank. Each hoof glinted, startlingly black. Absurdly, from somewhere beyond the surprise and the anger, he found himself considering this detail, the blackness of the hoof, thinking, *I never knew deers' feet were so black,* and then, just as surprisingly, hearing himself shouting at the man.

"Jesus Christ, mister. Is everybody around here crazy? Why do you all get so worked up over me?" The man said nothing. "I'm trying to find my mother, Allie Morelock, and I don't mean any harm to anyone. That's all. Find my mother."

"You aint from around hereabouts are you?" said the man, balefully.

"No, thank God," said Jim. "I'm not from around here. And I'm beginning to think I made a mistake coming down here."

The man began to laugh, a slow, baleful snarl of a sound, rising and growing into great gulping haws. At last, he mastered himself, taking several long breaths, and saying, "Well, I reckon you're right about that." He laughed again, low and muttering. "I be god-damned. Now you're a thinkin right." He leaned toward Jim, his eyes narrowing. "Now you tell me a thing," he said. "You ever seen Allie Morelock? Ever?"

"No. Listen," Jim said. "I'm trying to tell, I've been trying to tell you all. I was adopted in Roalton and I found her name on the adoption papers. Allie Morelock from Shaleen Prong. So I came looking."

"Shaleen," Johns Morelock said. "Hell." He looked back at the door, as if he were expecting someone. He gave a long sigh. "Well, buddy, Allie Morelock don't exist anywheres and they aint no use in you tryin to find her, here. Or Shaleen neither, you hear?" He leaned forward, pressing his chest against hands that gripped the curved bow of the chair back. "Hear?" he said again.

"So you know her. Knew her, anyway," said Jim.

The door opened and Paul Morelock entered, still carrying the rifle slung into his elbow. Jim watched him through the veil of his own fear and anger. *Good God, how could Leela marry such a man?* He turned back to the man on the chair.

"You knew her?" Jim said again.

The man said nothing, cocking his head back to look at Paul.

"Nothin in the car," Paul said. "He don't seem to be a cop." He walked in and stood over Jim, looking down. "What you after, anyways?"

"Do I have to say it again?" Jim said. At once he realized what Paul was talking about. "You searched my car?" he asked, incredulous. "You know, I do believe you people are all crazy."

"What you after?" said Paul, again, leaning toward Jim, peering at him, threat in his eyes, his stance, everything. Again, though, Jim felt a rush of anger through his fear. He'd not known he could respond to danger this way. Because no one had ever threatened him before; he'd never so much as spoken to anyone like Paul or Johns Morelock. Never. And so he startled himself with the aggressiveness of his own response, hearing his voice, outraged and demanding, with the thin tone of fright layered over the top.

"Isn't it just conceivable that I'm doing exactly what I say I'm doing, looking for my mother, for Christ sake?"

"Conceivable," Paul with the air of a man who had as never heard the word before and was trying out the sound of it. He laughed, quick and mirthless.

"He's after us, somehow," the older man said. "I believe he's really after us. How in hell would he know about her if he weren't already lookin for somethin on us?" The man turned back toward Jim, again pressing against his own hands. "Well, buddy, they aint no Allie Morelock no more. You may as well go home."

Paul stepped forward, brandishing the rifle.

"Okay," said Jim. "So I guess I've found out all I can from you." He stood up, facing Paul, close. "Thank you for your time." He waited for Paul to move out of the way.

"You get on out, now, or I'll have to run you out," Paul said, pushing a blunt forefinger into Jim's chest, nearly pushing him back onto the couch.

"All right," Jim said. He could hear the shaking in his voice, the sound of trepidation winning out against the anger. "That's enough. I'm trying to leave, aren't I? Just let me go, all right? And stop pushing me around." He really was shaking, he realized, shaking all over. He was scared and wanted out, but, to his own amazement, he found himself angry again, again challenging this man. "You know, you can't just push everyone around. I'm not your wife, you think you can beat up whenever you want. So don't you threaten me."

"What you know about my wife?" Morelock said, his voice rising. He lifted the shotgun, holding both ends crosswise, like a cudgel. "My wife aint no concern of your'n." He took a deep breath, working his hand around the double steel barrel. "I know you been nosin around with that brother of her'n, ain't you? I know it, goddamn it. Well, you might've stepped into more shit than you figured on, you know that, city boy? You tell that brother Sam to mind his business and send my goddamn wife back home where she belongs, you hear?"

"She's not here?" said Jim. "Not here?"

"What makes you think she's here?" said Paul. "Don't you never mind where she is. Iffen she aint with that brother of her'n. It aint for you to watch her."

"Your wife is one hell of a lot better off with her brother," said Jim, still listening to himself with amazement, hearing himself trying to stand up to this man. "Why don't you stop hitting women, tough guy?" He saw Leela in his mind's eye, bruised and hurt by this man, this thug, and he felt the strength, the bravado of his anger. "What's the matter with you? You afraid to hit a man?"

"Nossir," said Paul, slamming the gun barrel, hard, into Jim's face, knocking him down, between the couch and the older man, who watched impassively, still straddling the chair, the childlike hands grasping the curved wood. As Jim tried to rise, Paul kicked the side of his head, so that he keeled and dropped onto the floor.

"I ain't afeared," Paul said. He leaned forward, grasping Jim's collar, and dragged him upward and out, the exact way he'd been dragged into the room, so this looked like some film scene shown in reverse, back toward the door, which Johns Morelock kicked open, while Paul hefted Jim and heaved him out, pushing him once, as he staggered on the concrete steps, so that he fell, sprawled, into the yard. Paul spat at him, then turned back toward the interior, calling over his shoulder, "You get the hell on outen here, now. Or next time, I'll use the bidnits end of this blowbellers on you."

Sam sat at his desk, writing furiously on a yellow legal pad. He set his pen down, picked up a glass, and said to it, "Shaleen to Roalton to Shaleen to everywhere. Seek and ye shall find." He whistled softly.

He heard a car pull up outside, too fast, the wheels thumping wildly against the curb. Sam stood and moved to the front window, easing the slats apart.

It was Jim's car, though he had never seen it driven so wildly. *What's our boy been up to? Been on a toot? Went drinkin with Paul Morelock?* He saw the shadowy figure emerge from the car and he turned into the room, heading back to the desk, when he heard a heavy thump against the door. "By God, you have been on a rampage," he yelled at the door. "Just a minute."

When he swung the door open, Jim nearly fell through, into his arms.

"Jesus Christ," Sam said to the battered face of his friend. The side of Jim's head was deeply bruised, one eye swollen shut, an ugly contusion on the cheek. "What in the hell happened to you?"

Sam was behind his desk again, this time doing nothing, staring vacantly at the big map on the wall. He'd put Jim upstairs, in his own bedroom, the wounds cleaned up as well as Sam could do it. And now Sam was wondering *what have we got ourselves into?* He tried to retrace the course of the week. *Where did this go from a mild-mannered city feller lookin for his mother to a bust-head free-for-all involving the whole goddamn Morelock clan, not to mention the drugs, and that gal, Lindee? Nor Leela, tryin to get clear of that thug.* He shook his head. *And then decides she's got to go back there for something all to help Jim find his mommy. Where the hell is she, anyway? And then, Jim has to go off there to help her, keep her from getting herself beat up and he gets his own self pert well mashed by the same sonofabitch.*

He swiveled his chair around and reached into the liquor cabinet, drawing forth a jug. *Day he got here, I asked him how sure he was that he wanted to find his family. And now it appears he has and they's nothing but a bunch of drug runners and head busters. Boy howdy: he sure walked into it, didn't he? About three generations of it, seems like to me. And everything was pert calm and peaceful around here until he showed up. Maybe he's the troublemaker.*

The front door crashed open and Leela ran in, breathlessly waving a large, thin sheet of paper, already talking.

"...got it," she said. "It's here, I think. I couldn't tell too good in the dark, but I think it's here, Jim's momma's name, right in the Morelock family bible."

"Where the hell you been?" said Sam.

"I went to the house," she said, her eyes shining. "Broke in. Went in through the window. And I tore out the page from the family bible. Good thing nobody looks in it no more."

"You were there?" said Sam impatiently.

"Yes," Leela said, still breathing hard, still full of her own story. "Look," she said, spreading the sheet out on Sam's desk. "Here's the whole thing. The entire Morelock family from Anse and then Cuddy on down. She's got to be here, Sam."

"Nevermind that," said Sam. "If you were there, how come—"

"Nevermind!" Leela exclaimed. "After I went crawlin through the woods and climbed through the window and took something they'd kill me for takin if they ever knew I done it? Look at these clothes. I'm going upstairs and get cleaned up, get into my nightshirt, and then we'll look this over. And the name, Sam. The name's got to be here. I think she was Johns's wife." She stood straight, looking around, suddenly. "Where's Jim?"

Jim had lain for a while listening to the thudding throb in his head, testing the swelling with his fingers now and again, hearing the night sounds, and playing back the fight—if that's what you could call it—in his mind. Gradually, the moving figures, the swinging gun barrel, and the harsh laughter of Paul Morelock began to swirl and blur, and he was floating, overhead, out of reach of the fists, sailing somewhere up in the clear sky above the dark mountains and just dropping into sleep, when a knock at his door jerked him awake.

"What!" he shouted, too loud, frightened by the sound of his own voice.

"Oh, Jim, I'm sorry," she said, very softly. "I'm sorry; I thought you was awake. I thought I heard you tossing around."

"Leela? It's okay," he said. "Okay. I was just dozing off. But I couldn't really sleep, not with this shiner aching like it does."

She spoke through the barely opened door. "I should leave you alone."

"No," he said, hoping his voice would convey the real desire he felt to have her here. "No. Come in. Please."

"Well, I think I got some information on the whole family matter. But never mind that for now. I brought you a washrag and some ice water and salts. You can just soak the cloth and wring it out and it'll feel good on that bruise."

"I'd like that," he said.

So she came in, into his room, and he saw for a split-second the outline of her body through the gown, silhouetted by the hall light. Her hands held a shadowy object that glinted a round center: a stainless bowl. He turned on his side, leaning, and snapped on the bedside lamp.

"Hurt bad?" she asked him, setting the bowl on the end table and dipping a faded blue washcloth into the water. She leaned over him, looking. "Yep. That's a bit more than a shiner, I'd say."

"It throbs something awful," he said.

"He hits pretty hard, don't he?" she said, wringing the cloth and extending it, spread across her open palms. "You want me to do this, or would you rather?"

"You," he said, tipping his face to catch the cloth. The room went black as she draped the washcloth carefully across his brow and eyes, letting it fall lightly over the hurt flesh. It was very cold, and he caught his breath sharply, but then it eased and felt wonderful, cold and drawing. "My god, that's nice," he said.

"Yes," she said. "I know. I believe the cold cloth and the salts have gotten to be my favorite thing about my marriage."

They both laughed. He felt the tug of his smile against the swollen skin, turning his *hah* into an *ouch*.

"Sorry," she said.

"Well, I'm glad we can both laugh a bit about it," He said, drawing the cloth away from one eye and blinking up at her. "You're right: he does hit pretty hard. How's yours? By the way."

"Still got some color yet," she said. She turned her head and he saw the bruise, yellowing around the edges, a ring of deep burgundy lining the eye socket. "Ain't we a pair?" she said, smiling ruefully. "Give me that, I'll wring it fresh," and he tilted his face again, feeling the tingle as the cloth came free. She was standing by the bed, dipping the cloth, the cotton gown bright in the close light of the lamp, shadowing only a little where it dipped between her small breasts that stirred with her movements. She turned and reached the cloth to him again.

"Here," he said, scooting over. "Sit down." He patted the bed, then turned his head up again to receive the cloth. She remained standing, draping cold relief over his taut skin. Blind, feeling the ease and draw of the wet cloth, he patted the bed again.

"I will," she said. "In a minute." He heard her turn and he lifted the cloth, again, watching her move to the door, the slight curve of her flanks. "I got something else for you," she said, going into the hall. "Part two of the treatment."

He lay back, again feeling the heat pulled out of the bruised flesh, into the cold cling of cloth, hearing her say, *He hits pretty hard don't he,* thinking, *She sounds good. She sounds so good. Better, I mean. She wouldn't have talked about it that way a few days ago. She's easing back into herself, like the easy draw of the salts,* and he saw her white gown, the breasts under the thin cloth and he realized he'd been watching her for a long while, watching her move, waiting to hear her speak. He liked to think about her.

He heard her bare feet swish through the door, and he pulled the corner of the cloth up. She was carrying two white bowls, curved cold white china against warm, curved white gown. He thought of Wallace Stevens's, *A bowl of white*, remembering, *Cold, a cold porcelain, low and round.*

"Ice cream!" she proclaimed. "Butter pecan ice cream. Part two of the cure." And she eased herself down, sitting on the bed, balancing the bowls, while he thought of Stevens, again, *Kitchen cups* carrying *concupiscent curds.* And then another: *We make a dwelling in the evening air.*

"Whoops," she said, turning toward him, pushing the bowls at him. "Take these. I forgot the dern spoons." And she was up again, moving, and he watched her, again, thinking, *she is better.* Thinking, *how could she be any better?*

When she had gone, he found himself saying her name, not the married name, but the real one, *Leela Lofton,* the four syllables, soft as a sable brush.

They sat, eating their ice cream, talking and laughing, easy and fun, like two kids having a sleepover. He tossed the washcloth into the stainless bowl and they sat, facing one another, knees up, watching each other eat the ice cream that tasted so good against the bruise and the hurt, sharing the pleasure, because they'd both been hurt, easy with one another because of the grotesque truth that they'd both been beaten up by the same man. *Is that it, really? She, we, are so comfortable because he's hit us both?* Hearing her, again, saying, *He hits pretty hard, don't he?* And thinking, *Yes. Yes. God bless the luck to have walked into his gun barrel today. God bless Paul Morelock.*

"I need to show you what I got," she said at last. "I went there and climbed in the window. Lord, it must've been you that drove in." She put her hand to her brow. "God. I'm sorry. You made the distraction that got me into the house. And then I just took off, while you stayed there and got beat up."

"What is it?" he said. "What did you get?"

"I took the page out of the family bible," she said. "Where they write down the family tree? All the marriages and births and all. And I think your mother's name is in there. I think she was married to Johns. Her name was Eleanor."

"Eleanor," he said, feeling a rush, like falling through air. "Not Allie. It just sounded like Allie. Eleanor: Ellie."

"Right," she said.

"So does that mean it's the woman I saw on the mountain? You got Evelyn mixed up with Eleanor?"

"I don't know," Leela said. "But it could be her. I might have gotten it confused with Ethlyn and so came out with Evelyn. But it might not be Evelyn. Eleanor. I don't remember. We'd have to go up and see."

"I'm not sure our faces could take another whooping," he said.

"I can see your point," she agreed.

"So, anyway," Jim said ruefully, "I just got beat up by my brother?"

"Half brother," Leela said. "Johns married again and had the two boys, Paul and Pierot."

"I knew I was getting close by the way they acted." he said.

"Who? Paul? Why in the world do you say that?"

"I don't' know. Both of them. They don't like me asking about it." He paused. "And they seemed to recognize me. Just like the old man up on Shaleen. I still don't see how they could, though."

"Well you sure don't look like no Morelock to me." She laughed. "Good God, brother to Paul. Lord help."

"Sam said you all were Hamptons, even."

"We are, far off cousins of some sort. So I naturally wasn't making sense marrying Paul Morelock, was I?" She shook her head, suddenly serious, sad. "God, what was I thinking, any-way?"

"We talked about that, remember?" he said. "Childhood and

the decisions we make. I understand that, I think. We can't have them back, so we'd best forget them and move ahead, right? I can see, besides, a bright, vibrant young woman getting stuck with exactly the kind of man he is."

"What?" she said, arching a brow. "Why in the world?"

"Because he would stand out, wouldn't he? And in this place, this dark mountain place, he'd seem bright, too, flashy, at least, and cruel, which sometimes stands for bright and strong, to a young girl."

"Ladies love outlaws?" she said, smiling sadly. "Sam says that."

"Something like that," he said.

"Well, I reckon so," she said. She looked at him. "Why didn't you never get married?"

"I don't know," he said. "I've known lots of women, some of them pretty close, pretty domestic. I lived with a woman for a few years. But I always felt lonely. I have always felt that way. And you can't much build a marriage if you're lonely all the time. Can you?"

"Lonely," she said, testing the word. "Lonely. Ain't that why people get married? So they won't be alone?"

"Not solitary," he said. "I like solitude. Crave it, in fact." He took a last spoonful of ice cream, scraped the spoon around to pick up the meltings. "But lonely is something else. Lonely eats at your soul."

"That's why you're looking for your mamma, ain't it?" she said. "You think if you find her, maybe you'll find a cure for the loneliness? That it?"

"Maybe," he said. "I don't know."

"Maybe you will," she said. She leaned forward, touching his arm. "I hope you do, Jim. I really do."

He shrugged, a rueful smile. "It seems I'm going to find out I'm a Morelock. Which means Hamptons like you ought to be shooting me, instead of sitting on my bed, eating ice cream with me."

"I like it fine, right here," she said. They sat, silent for a moment. "You know you have pretty eyes?" she said, leaning forward again. The gown came away from her throat and he saw the pale curve of her collarbone, the soft skin below, dropping off into shadow. He felt himself flush and he turned away. "I mean it," she pressed. "Big and blue."

"Black and blue, you mean."

"No. Really. And they're...expressive, I guess you'd say. I don't mean to embarrass you."

"Well, I guess you do," he said. "But thanks."

He watched her eat the last of her ice cream, the graceful hands, the sleeve of her gown falling back, showing her elbow, the curve of her upper arm, a blue vein running upward, into the dark sleeve. "You don't look so bad yourself," he said, coloring, again.

She broke the tension. "For somebody who just got a whoopin," she said. "Well, thanks, too. It's nice to hear. From such a pretty feller." She laughed. "Who just come in second in a fist fight."

She sat back, dipping the spoon into the melting lump of ice cream. They sat in silence as she finished, eating slowly, glancing at him now and again, then lowering her eyes, so that the soft lids, the dark lashes, the bruised cheek made her seem small and fragile, like a girl.

And when she had finished, he put his bowl on the table, and she set hers on the floor and he took her hand, drew her to him, and kissed her, framing her face in his cupped hands.

"Ouch," she said.

"Ouch is right," he said, drawing away and touching his face gingerly. She put her hand behind his head and pulled him back closer. "We got to stop seeing that man," she said.

They laughed into each other's mouths. Kissed, again. Said "ouch," again.

"I think there might be some places we can touch that aint hurt," she said, moving her lips against his. She reached for his hand and placed it on her leg, sliding him under the gown, just above her knee, on the soft skin. They both sighed into each other's mouths. She kissed him again, and said, "Wait."

She rose onto her knees in front of him and lifted her arms, inviting, and so he drew the gown upward and over her head, baring her, seeing her small breasts, fuller than he had expected, and the small bulge of her belly, unspeakably beautiful, the fluff of dark hair, the soft hollow at the join of each thigh. She leaned forward and kissed him as he reached for her. "Wait," she said again.

And she pushed him back, brushing her nipples across his chest, and undressed him, opening the pajama shirt, and then kissing downward, pulling the elastic of the waistband up and over his erection, then stroking and tasting, and back up, pressing the length of her naked skin against his, and they turned together, rolling over until she embraced him with her thighs, around his back, drawing him in.

And so it began. Later in the night, he awoke, and pulled himself up behind her, spooning, feeling her soft backside against his belly, his arm reaching around, hand spread to span her stomach, moving up across the soft breasts, then down, his palm closing, to touch her with his outstretched fingers, testing, feeling the wet heat of her response. She, a spoon too, pushed back against him, fitting his erection between the long split of her buttocks, nestling him. And then she brought her hand around, finding him and caressing along his length, drawing him down and in between, to the place where their hands met, hers behind, guiding him, his in front, opening her. As he moved into her, she moved back onto him, so they couldn't tell who was doing what, moving together, slowly, carefully, as if they really were afraid of hurting each other, merging with a long sigh. And then, all at once, they both began to weep, quietly, not from the physical pain, the bruises, but from the long loneliness, weeping for one another, and moving together, while the tears mingled, sad and hurt, and lonely, and in love.

THREE

"Everybody up?" Sam shouted, ranging through the hallway on Saturday morning. "Let's rise and shine, we got places to go, things to do."

Jim's door opened a crack. "Just a minute. Go on down and start the coffee and we'll—I'll be right down."

"Coffee's started. Come on," said Sam. "I'll get Leelie."

Down the hall, Sam rapped on Leela's door. "Come on, sis," he said. "Time's a wastin'." He waited for her answer, and, when none came, he turned the knob, opened the door and looked in, saying, "Rise and shine, baby sister."

The room was empty. The bed had not been slept in.

Sam swung around and returned to Jim's door. "Goddamn it," he shouted through the wood. "She's done gone back to that sonofabitch. Can you believe that?"

Jim's door swung open. Leela stood there, a pale figure in her white cotton gown, her eyes soft from sleep, her hair tousled.

"I'm here, brother," she said, tilting her head, looking at him, her eyes showing a touch of embarrassment and more than a little bit anxiety about being found here by her older brother. "I been here," she said. Her arms moved away from her hips, palms out-turned, a gesture either of confession, *yes, brother,* or of fatalism, *what can I say? Here I am.*

Sam whistled, low. He scratched his head, then leaned by Leela, looking into the room, watching Jim climb into a pair of jeans, his chest bare. Sam whistled again. Jim's face was livid with the bruise, his left eye swollen completely shut. He looked up at Sam.

"What?" he said, challenging.

"Oh, I didn't say nothing," said Sam. "Don't mind me. I aint but a guest, here, a sleepin down on the couch. Or maybe the innkeeper, a tryin to manage the establishment. Trouble is, I can't even keep track of who's in what room." He scratched his head again, and turned, heading for the stairs.

"Sam," Leela called after him. "Sam, it aint…"

"Oh, don't mind me," he answered, waving a hand in the air, starting down the stairs. "This here is a bed and breakfast, if you all want coffee and a bite before we head out."

Jim was at the door, now, tucking in a blue work shirt. "Go where? Where we going?" he asked, putting an arm around Leela's shoulder. She leaned very slightly into him, letting him feel the weight, the warmth of her body.

"Goin to Glen's," Sam shouted from the bottom of the stairs. "She called, says she's got somethin for you to see. That is, if you're still lookin for anything you aint already found."

They rode in Jim's car. Sam grandiloquently swung the passenger door open for Leela, brushing the seat off, bowing to her. "Just let's go," she said, opening the rear door. "You set up there, tell him where he's going."

"By the way, where are we going?" said Jim, climbing into the driver's seat.

"I told you: Glen's," said Sam. "We need to find out who you were lookin at up there on that mountain, don't you think?" He fired up the car. "Might've been your grandpappy." He turned to Jim. "Unless, of course, you don't want to look no more."

"Just let's go," said Leela. And they were off.

* * *

"Well I don't know," said Glen, peering at the bible leaf. "Don't know what all this is going to tell you all, for one. Don't know as I like the idea of tearin a page outen a family bible, for another. Don't care who they is. And even if I did like it, I'd be afeared to do it to this family, kindly, in particular."

Five miles away, up the mountain in the other direction, Paul and Johns Morelock stood at either side of Johns's coffee table, staring at the opened bible, their thin eyes flashing with rage and wonder, looking at the place where the page had been.

"Who in the hell tore out the whole goddamned family, I'd like to know," said Johns. "I'll kill the son of a bitch that's violated this here book."

"You know goddamn well who done it," said Paul. "Or who it was done for."

"Okay," said Glen, running her finger along the page. "Here's Anse and Cuddy. That's the main line. And all Cuddy's boys, Vernon and Kinnie and Jessum and Claude and all." She traced her finger along, calling out names, until she got to Johns. "And this here's been wrote in and then erased."

"It says 'Eleanor,' said Leela. "If you look close to it, you can read it."

"Sure it does," said Glen bending close and peering. "Sure enough. Now, I told you there was an Eleanor. But I don't reckon I understand all that I know about this."

She straightened back up. "And there aint no baby's name. They'd have wrote the baby's name in, even if they was to scratch it out later, too. They wouldn't have just let it go." She shook her head. "Bad luck, if it aint wrote down. And even if she'd left, she'd likely come back to have the baby, I reckon. Unless she'd got too scared of Johns, or had made arrangements in town, somehow."

"She ran off," Leela said. "To Roalton."

"Well, now, I reckon she might," said Glen. "But she come back, right quick, anyways, because my momma, she saw her right here, buying supplies. Hardware and food and all. I asked her about the women, and she remembered Eleanor, though we didn't think nothin of it at the time, being as how you was lookin for Allison. She remembers because she says it was a rare thing to see Eleanor Morelock at any time. She was kindly nowhere to be seen. So between all the supplies—food and lumber and tools—and just the plain fact of seeing her, Momma'd remember that. So she was back some time. Don't know how long she stayed."

"So either she had baby Jim, here," Sam said, "and then got scared…"

"Or hopeful," Leela said. "It might be she had the baby, and that gave her the courage, or the hopefulness, to leave."

"Okay," said Sam. "Scared or happy, either way. She had the baby and that gave her a reason, one way or the other, to leave town. But she was all alone with the child, couldn't really take care of it, didn't want to go back, so she gave him up for adoption."

"Makes sense," said Glen. "Except the baby aint wrote down in the book."

"Or maybe she didn't know she was pregnant when she left, so she ran off, until she found out she was going to have a baby. But then she knew she couldn't take care of a child, so she came back and had the baby here. That would account for Glen's momma seeing her. But then she realized it was a going to get worse and didn't want to raise this child with the real father, Johns Morelock, nohow. So she took and run off again. Found out she still couldn't care for the kid and so arranged to give him to the physician. That makes sense, don't it?"

"Or she ran off, found out she was pregnant, had the child—that would be me—in Roalton, and gave him—me—up after that."

"Then why did she come back?" Leela said.

"Well, maybe she just gave up after that. Or maybe Glen's mother was mistaken."

"My momma don't make a lot of mistakes," said Glen.

"We're stumped, then," Sam said, after they'd returned and were sitting again in the office. "Either we've found out what there is to find, and you're the son of Johns Morelock, and Allie, or you're something else we aint never going to know about. Because there aint nothin more to find."

"I don't believe it," Leela said. "I don't care what you say, he aint Paul Morelock's brother."

"Half brother," Jim said.

"Correct me if I'm wrong," Sam said, "But weren't it you that went and tore out the page from the bible that shows us he is Paul Morelock's brother?"

"Half brother," Jim said.

Sam tossed the file onto his desk. "Look," he said. "I know neither one of you wants him to be Paul Morelock's brother, and I know you want to make up some better story to tell yourself. But wanting it don't make it true, does it? And we've got three versions of what went on and every damn one of them says Allie Morelock was married to Johns Morelock, until she left town. And she done that sometime before Jim was born. And two of the three say she come back for a week to have a baby and then left again. And if that baby wasn't you, then you wasn't born in 1973. Not by that woman. Not unless God come down in the shape of a swan and loosed them thighs."

"Shut up, Sam," said Leela. "Let's talk over this one more time, anyway."

"What for?" Sam said. "We got the family history and the bible and the adoption papers. We got Jim, here. We got momma and pappa and baby brother, here, even if we don't like baby brother too much and he damn sure don't like us."

"Baby brother, who's involved in some illicit activities, to boot. Don't forget that," said Jim. "We are on the trail of a dope ring, if nothing else."

"Yes, and we'd best decide whether we want to muss up all that or just leave it alone." Sam pointed his finger at Jim. "I reckon maybe we've done all we can do and ought to let the whole thing go."

"You're going to quit on me now?" Jim said.

"You know what, cousin?" Sam said. "I've been tryin' to tell you this since you walked in the door, and you aint wanted to hear it once." He picked up the file of papers and slammed it onto the desk again.

"You come down here because you wanted to find your mamma, and the day you got here I asked you was you sure you wanted to find out who she was, no matter what? You remember that?"

"I remember that," Jim said, sighing.

"Hey, cousin, you can give as big a sigh as you want, like to say, 'Oh is he going to start on that again?' Well, don't stop listening to me quite yet. I know you'd just as soon go out there and get your skull split open again, maybe try your manhood against Paul Morelock, again, so they can shoot you, put you out of your goddamn misery. And that aint no problem, you want to do it. I aint a goin to stop you."

"So what's your beef?" said Jim. "Why does it matter to you whether I do or don't?"

"Because before you come into this town, everything was pretty quiet around here. You ever think of that? And you come in not wanting to make any trouble, just a lookin for your long lost mamma, didn't you? And what happened? All hell broke loose. You come into town and all hell breaks loose and now you want to go after the bad guys that started all the trouble? Are you kiddin me? Seems like maybe you're the one started all the trouble."

"You're bein a mite unfair, brother," Leela spoke up at last. "It was you decided to be a big-time reporter, get the goods on the bad guys, weren't it?"

Sam stood abashed a moment, while Jim nodded enthusiastic agreement. "That don't mean nothing," he muttered, ruefully.

"Besides," Leela said. "There aint really all that much trouble. Not really. Is there? Paul's all steamed up, but that would have happened anyhow, with me leavin for good, whether Jim was around or not."

"There's more to it than that," Sam said. "There's the connection with Trapper. And anyway, we've found out what there is to find out about Jim, aint we?"

"No," Leela said. "It's full of holes. And it seems like to me we aint looked in the right places, yet."

"What other places are there?" said Jim.

"He's the big-time investigative reporter," she said. "Whyn't we ask him?"

"Look," Jim said, "we're not getting anywhere shouting at each other." He turned to Sam. "Let's have a cup of your stump-blower and try to think this through. Fair enough?"

Leela threw her hands up in the air.

"Fair enough," said Sam, brightening.

So they sat in the office, Jim and Leela on the couch, Sam behind the desk supervising the distribution of drink, and making a scribbled series of doodles on a paper.

"Here's what we've got," he said. "You were adopted in 1973 by a wealthy physician in Roalton named Thorwait. The transaction was done in private—probably a slightly shady undertaking, even in those days—but given the whatchacallit, sinecure, of a lawyer's representation."

"Or at least a lawyer's fee," said Leela.

"Which is more likely the ultimate mark of legitimacy," said Sam. He wrote *Adoption, 1973,* on the paper. "We know the mother was named 'Allie Morelock' on the document, though we think, now, that she was Eleanor Morelock, and that she was no Morelock at all, except by marriage to Johns Morelock."

"Of the Shaleen Creek Morelocks," said Leela.

"Of the badass, bust head, whoop-yer-ass Shaleen Creek Morelocks," said Sam. "That, if local legend is true, has always been the baddest family around here, and always run the whole damn show when it come to moonshine liquor or anything else you, or," Sam cast an eye at Leela, "your teenage kids, haply, might want to get involved in, that you shouldn't ought to."

"Okay, Sam," said Leela. "I got hooked into a bad thing because I was a stupid, rebellious kid. So what's new? What's that got to do with anything?"

"You got involved with the big bad Morelocks as a teenager because they was glamorous. When really they was just greasy. And got yourself knocked up."

"Sam!" Leela said, standing up. "Just shut up, Sam."

"What?" said Jim.

"She didn't tell you?" said Sam. "Oh." He cast a look at Leela, again, who slowly sat down, her eyes blazing back. "Well, yes, Paul Morelock got our sister great with child, which was why she decided she had to marry him, even after she'd begun to figure out that he was a no good, bust head...all them things we just called him."

"Okay, Sam," said Leela. "So I did." She turned to Jim and squeezed his hand. "I'm sorry I didn't tell you."

Jim was dumbfounded. "You're telling me you have a child?" he said. "Where is it?" he asked, puzzling a moment. Then he turned toward her, shocked. "Don't tell me you gave it up for adoption."

"No," she said. Then, flashing her eyes, said, "Why not? Wouldn't that be the right thing to do?"

"I'd think you'd have told me," Jim said. "Under the circumstances."

Leela stopped, squeezed his hand again. "I'm sorry, Jim. I

should have told you this."

"She had a miscarriage," said Sam. "The first of two. Which is probably the Lord's greatest blessing because Paul Morelock has given up on trying to make babies out of that marriage. He's stopped tryin to knock her up and taken to just knockin her down, I reckon."

Leela began to cry. Jim put his arm around her.

"That's enough, Sam," he said. "Why are you doing this? Why drag Leela through all this?" Jim pulled Leela closer, her weeping head resting on his shoulder. She hugged herself to him. "Are you just being drunk and ornery, or what?" he asked Sam.

"I'm thinking Morelocks once might be Morelocks twice," Sam said. "How did Eleanor Morelock get hooked in with these bastards, too? How did she wind up gettin married to Johns Morelock, who, all things considered, is just the earlier generation's worth of Paul Morelock?"

"You think he got her pregnant?" said Jim.

"Could be," said Sam. "Could be she saw him as a romantic outlaw, too, and then got herself in trouble, found out she was a going to have a baby."

"Maybe she just wanted that sort of thing. Maybe she's just as mean as they are," said Leela, raising her head, still sniffling, but back into the discussion. "Maybe she got what she wanted."

"Then why run off as soon as you've got a kid? Or maybe when you find out you're about to have one? Why run off at all? No. She's more like you, sister; she got tricked into it, somehow and got trapped. And at some point, she got out, probably, like you, again, the first time she felt she might really have a chance to get away."

"Okay," said Jim. "Okay. Let's assume what you're saying is right. That Ellie Morelock had a similar kind of problem as Leela had: she got lured in as a young girl. Okay. Then what?"

"She was only seventeen, right? When she gave you up," said Leela. "Same age as I was when I started…started in with him."

"And let's assume," Jim continued, "that Johns Morelock was

as abusive, not to mention criminal—as his son, Paul. So what?"

"And that he'd be just as sure as any Morelock ever was not to give up control of his own operations to nobody else," said Sam.

"Okay," said Jim. So what?"

"If you're a young wife with a new kid—or fixin to have a new kid—and you're tryin to get away from your sonofabitch of a husband, but you feel trapped and scared because he's got his hand on everything that happens around these parts, and aint likely to be any too happy if you just pick up and walk away. And you aint had the good fortune to have a miscarriage. So you stay put, because you don't see any way clear of the long arm of the Morelocks. So?" said Sam, expectantly.

"Something must have happened to make her go," Jim said. "Something that either made her think she could get away, now, or..." he stopped. "Or what?"

"Or something bad enough that she had to go," Leela said. "She was scared or desperate enough because of something that happened that she had to run. No matter what. Or wait. Maybe something else, like we said at Glen's. Something that made her want to get away, care enough about herself to want it. Not the baby, not yet. Something else." She stopped. "I don't know. I guess I'm just tryin to read myself into her."

"Could be history repeats itself," Sam said.

"Eternal recurrence," Jim said. "One generation after another."

"Could be," said Sam.

"Okay," said Jim, again. "I still say, so what?"

"We need to look and see what happened back here around 1973. Besides just a baby—no offense, Jim. What might make a timid young girl like Leela—sorry...like Eleanor—pick up and get away." Sam set his glass down and stood up. "We're a going to the back cells," he said. "This operation has been a newspaper for fifty years, one way or the other. And when they moved in here, they dumped all them files back in the old jail cells. If we're lookin for local news from 1973, that's where we'll find it. Come on."

"What are you saying?" Jim said. "Where are you going?" But they were interrupted by a loud, insistent knock on the door.

"I'll get it," Sam said, going into the hallway, followed by the others. He opened the door, half expecting to see Paul Morelock, though he probably wouldn't have knocked, would have just barged in, swinging. Still, the anticipation confused him, so he didn't at first recognize the middle-aged woman standing there.

"I need to talk to you all," she said, hurriedly. "They're up to something."

"Somethin?" said Sam, "What somethin?" He peered at her. "Who in the hell are you, anyway?"

Jim suddenly realized who she was, the woman he'd seen up on Shaleen Prong, in the dugout cabin, tending the strange, wailing old man. Then she looked away from Sam toward Jim and stopped, struck still. And the recognition appeared, too, in her eyes. "Oh my lord," she said. "It's you."

"Who is up to something?" said Sam, exasperated. "And I'll ask again, who in the hell are you?"

She reached out a trembling hand and touched Jim's cheek, running her fingers along the line of his jaw. And Jim turned to Sam.

"I believe this is Eleanor. Ellie Morelock," he said. Looking back at her, he said, "My mother."

"You got to stop them," she said, again. "You got to do somethin. They's up to something bad, and I don't want…" Her chin trembled. She looked at Jim. "I don't want you to get hurt."

"Okay, okay," Sam said. "Let's just calm down for a minute." He put his hand on Eleanor's shoulder and piloted her into the office. "Just set down and tell us what's going on. Who's up to something, as if I didn't know?"

"Johns," the woman said. "Johns and Paul Morelock. They're

fixin to do somethin.”

“As if I didn’t know,” said Sam, again. He held a hand up, a calming gesture. “Now let’s just take her easy. What is it they’re fixin to do, exactly?”

“I don’t know,” Eleanor said. “But you got to do something. They’re a going to hurt somebody, and I don’t want…”

“Okay,” Sam said. “You don’t know what they’re going to do, but you want us to stop them. Just how would we do that?”

“I don’t know. You got to go there, get them. Stop them.”

She had walked—half running—all the way from Shaleen Creek. In her worry, and in the shock, now, of seeing Jim, she was in a state of near collapse. They could all see she had no real knowledge of what the Morelocks were doing. So they calmed her as best they could and reassured her that they’d hear about the trouble first thing in the morning and would help her in whatever way they could. And they put her to bed in what had been Leela’s room. There was a little awkwardness about where Leela would sleep, until Sam came back and said, “Look, we all know she’s putting two people out of that bed instead of just the one. Jim aint spent a whole night on that couch all week. He’s kindly been commutin.”

Leela began to protest but Sam cut her off. “Now, sister, it don’t do no good to pretend, even in front of Maw. You and Jim can just take my room and I’ll come down onto the couch. I got a paper to put out anyways, sometime or other, when I aint moonlightin as a rest home manager and social director.”

So they agreed, calmed Eleanor, and settled her in, upstairs, assuring her that they’d take care of whatever they could in the morning.

Upstairs, the woman stood diffidently at the door to the room and said to Jim, “I aint slept in a proper bed in a hundred years.” He beckoned her in and tried to make her feel welcomed and comfortable. She had looked around the room, feeling an odd mix of relief and anxiety. Noticing the old photo on the wall, she looked it over closely, and said to Sam, "He looks just like you. Is he your daddy?" They all laughed lightly, and Sam said, "Well, I reckon that makes you an official resident."

Jim had helped her work the shower, then left the upstairs to her, saying, "Don't worry, now, none of us will be up here until you get all settled in." But she hadn't trusted them, had pushed the laundry hamper to close off the bathroom door while she showered. Later, she did the same with the table in the bedroom, sliding it over to block the door closed before she got into bed.

Several minutes later there was a quiet knock at the door, and she thought, *I knew it*. She got up and walked to the door, saying, "I'm abed. I'd as soon you don't come in."

Jim's voice answered. "I'm sorry to bother you." Then he said, "Mother." She put her hand to her throat. "I just want to ask you again what we can do, what you expect us to do about Paul and Johns Morelock, and whatever they're up to." He sounded hesitant, tentative, but she knew the answer and didn't wait. The vehemence of her response shocked and frightened Jim.

"Get them," she said, fiercely through the door. "Get a gun. Get a bunch of guns iffen you need to. Kill them, if need be. Just stop them before they can hurt you, too."

Jim was stunned, appalled. "You don't mean that," he said.

"Kill them both," she said again. "Afore they kill somebody else again. And again and again," she said, beginning to weep, beating her hand on the door as she repeated the words.

"Your husband? My own father? You know what you're asking me to do?" Jim said, his voice hushed, frightened. "You're asking me to kill my father. My own father. And my half brother as well. How can you ask that? How can..."

The door flew open and he saw her contorted face, thinking, at first, that she was in a rage, about to attack him. Then he realized with a shock that she was laughing.

"Father!" she shouted. "Johns Morelock? He aint your father. Not by a long sight." And then the laughter subsided and she leaned against the door and began to cry, again, this time softly and quietly. He touched her shoulder and she reached out and ran her fingers along the line of his jaw, like she had before, and, still weeping softly, said, "Oh no, son. He aint your father."

So Jim sat with his mother on the bed, as she told, hesitatingly—groping for words and explanations—the story of her flight to Roalton, a poor, half-aware mountain girl on the run from a savage family. She told how she had gone to a sister, begging for lodging and help, and how the sister had taken her, the very next day, to an agency, which had placed her in a domestic cleaning job.

"So I went to work for the doctor. Cleaning his house and his offices, both," she said.

"That must have been hard to do," Jim said, sympathetically. "Especially for a pregnant woman."

She shook her head.

"Oh, I weren't pregnant yet."

Jim stared at her.

"You mean the father—my father—wasn't from around here?" he said.

She waited a moment, looking back at him, as though she were thinking, planning, how to tell it. When her answer came, it was whispered, nearly inaudible.

"Oh no," she said. "He weren't from around here."

"I don't believe it," Jim said. "I've been nosing around here, looking for him, and he wasn't ever here in the first place?" He put his hand over hers, thinking, *Well, mostly, I've been looking for her. Somehow, it's always been like the father was irrelevant, like the thing I had to do was find her, then the whole mystery would clear up. I suppose it's because I had her name—or a version of it—and no reference at all to any man. Except, of course...*

Oh no. It couldn't be. He felt like he'd been hit. His head literally snapped back with the realization; his eyes stung. His hand tightened over hers. "Wait a minute," he said. "Wait."

She responded with a sad smile.

"Wait," he said, again. Up to now he'd felt as if he'd been swimming across a sea of unknowns, yes. And it had been a frightening enough place, all along. But he'd swum strongly, steadily, for all these days, sure of the surface, sure of what the effort was all about. And now, suddenly, he found himself drowning. He felt he would be overwhelmed at once if he let her speak again, as though her voice would come in an enormous swell that would knock him into the depths of the strange, indefinite question, the one answer he'd not really ever sought, perhaps because he knew that underneath the undefined surface of mystery was a certainty more powerful than any question. Perhaps he had felt it lurking beneath, like some monstrous animal, or brooding, watching him emerge from the same depths. So he'd thought he'd been breasting the surface, when, all the while, he'd been a part of the very element he thought he could control. And now, as he watched this weathered, tired woman who was about to tell him what he now believed he had known all along but had refused to see, he found himself, ridiculously, hearing words running through his mind, the words his physician father would recite, at times, late at night, when the man would sit in his darkened study and drink bourbon, speaking the poetry into the dark room to no one: *But I beneath a rougher sea.* A boy, Jim would creep down the hallway in his pajamas and peek into the unlit room, seeing his father's shadowed bulk sitting in the big oak chair, looking outward at nothing. And the man would hold his glass up, toasting a nonexistent presence, reciting melodramatically. *Was whelmed in deeper thoughts than thee.*

And Jim said, again, "Wait," thinking maybe he needn't hear this, thinking perhaps he could put the mystery back, leave this part unsolved. And he thought of the flimsy adoption paper that had borne her name—and the scrawled initial, *M*, followed by the two signatures: his father's and that of the attorney-witness.

And he realized with a start that his mother—the physician's wife—had not been mentioned anywhere on the document. He felt a deep, physical tug somewhere inside when he realized this. *I've been wrong all along. Because the missing mother hasn't been Allie, or Eleanor Morelock at all. It has been that other one, the one who appears nowhere on the adoption agreement, as though she didn't exist at all, as though this was only a transaction between James Thorwait and Ellie Morelock, something they'd talked over, agreed upon, as if the child was a matter of concern only to the two of them. And not to the woman who would raise and feed and worry for me, that adoptive mother who had somehow been left out of the negotiating, the figuring, the agreeing.*

Nancy was her name. She had been raised in a well-to-do family, destined to a comfortable, high-society life; she may as well have been selected in the cradle to marry George Thorwait. And he—Jim—had called her "mom." She had died a decade ago, been mourned as a mother, and then, once again, disappeared from his life, while he searched for this other, this *Ellie* not even noticing until now that she—Nancy Thorwait—had been left out of her place in the adoption document itself, replaced by this woman, Allie Morelock, just as—he now dared think the thought for the first time—she had been displaced in his father's—George Thorwait's—affections. *Or at least his bed*, Jim thought, with a new bitterness.

And, thinking the thought, he was able to speak it. He took his hand away from his mother's and said, "So it was there, in that house in Roalton, all along. I was conceived there. I am the son of George Thorwait."

She nodded slowly, turning her eyes from his.

"Your father," she said, simply, "was your father."

FOUR

They sat in silence for a long time, until Jim stood up and walked slowly toward the door.

This time, it was Eleanor's turn to say, "Wait."

He turned. "What?" he said.

"Don't you see, I wanted what was best for you? I gave you up. I gave you to a man who had the money and the, the connection to you, who would care for you."

"What are you talking about?" he said. "You weren't thinking of me. You couldn't have been. You didn't have me to think about yet. I wasn't even conceived when you went into his house for the first time."

"No," she said, falteringly. "I reckon not." She tried again. "But I hadn't had nobody, since my folks died. And here I was in a big town and there weren't nobody there, neither. Except him. He was nice to me and he give me extra cash."

"I bet he did," Jim said, dryly.

"You're right," she said. "You're right to think I aint nothing but a…aint nothing. But him, he was a good man and I knew he'd take care of you," she hesitated, "after you were coming, after I knew we'd, we'd made a baby. I knew he would be good to you. And your momma."

"I thought you were my momma," Jim said tightly. "But then, this is the first time we've bothered to mention her, George

Thorwait's wife, isn't it?" He laughed, unpleasantly. "So I guess you got the rules switched, both of you—my father and his cleaning woman. Because you became the lover and she became the caretaker, cook, and cleaner. Right?"

He felt the anger and bitterness burning at his cheeks.

"Was it because you saw a chance for that extra money? Or because you thought it would be a thrill to seduce a wealthy man, a successful, city man? Or no," he said, holding up his hand. "No. It's more likely he seduced you, isn't it? The rich, powerful householder taking his pleasure with the maid? Like some son of a bitch in a bad Victorian novel."

"No," she said sharply, suddenly, still looking away from him. "No. You got it wrong. It was me. I reckon I just wanted him. I found a time and a place where he'd be alone with me, and I kindly threw myself on him. Made him to kindly react to me, you see? It weren't him. I planned it all, you see? And it weren't that he didn't care about your momma. He felt terrible after." She looked at Jim, now, pleading. "You got to believe that. They loved each other, and I was the one that tried to come between them. I kindly forced myself on him."

"So you're telling me you're some common slut who took a chance with my father," Jim said, flatly. "And got pregnant with me, and gave me over to him because,"

"Because they—your father and your mother—they were the ones who needed a child, wanted a child. Not me."

"Not you," Jim said, "So you're saying you didn't care about the baby. About me."

She shuddered, then pulled herself up with an obvious effort. She looked at him, her eyes wavering, then, as if by an act of will, looking directly into his.

"Didn't care a thing about you," she said. "I just wanted rid of you. It was them that wanted you. Them's your parents," she said. "Daddy and momma."

* * *

He stood in the doorway, looking at her, feeling the hatred begin to well up. He saw this woman now through the medium of that deed: seducing the mild physician, on a whim, or because she wanted to have the man, see what success felt like. Engendering a baby and then handing him over, because she hadn't wanted that, had only wanted the brief shudder, the cry of passion. But not the child, not himself.

And he should have known it. He'd always been told "you have your father's eyes." Always known it. But he had refused to see even this, believing the congruence of blue eyes to have been pure coincidence, an ironic joke played by the father to help keep the secret of the adoption, keep the boy believing he was who he was being shaped to be.

And worse, he'd thrown all of it over the moment he saw the document, the name of this mother, *Allie Morelock,* this woman who had at last come back to seduce him as well, bringing him off on this hollow quest to find her, because he thought she held the secret to some "real self" that the adoption—the powerful father's powerful secret—had betrayed. And now she had turned up, again, this time to tell him the quest itself was pointless: there was nothing to find in these dark mountains. Nothing but the pain he'd already endured, the wounds themselves, and the throb of feeling as if he were wandering around a strange, dark place where he didn't belong. Well, that much was true: he didn't belong here. He had no connection with the place, after all. He was no Morelock, no lost fragment of mountain consciousness. That had all been romantic posturing. He was the son of a Roalton physician, gotten in an impersonal act of lust, forever regretted. But raised like a son by the mother he'd erased from all of this: Nancy Thorwait. He loved her intensely at this moment, as he felt the hatred for this other woman, this *Allie Morelock,* surge and seethe.

He turned away abruptly and nearly threw himself down the stairs, in his desire to get away from her, this woman, the answer he had sought so avidly. And now, to his disgust, she followed him, the weary body, the longing eyes, trailing him down the stairs into the office, where he turned upon her, asking, harshly, "What do you want?"

And she stood there, silent, looking at him. She lifted a hand, then let it fall. "Nothing," she said. "I reckon they aint nothing more to say."

At that moment, the kitchen door swung open, Sam bursting into the room, his eyes bright with discovery and announcement, Leela following him saying, "What is it, Sam? Show me what it is, damnit."

All four people stood there, like a tableau, Sam in the middle of the room, holding up a yellowed, brittle news clipping, Leela imploring him to "show me," Jim and Eleanor Morelock still facing each other, the disgust and hatred showing on his face, the weariness and loss on hers.

"Wait til you see what I got here," Sam said. "The goddamn mystery is solved."

"You're too late," Jim said. "She already told me."

Sam let his hand fall. "Damn," he said. "I thought I had the scoop right here."

"What is it?" Leela said, exasperated. "Damn it, Sam."

"It's the proof of who this boy's daddy is," Sam said.

"I know who my father is," said Jim. "My father is my father, as this woman said. My father is George Thorwait, physician and civic leader of Roalton, Tennessee. And I don't belong here," he added, feeling a new layer of defeat, feeling somehow that this soured everything he'd done this past week, the searching, the fighting, even Leela's embraces. Everything. "I'm the son of a Roalton physician," he said. "And his loving wife," he added. "By default, since the mother simply gave me over to them, not wanting me. After she'd enjoyed the man, my father."

"What in hell are you talking about?" said Sam, holding up the clipping, again.

"She told me," Jim said, pointing angrily at Eleanor Morelock. "She wasn't pregnant when she left here. Wasn't pregnant when she went to Roalton. Wasn't pregnant," he said, sweeping his arm wide, "until she seduced George Thorwait. Got a baby and gave him away. To the people who wanted him." He turned viciously upon the woman. "Isn't that right?" he said, his voice sharp and clipped.

She nodded.

"Good Lord," Leela said. She reached to touch Jim's arm, but he jerked away.

"Never mind that," he said. "Never mind any of this. I don't belong here."

They stood silently, in tableau again. At last Sam spoke.

"That's about ten pounds of bullshit in a five-pound sack."

They all stared wonderingly at Sam. He handed the clipping to Leela. "Take a look at that," he said.

She studied the faded, fragile paper for a moment. "What's this?" she said. Then she said, "Oh my word!" She looked up, wonderingly, her eyes moving from Jim to Ellie Morelock. She said, "Sam's right," and passed the paper across to Ellie.

Jim's mother looked closely at the clipping a moment. Then she leaned back against the wall and slid slowly downward, her body folding itself, until she knelt on the floor, the tears spilling. Jim came down next to her, looking quizzically into her weeping eyes.

"What is it?" he said. "What is it now?"

She reached a hand up and touched his face.

PART FOUR

ELEANOR

The ground over our bones may grow better
covers inside our bodies than any
we can imagine against the ridges
of our lives, our innocence in a basket
full of eggs waiting to break for space.
—Shelby Stephenson

ONE

She sat on the floor of the office, touching Jim's face, looking into the blue eyes, feeling the slight softness along the line of his jaw, and the breadth of his forehead, features no one else would have particularly noticed, but that somehow made the strongest pull at her heart. And later that night, upstairs in the dark of the bedroom, she ran her memory over Jim's face, like a hand smoothing the page of an album. She looked toward the photograph on the wall, seeing the blank gleam of the glass in the darkness, and she pasted her own images on its pale surface, blinking her eyes to turn the pages.

She had been born just after World War Two, in a two-room cabin on Elk Creek, so far back in the mountains that the land available for cultivation was not enough to get the family by, and they had lived as nearly like original settlers—hunting, trapping, gathering wild foods—as was possible near the middle of the twentieth century. Rural electrification had never come this far up the hollows, so her girlhood was lit entirely by coal oil and paraffin. And, of course, there was no radio, no pump for running water, no refrigeration beyond the water box in the springhouse, where they kept their milk and butter. There was a dilapidated, 1936 Ford flatbed. Her father treated this truck as though it were a glorious, mythical beast. He patted it whenever he walked by it, and he washed the engine every week, scrubbing it with an old horse brush.

They had grown a bit of tobacco, for a few dollars of hard cash, and had otherwise made do with a few chickens, a cow, a hog or two, and a brace of tough little mountain ponies that could handle these steep rocky slopes almost like goats. She could remember the times when they actually used three-piece wooden saddles, though that had been in her extreme youth. By age seven, she could ride these horses, could spin and sew, tie off a hand of tobacco, and skin a raccoon. At twelve, she could drive the truck, butcher a hog, and grade tobacco. She had never spent a full year in school, had never learned to read or write. Nevertheless, she liked to learn the skills of mountain living and was an avid helper all around the place. The youngest of ten, she had seen her older brothers and sisters marry and leave, until there were only three left at the house, then, rather suddenly, the two boys were gone, and she was alone with her parents. She was graceful, intelligent, and energetic. And she loved the place, the deep hush of the hollow, where the cabin tucked into the mountainside, so the night winds boomed and bellowed overhead, like distant thunder. She loved the work, even, being up before dawn watching the hollow gradually lighten, while she felt the weight of the spring water she carried pulling at her shoulders, the sun still down behind the high wall of the mountain, until, later, it would appear overhead, flecking yellow on the leaves and rocks.

The family went into town now and then, though not each Saturday as the folks lower down the mountain did. Perhaps three times a year they would go in, walk the streets, see the sights. Once or twice she went to a movie, and she was breathless with wonder.

Just before her fifteenth birthday, her parents were killed running a load of tannin down to the railhead; her father had insisted on taking the bark in their ancient, single tongue wagon because he hadn't cleaned the engine on the truck that week, and they had been struck broadside by a speeding car. The next day, the high sheriff had made his way up the mountain and told her the news, offering to take her into town with him, so she could "make arrangements." But she had refused the offer, saying, "I'll get up tomorrow and come on in myself." She asked him, though, to telegraph her siblings, since she didn't know how to do this, and she asked, hesitantly, what it would cost her.

"I'll take care of it, miss," the sheriff had said, looking around the two-room cabin. "Don't you matter about it." And so she had shown him a slip of paper with the addresses. She couldn't read it; her older sister had compiled the list, drawn four houses and four stick figures on it, so the folks would know what it was, and had sent it to them. The sheriff had copied the information and handed her back the note, saying, "You be careful, now, hear?"

That evening, she took a spade and a sack and hiked up Elk Creek to a spot where the course switched back sharply, a place they all called the Elbow. She found the uneven stone, slabbed with mica, and rolled it, digging beneath until she unearthed the small tin box holding the family's emergency money. There were fifty-dollar bills and one old twenty-dollar gold piece, and she wrapped these carefully in the sack.

She sat on a rock by the creek, listening to the rushing water, watching the dusk deepen into the hollow, the sky still bright blue overhead. Then the cove-light shifted, all at once, to a deep purple and the sky overhead turned pink. There was an oak seedling growing improbably through the tight space between the rock where she perched and the next outcrop of granite, and she reached her hand to it, stroking the light green leaves. Then she peeled two small branches from the slight stem and dropped them into the water, where they tumbled almost instantly from sight, down the plunging stream.

Next morning, she killed and dressed all the chickens, wrapping them in wet flour sacks. It was still barely dawn when she put the sacks into the bed of the truck. She went to the hog pen and stood for a moment, wondering whether she could get anything worthwhile out of killing a hog in the summer. At last she decided against this and, instead, set the sides on the truck, led the hog up on a halter and, using an oak switch, drove the animal up a ramp into the bed. The ponies were gone, killed, no doubt, pulling the wagon her parents were riding. So she let the cow from the barn and turned it loose to graze, hoping it would find its way across the hollow and up to the small meadow. *If she don't*, she thought, *they's plenty to eat in the garden*, and she set the gate wide open for the animal. She returned to the cabin and searched it, looking for anything of value and finding nothing but a large knife and two cast-iron cookpots, which she lugged out to the truck. She returned and considered her mother's chestnut dresser, the pride of the homestead, for a moment, then gave up the thought of trying to get it into the truck. "Can't drive a dresser with a oak switch," she said, aloud. She took the feed sack with the money in it and filled it with her clothing, rough cotton shirts, and two pairs of overalls. She had no shoes.

It was full light by the time she cranked the truck and headed down the hollow. She knew her way into town, though she had never been there alone, had never driven the truck on the high road, even, and didn't know where she would be going once she got to town. She figured she'd just ask around for her folks and someone would know where the bodies were and could tell her what to do. *It won't be no trouble sellin the hog nor the chickens. They's always somebody wants to buy a fresh chicken, and that's a good hog, healthiest hog he'd ever raised, Daddy said.*

She wasn't afraid, wasn't particularly sad about her loss. She was busy. She was working her way along a process she knew nothing about, driving into a new world to find the bodies of her parents and send them off to another world. Then she would learn how to sell the things and work out how she was going to live on a mountain farm by herself. After that, perhaps, after that, there would be time for the luxuries of fear and grief.

She didn't like the feel of the rubber gas pedal under her bare foot.

Several miles down the high road, just as she began to relax, the truck died out, and she sat in it for an hour, calmly trying to figure how she would get herself, not to mention the hog and the chickens, into town. At last she got out and began to walk, carrying the sack with the money and her clothes.

Some time later a new pickup stopped for her and a young man offered her a ride. She stood silent for a moment, looking at him. He had a rough, homemade-looking crew cut, a heavy brow, and narrow eyes. He was chewing tobacco and he pushed his head out the window and let a gob of spit fall to the asphalt. He smiled at her. "Come on and get in. I'll take you where you're a going."

She stood, watching him impassively. Finally, she opened the sack and offered a bill. "Could you see clear to haul a hog and some dressed chickens to town?"

"That's your flatbed up the way?" the man asked. She nodded. "It's about ready for the trash heap, aint it?" he said, and spit again. She nodded again and thrust the bill toward him.

"Get in," he said. "We'll see what's to see." He leaned over and pushed open the door. She climbed in, and, immediately, he backed and turned the truck and punched the accelerator, spewing gravel. The tires caught and the truck leapt uphill.

"Mercy," she said.

"This here's a souped-up little number," he said. She had no idea what he meant by that. He winked at her and said, "You look like you could be souped-up a mite, too, if somebody were to try." Again she didn't understand, though she heard the leer in his tone and held her clothes sack tight against her chest.

"Where you comin from with all that stock?" he said.

"Up to Elk Creek," she said.

"Elk Creek? Aint nobody up on Elk Creek."

"They's a few," she said. "Was."

"Way on up there?" he said. "Lord God, honey, you're from bear country, aint you? I bet you don't even got electric up thataway, do you?"

"I reckon not," she said. After a pause, she said, "I been in town before."

"I bet you have, honey," he said. He reached across and touched her leg.

"Please don't do that," she said.

"Suit yourself," he said.

He didn't touch her again until they got to the truck. Then he cut his engine, spat out the window and reached over to her leg again.

"You don't have to pay me nothing if you'll give me a little kiss," he said. He squeezed her leg, and she moved, drawing away.

"I reckon I'd rather pay," she said.

"Suit yourself," he said.

He didn't have a ramp for the hog, so they stood and looked at the animal awhile. "That hog aint going nowhere today," he said.

"Maybe you could drive me into town and we could send some folks up here for it. Maybe sell it and let them come pick it up."

"Who's going to run all the way up the mountain to fetch a scrawny hog outen this wreck?" he said.

"Seem like to me this is pert near all the way down the mountain," she said. "More than halfway to town."

He spat. "Is if you're comin from Elk Creek." His laugh sounded like a sneer and she colored slightly. He looked her up and down, mulling a moment. "Wait a second, honey. Whyn't we go on to my folks' place? It aint but a mile or so from here, up to the Shaleen breakout. We can get you a bite and put you up and send my daddy down for the hog. He's like to buy it outright," the young man said, encouragingly. "And I'll be durned if he don't pay you a good price for them chickens."

"Can't," she said. "My folks is dead, in town. I got to go make arrangements."

"You come on up and we'll send down, save you all that trouble. You probably don't know which way to turn in that big old town, do you? You'd just get yourself confused. You come on up with me and my folks and my cousins, they'll take care of everything."

"I don't know," she said.

"It's fixin to get dark," he said. "I reckon I can leave you here, if you want to spend the night on the road. It's pert dangerous though, settin out here where anybody could swarve into you."

She thought of her parents, the wreck on the highway.

"All right," she said. "I reckon your mother could help me think out the arrangements, couldn't she?"

He laughed and started the truck, punching it onto the road and up the mountain.

"My mother's dead these six years," he said, touching her leg again.

Ellie shrank away. Years later, she would remember this as the moment she realized she would never see Elk Creek again.

On the way up to Shaleen, he started bragging, trying to impress this pretty mountain girl. Johns Morelock was his name, he said. He was damn proud to be a Morelock, he told her, as though he thought she might challenge him. "We run every damn thing there is up thisaway," he said. "Folks gets in our way, we run them clear out of the country," he said. "My pawp, he's Jessum Morelock, and I reckon he's killed more than one feller tried to get in our way. Wouldn't mind if he done it again."

Ellie was frightened but she was determined to "abide," as her mother had told her to do in hard times, with that fatalism that had seen generations of deep mountain people through trials and horrors enough. "You just abide, lessen you make something worse," her mother had said. "Aint nothing so bad it can't get worse. Don't you forget that." Ellie remembered her mother's calloused hand stroking her cheek. "But iffen you can just abide, they aint nothing so bad it can't get better, neither."

So she thought of this, as the young man rocketed the truck up the mountain. At a switchback, before she could see where the big stream came down, he drove straight across, so that she thought he was going to take them over the ledge. But it was a lane, cutting sharply off the high road and rising upward, steeply, so that the truck lost its momentum and rolled to a stop in the deepening dusk of the woods. The creek roared somewhere off to the left. Ahead was a clapboard house, with a low porch stretching all across the front.

"This here's the place," he said. "Aint no place but this place around the place."

She was frightened by the one-armed man with the glinting eyes. He looked at her dispassionately and said, "Fetch her a bite to eat," in the same tone of voice someone might have used to say, "Kill her."

She was in the large, wood-framed farmhouse, sitting at a velour couch fronted by a glass coffee table. She had never been in a place quite like this and, as nervous as she was, she found herself looking with pleasure at the shiny furniture, the big mirror over the hearth, the bright yellow carpeting on the floor, into which she wiggled her bare toes as she sat placidly, abiding, watching the men come and go. A radio played loudly in another room and she heard a man's voice wailing a song about a whippoorwill that was too blue to cry.

They had been nice enough to her, in an overbearing kind of way. The young man, Johns, had brought her into the house where three men were sitting, drinking beers. They all looked her over.

"Lord God, boy," said a thin, graying man with big hands. "What'd you use for bait?"

This was Snide, she learned, an older man, cousin to the one-armed man, second cousin to Johns. He seemed tense, fidgety, when he looked at her, "strung like a banjar," her father would have said. Next to him sat a morose man in his thirties, another cousin, who watched her body closely, but would not meet her eyes, and said nothing at all. This was Reuben, she learned. The one-armed man was Johns's father, Jessum. Alone among the men he didn't appear to be watching her, barely seemed to notice her. And then he had barked out that command, which sounded like an execution order: "Fetch her a bite to eat."

They had done so, while Snide and Johns went off to see about her truck and the hog and chickens. At some point, she'd said, "I'm thankful for your help" to the one-armed man, who had taken her by the shoulder and looked at her with those glinting, narrow eyes. "It aint help," he had said. He released her with a small shove and walked on by, leaving her wondering.

Reuben ate with her, the two of them sitting at a worn oak table, scorched with flat iron burns, the first familiar mark she'd seen around this house. She brightened when she saw these. "I could iron you all's clothes, if you've a need," she said. "By way of payin back. Iffen you all have a flat iron." Reuben had guffawed thickly and said nothing. When she got up from the table to put her dishes at the sink, he had watched her every move, chewing his food slowly, swallowing, savoring, his eyes on her all the time.

Later, Jessum took her by the arm and led her to the hallway, where he placed her in front of him and said, "Go on." He prodded her gently and she walked along until they came to a door, where he said, "Here," and ushered her into a small room that was filled almost completely by a heavy walnut bed and a mirrored dresser. He flicked a switch by the door, lighting the room. "You sleep here," he said and turned, going out and shutting the door behind him.

She stood in the room, thinking, *This must be the way the man who was "sailin out on the ocean" felt. Many a mile from home on the sea.* She knitted her hands and took a full, deep breath. *How in the world did I come to be here?*

The door flew open and the one-armed man, Jessum, thrust

his hand in, holding her sack. He threw it onto the bed and left, pulling the door closed. She stood a moment, then went to her sack and rummaged around for her cotton nightgown. She unclasped the bib of her overalls, letting it flop over at her waist. Then she stopped, pulled the bib back into place, and fastened one side, realizing the man would be back one more time.

A moment later, he kicked the door open and entered awkwardly balancing a white enameled pan full of water on his one hand, like a waiter with a tray. He turned to the dresser and stood, holding the pan high, looking at her. She realized with a start that he couldn't set it down and she took it off his palm, placing it on the dresser and saying, "Sorry. Thank you." He pulled a cloth and a towel out from under his stump, and drew a square white bar of soap from his pocket, placing it next to the bowl. He left the room, saying nothing.

"Good night," she said to the closing door. "Thank you."

She knew he would not come back now, so she undressed, folding the clothes carefully, decorously. She washed herself, *thinking top to bottom*, and hearing her mother's voice, teaching her to wash out of one pan, cleaning her face, her armpits, her privates, then her feet. After she had dried herself, she turned and said, "How in the world did you get to be here?" to the thin, naked young woman in the mirror.

She drew on the coarse, homespun shift and lay down on the big bed. It was very soft, like falling into water, and she rolled a little, feeling the fluffiness. She lay on her back for several minutes, then, remembering, got up and went to the wall, flicking the switch down. In darkness now, she felt her way to the bed and crawled in, pulling up a feather tick that smelled of cedar, and home.

She had a dream that she was driving the old wagon, full of dressed chickens, chucking the horses along, when her father and mother sat up out of the bed, saying, "Where in the world are you going, Ellie?" Then the wagon had dropped off into the ditch and she heard the load of meat falling, slewing off the side of the bed, and her parents falling with it, into the dark ditch, making a terrible crashing noise.

She awoke, still hearing the noise and realized the sound was coming from outside her door. She heard the *thoom* of heavy shoes on the wood floor, and the low grunts of men struggling, the thud of a body against the wall. She heard a breathless voice saying, "goddammit," then the sound of a fist striking flesh, twice, and, again, the body against the wall, sliding down and crumpling on the floor like an echo. From further away, she heard a voice calling, then, close, a man saying, "You want some of this too, old man?" Then there was silence.

The door creaked open and she heard the man come into the room, approaching the bed. She was afraid to look, so she lay on her back, staring straight upward, watching the grain on the oak ceiling, listening to the shoes on the wooden floor, so much louder than the bare feet of her parents, brushing the floor as they finished the cleaning up while she lay, a little girl, in the high loft, where the warm smoky air collected and soothed her to sleep. Here, in the thin air, the man's shoes clumped, approaching like a big storm, closer and closer.

She could sense his bulk at the side of the bed, and she knew it was Reuben, the thick-waisted man who had watched her, silently, all night. She began slowly to slide her body away, toward the far side of the bed, feeling ridiculous, forlorn, knowing there was nothing at all she could do, trying to tell herself, *abide, abide*, trying to hear her mother's voice, but hearing nothing, now, except a roaring in her ears. Then she felt the tick flung back and the wash of cold air and she rolled away faster, but his hand came down and yanked her back, then his face was next to hers, smelling of liquor and tobacco, mumbling something she couldn't understand, then a hand sliding down the scooped neck of the gown and fondling her breast and the wet lips sucking on her neck while his body dropped heavily onto hers, his thigh pushing at her.

The light came on like an explosion.

She felt Reuben's weight jerk from her, and saw, at the door, the man called Snide, holding a pointed rifle, motioning the barrel to the side, directing the heavy man off the bed. "Git," Snide said.

Reuben rolled himself from the bed and stood, saying, "What in the hell?"

Snide strode into the room, lowering the rifle across his body. When he reached Reuben, he swung the gun stock upward, catching the heavy man in the jaw and dropping him, unconscious and bleeding, to the floor.

"Now I reckon he'll leave you alone," Snide said to Ellie, turning and propping the rifle in the corner.

"My Lord," she said. "Thank you."

"That's all right," he said, stepping over Reuben's bulk and leaning on the bed, over her. He reached his big hand toward her and grasped her gown, pulling so hard she thought at first he was trying to lift her. Then the fabric tore and he flung her back, her breasts and belly bared. He stood up again, straddling Reuben's insentient form.

"Let's us do this right," he said, unbuckling his belt.

TWO

Next morning, they had sent into town and made arrangements for her parents to be buried in the Methodist lot, telling the sheriff they were "relations" and would look after the daughter. They had even taken her to a funeral, where one of her older brothers had appeared—a virtual stranger to Ellie—and Snide had told him she was married to Johns and was well taken care of.

The brother left that same day.

By the end of the first week, all of the men had had her, the sole exception being Jessum, the one-armed man, who viewed her with some kind of fatalistic detachment, caring for her—he brought her water and towels each day, even though there was a bathroom and running water, and he saw that she was fed—without any emotion beyond a vague disquiet, as if she were a foundling kitten that he knew would run away, someday. Snide had attempted to claim her for his, "after you all have your fun," but the one-armed man had overruled him, declaring that it was only fit and proper that she belong to his son, Johns, who was young and had found her in the first place, and that she be his wife, "before you all beat her up too bad."

There had been a sporadic series of fights for two days, then it was settled. The other men left her alone and she was married to Johns in a strange ceremony performed by a gaunt, raging preacher in a worn coat on the front porch of the house, and attended by three or four families of people she had never seen. Johns had put a fat, gold ring onto her finger. When the thing was ended, several of the women approached and hugged her automatically and one—a graying woman in a faded bonnet—opened the huge family bible and penciled in her name next to Johns's, saying, "Well, here you are," showing Eleanor the page written over with names, interlinked with straight lines. Ellie couldn't read them of course. But the woman acted as though the odd scrawl she'd written in the bible was more real than Eleanor herself.

Later that day, Johns had taken her up the creek, telling her this was the honeymoon, had stripped her and forced himself into her as she lay sprawled across a fallen birch. And she had entered into the round of life she would endure for the next two years. She had just turned fifteen.

She knew the day she first came here that these men were not farmers, and she had wondered over the succeeding days how they managed to keep this big house, and these shiny cars and trucks. She found out soon enough that they were driving moonshine into Roalton and swapping that for cash they would run into Asheville, where they would buy drugs, hopscotching state lines the way they'd learned in the old prohibition days. Now it was bonded liquor into the dry counties in Tennessee, and "bennies" and "goofballs" into the big market in the coal fields to the north, over the Virginia line, and across Cumberland Gap into Kentucky, so now they were jumping in and out of four states, without out traveling more than sixty miles on any run. They put her to work counting pills, wrapping them into tin foil squares, twenty and fifty and a hundred pill lots, before she had any idea what this was all about. She cooked for them and kept the place. She wasn't happy, but she thought of her mother, and the imperative to "abide." She waited.

* * *

On odd occasions, Johns would take her into town, and, some nights, to a ramshackle dance hall over the mountain toward Roalton. It was a "dry house," but alcohol—Morelock alcohol—could be bought under the counter in the snack bar, or the men would carry silver flasks, or quart jars, and they would bring their girls out to the cars in between sets, where they would sit in the back seats, drinking from quart jars and fumbling under each other's clothing. Inside, the hall was dark and smoky, and the music echoed disconcertingly, so it was difficult to dance in anything like proper time. Ellie didn't know about this kind of dancing anyway, so she would allow Johns to drag her clumsily around, his arm crooked about her neck like a headlock. The band was good—even she could tell this—playing a hot brand of hillbilly country music from a slightly elevated stage at the end of the long hall. There was always a knot of people standing close to the stage, where the music could actually be heard, watching the men play, nodding heads and tapping feet, the couples holding each other around the waists, swaying back and forth to the music, singing along to "Little Red Wagon," and holding up pint flasks in mocking salute as the band played "Drivin Nails in my Coffin."

She liked these dances, liked the music, especially, and tried to persuade Johns to stop dancing, so they could go over and listen close. She'd never heard electric guitar or lap steel back home, of course, and she was thrilled and moved by the volume, the driving beat, the vertiginous swoops of the steel guitar. Johns would usually ignore her pleas, particularly if he'd had a lot to drink, when he would drag her around the floor a few times then head out to the parking lot for more alcohol.

There were fights, usually over a woman or a supposed insult. These were brief, ham-fisted affairs that were over quickly, bystanders stepping in, the two combatants walking away from each other, cursing and threatening, a little bruised. At times though, they would be worse. The men would meet again outside, where the spectators wanted to see and didn't interfere, and where the fighters would try to hurt each other quickly and seriously, gouging eyes with fat, stiff thumbs, or slashing with knives, or trying to gain control: wrapping an arm around the other man's neck and pummeling away at his face until he began to convulse.

Johns was a big man, with a reputation, and the others usually steered clear of him when he became belligerent, allowing insults and provocations that would surely have been answered, had they come from anyone else. At times, though, when he had consumed enough to become belligerent, or, especially, when he was "hopped up," mixing the drink with bennies, he would become involved. He usually won the fights handily, and it would arouse him, so he would strut away from the crumpled body of his opponent, wiping bloodied hands on his jeans and grabbing Ellie by the arm, pulling her to the car, laughing, saying, loud enough for everyone to hear, "Come on, hon, let's have a drink and a feel."

On this night, though, he had not marched up to Ellie, but had stepped across to his vanquished foe's woman—a large-breasted girl with vacant sheep's eyes—and had curled his arm around her waist, saying, "Now you come along with me," taking the girl off behind the building as the spectators wandered away, and Ellie stood, alone, in the pebbled parking lot.

That was the night she met Morgan Hampton.

She was standing in the lot, hugging herself against the damp, wondering what to do, when a man said, "You need some help?" and she turned to see the deep blue eyes, the broad forehead, the soft jawline. She recognized him at once as the lap steel player in the band, and she heard herself asking, oddly, "Aint you supposed to be playin music?"

He laughed and said, "We're on break. I come out for a smoke and seen the fight." He looked at her. "But the fight's all over, and I seen you a standin out here all alone. You okay?"

"I reckon," she said. "My husband, he..." She stopped, not knowing what to say. Still hugging herself, she said, "I'm all right, thanks. You just let me wait for him."

"That was him went off with that woman, weren't it?" he said. She turned back to him. His eyes were a deep, dark blue, expressing sympathy and concern. She was drawn immediately to this man, but she was worried, as well, lest Johns return and cause more trouble.

"You'd best just let me wait on him," she said. "He'll be back." She began to feel anxious about this man's safety. If Johns came back, wild and drunk as he was, he might decide he didn't like her talking to a stranger, especially a young, sympathetic man.

But he refused to leave her alone, saying, "Whyn't I just go around here and see can I find your husband?" She shook her head, but he was already moving, heading around the building where Johns had disappeared with the woman. "You wait here," he called back. "Watch and stay away from that feller on the ground," he added, referring to the broken man who lay, abandoned, too, about ten yards away from Ellie. "I'll be back," he said, and disappeared around the corner of the building.

A few minutes later, he returned, his big eyes looking sad, or worried.

"You come on in with me," he said to her. "I got to get back to work, but I don't think you ought to stay out here. You come on in and I'll help you when we finish. Your husband, he's…he's kindly got busy. You come on with me."

"I reckon I better wait," she said.

"You come on," he said, firmly, taking her elbow and nudging her gently toward the door. Later, she would think of the combined feeling of gratitude and fear as "dizziness." The entire Morelock phase of her life had begun with a young man offering to help her, and she had no reason to trust this stranger, either. Still, because she had seen him in the band, had enjoyed his playing, she felt a strange sense that she knew him much better than she did. And there was the way he looked: the big, deep eyes, the gentle softness in the line of his jaw, the intelligent forehead. She knew she probably shouldn't respond to him, but she did. And she was alone; she had no idea how she would get home. She realized Johns Morelock had probably forgotten all about her in his drunkenness, his pleasure at having beaten the man so badly. And she knew he had taken the woman as some sort of prize, and had gone.

So she followed Morgan Hampton back into the hall, where he escorted her to the side of the stage and bade her stay there. He brought her a Dr Pepper and told her, "Don't worry. I'll be off in forty minutes. You just stay here. If your husband comes back, he'll see you up here. And if he don't, I'll help you get home."

As the music began again, she felt the fear begin to drain away, and she found herself listening, watching the young man work the bright steel bar along the strings of the strange lap guitar that looked no more musical than a grading board, but from which he drew such amazing sounds. She saw the strange metal picks on his fingers, the flecked, multicolored plastic pick on his thumb, the curve of his right hand, looking fierce and powerful, like a claw. But then the fingers would go to work and look as delicate as if they were stroking an infant, and moving as precisely as the hand of a woman tatting lace. She was surprised by how little each hand moved, while the complex, stirring music poured forth from the trivial, flat instrument.

Johns never came back that night. He had apparently forgotten her as thoroughly as he had taken over her life, virtually kidnapped her, only a few months before. Now she stood in the dance hall, watching this new protector, who could make her skin chill with the wild glittering slides on the strange, flat, unassuming instrument. It suited him, she thought, because he was unassuming himself, a quiet, sober man with sad, thoughtful eyes who had decided to help her. She thought perhaps she could trust him, and she felt her heart flutter the least bit.

He finished his set and packed up the instrument, letting her carry it outside while he took a heavier black box with knobs on it. In the parking lot she turned to see which way his car might be and found he had set the box down and was standing, looking out at the road, waiting.

"My paw will be along to pick us up," he said. "I aint got no car of my own, or I'd take you straight on."

"That's okay," she said.

"He'll be here directly," he said. They stood a moment in silence.

"You know," she said, "I don't even know your name." She felt bold saying this, as though she were flirting, or asking for something private, some intimacy.

"No, nor I your'n," he said, and looked back to the road. Now she wondered if this was a game, some ritual test to see who would reveal the name first, as though whoever held out longest would be the winner, and be in charge, somehow. But then he chuckled.

"I'm Morgan Hampton," he said. "From over Timb's Knob."

"Eleanor Taylor," she said, then, catching herself, "Morelock. Eleanor Morelock."

"Pleased," he said. "You're from the Shaleen Creek Morelocks aint you?" he said. "Just over the top from our old home place, I believe."

"I reckon," she said, though she wasn't too certain. The family had not told her much and she had never been allowed to wander freely around the mountain. She realized for the first time how little she knew about her own whereabouts, the people she lived with, the family that had captured her, brutalized her, then taken her to its bosom, in a manner of speaking, at least. Married her and written her name in the family bible, at any rate. Put a ring on her finger. She knew enough to say, "They's right proud of being who they are. Being Morelocks."

"Well I reckon so," he said. "They run most of my people clean off this mountain thirty years ago." He laughed. "Aint enough left of Hamptons around here for them to even notice, I reckon. My Pap, he come back and said he'd be damned if he wouldn't farm a little piece of the old family place. On down in the cove, since the old place is federal land, now."

They stood for a while in silence. "I reckon my husband aint a comin back," she said. "I reckon he forgot."

"I reckon he got busy," said Morgan, awkwardly.

"Maybe he's back home," she said. Again they stood a moment in silence.

"They's a path from the old Hampton place up over the knob to your place, did you know that?" said Morgan.

"What's that?" she said, "The old Hampton place?"

"It's some old busted down cabins where all my folks used to live," said Morgan. "Up yonder, beyond the ridge. Like I says, it's federal land, now, but I been up there, pokin around. My daddy grew up there, he and his brothers. They used to fight your folks, you know? Used to work with them, or for them, then something happened and they took to fightin. They was a bunch killed. Anyways, I went up there to look around and found a old trail runs right out from the back of the place up and over the knob and down to yours. Splits halfaways down, to an old mill, sawmill, and then the other way to your place. But I reckon you know all that. Anyway, I've hiked over there. I been there. I believe I've seen you there, once. Watched you out back tossin out dishwater, I believe."

She flushed at this, feeling the displacement again, as though she were a stranger in her own place, where this man she'd never seen could know his way around her own home place better than she did, could walk down and look at her. And she felt as though she had disappeared somehow when her folks had died. She hadn't even seen them die. They had just left and there she was, alone on Elk Creek. She thought of herself that day, digging up the money, killing and dressing the chickens, thinking, *I done everything right, everything I could do. And then come off the mountain and it all didn't matter. None of it: not Momma nor Daddy nor whether I'd ever lived nor done anything—worked in the field or learnt to tan a hide—none of it mattered a lick. I come off that mountain and I may as well have been a newborn baby for all I knew. And I let Johns Morelock take me home like he'd caught me in a dead fall. And I don't even know if my life ended when I come off from Elk Creek, or whether it just begun when I wound up at Morelocks'. Because now neither'un feels like it's real. I don't know.*

But she felt, too, as though this young man with the sad eyes had looked at her in the old way, as if he'd seen the person she'd been on Elk Creek, as though, somehow, his recognizing her had given her back a small piece of herself, the person she'd been before she became a Morelock. "Eleanor Taylor," she'd said to him, almost by accident, but she believed it was true.

A beam of headlights floated around the corner and she saw a big Dodge sedan slow and turn into the parking lot.

"That's Paw," said Morgan, lifting the box. Ellie grabbed the instrument case.

In the car, she watched the headlights swinging around the bends, saw the dark foliage rising up, the steep slopes of mountain, all around. She thought about Elk Creek, again, and the darkness there, untouched by beams of electric light, and thought about the amber glow of lamp light; her mother would put an open flame kerosene bowl on the scrubbed oak table each night, around which they'd gather to do their separate tasks, Daddy punching a new hole in a harness strap, while Momma flexed a split of oaks into a bowl of water, and she stuffed a pillow, all of them talking, telling each other the stories they already knew by heart or singing songs from somewhere they'd never seen, the words—"I'm sailin out on the ocean," or "I was born in Bingen, fair Bingen on the Rhine"—perfectly recalled in some inheritance beyond memory, so that she knew the sense and the touch of these tunes as deeply as she knew anything, though the words made no sense.

Somehow, this young man with the big sad eyes had made her think of these old times, though her family's eyes had been pale, light gray-blue, and distant, and she had never seen anything to match his figure, seated on the stage, the flat slab of instrument in his lap suddenly brought to life by the slight motions of his hands, that seemed to float above the instrument, like a preacher calling forth a spirit, or a dowser, looking for water. He moved the piece of steel in his left hand like floating a leaf onto still water.

His music sounded nothing like the singing back home. Lord knows, her mother would have bundled Ellie away from such sounds the instant she heard the slither of those notes, and the throb of the volume. But still, somehow, the playing had brought Eleanor back to memories of the singing back home, something she had lost in these months with the Morelocks, who had been able to keep her, but had never moved her, not in this place she knew was her own. So she saw, riding in the musty interior of this Dodge sedan, sitting by Morgan in the cavernous back seat, that they hadn't taken everything, that there was still a link to home and some real person remaining, whole, inside of her. And, later, she knew it was the young man with the big sad eyes and the delicate fingers, the floating slide of the steel, that had brought her back to this core. And she felt she could never give him up, after that, because he was her link to her own self.

But that was later. Tonight, the car pulled in and she saw a biggish man who didn't much resemble Morgan except for the eyes. She called him Mister Hampton. He reached a hand out to her, but it was not a particularly warm gesture, and she felt his reserve at once. She couldn't understand his reaction to her, but she knew it was not so much dislike as disapproval, or perhaps disdain. She wondered if he knew how she'd been taken by the Morelocks and she felt a rush of shame. Then she told herself that was impossible: even the women in the family hadn't known. So she let it go, deciding he must just disapprove of his son helping out stranded young women, or maybe he didn't like having his son playing lap steel at a dance hall. It didn't matter, she de-cided.

She and Morgan sat in the back seat of the old Dodge and they headed up the mountain in the dark night. No one spoke.

At last, as they approached the big curve into the hollow where Shaleen poured forth, she said, "It's before the crossing, up above the creek. The next turn out." Morgan's father said, "I know it," tersely, and swung the car into the turnoff a little too fast, so the tires spewed leaves and gravel. He stopped before she could see the lights of the house.

"Walk her up there from here," he said, in a clipped voice. "This here's as far as I'm a going."

They went up the curving track in the darkness. When she saw the lights shining on the long porch, she said, "This is far enough. I reckon I'll just walk on up from here, myself." When he pro-tested, she cut him off, saying, "He might could still be drunk. There aint no use in having no trouble."

So he agreed to let her go. He held out his hand to her, but she pushed it away and stepped forward, hugging him.

"Thank you so very much," she said. "I believe you're a nice man."

"You aint seen too many nice men, have you?" he said, qui-etly.

She didn't answer him, but said, "I'll be watchin the trail out back, next time." And she turned and hurried away, her head lowered, running toward the house.

THREE

Johns did not return at all that night, or most of the next day. When he did appear, he was drunk again, and he beat her because, he said, she could not have gotten home on her own, so she must have "found her a buck to rut." Jessum had watched all this impassively, sitting in his big rocker, while Johns held her by the neck of her shirt and hit her with his fist. Later, when Johns had finally passed out, his father ordered her to "get my boy into the bed," and she had dragged Johns to the room and left him unconscious on the floor. She sat on the bed, watching the man snore raggedly, touching her face to feel the swelling, testing the bruised flesh. She arose and went down the hall to the bathroom sink, where she bathed her face and looked at herself in the mirror, the eye nearly swollen shut, a deep spread of colors across her cheek and blended onto her temple, like dark paints smudged across a smooth palette. She turned to leave the room, then stopped, turned again, and slid the window wide open. Stepping onto the toilet seat, she raised herself over the sill, one leg across to the outside, and ducked all the way out, falling a few feet onto the soft earth.

She felt her way across the dark clearing, gradually seeing the way, as her eyes adjusted and she looked upon a pale wash of moonlight reflected blue-gray on the foliage, so that she could make out the bulk of the mountain rising before her, and could see, by its darkness, the place where the trees opened up slightly,

264

where a trail began. She entered the darkest place and picked her way up the slope, looking for blackness that told her which way the trail went, and when it would dip downhill for a moment before rising again. At one point, she missed a switchback and blundered into a thicket, the branches whipping like knife cuts against her bruised face. Further up, the trail went over a huge, flat outcrop of granite and she spent a long time searching to find where the path reentered woods and scrub on the other side.

Further along, the trail suddenly steepened, then, at last, she topped a curved bulge, a false summit, and the way opened up into the clear moonglow. It felt much brighter, now, after the darkness of the mountainside. The trail was eroded here, and she walked between shoulder-high walls of earth, her head swathed in moonlight, so her body seemed to have dissolved into the blackness below. Then she rose. The trail tipped out of its sunken path and she was on the brim of the knob, bathed head to foot in the blue-gray glow. At the top, she found a rounded granite boulder, flecked with quartz, and sat, her face turned upward, as though the glow were a fountain she could bathe in. She stood, suddenly, and began to unbutton her shirt. A moment later, she lay naked, bared to the sky, feeling the cold stone, the huge mountain beneath, pressing up against her back, molding to her form, so that she couldn't tell if the movement she felt was her own body, breathing, or if it was the mountain pulsing against her. The cold rock below made the moonlight feel like warm water pouring across her curved breasts and belly, and she believed it was pouring her own soul back into her hurt and derided body. She was alone, with herself, on the mountaintop.

She awoke as the sky was lightening in the east. She was chilled and, for a moment, felt a rush of fear, not knowing where she was, feeling, first, that she was cold and naked, and wondering how this had come to be. Then she remembered and the fear pulsed through her anew because she realized she'd not been home, and Johns would be angry. She could see him, storming around in that house that had never really been hers, but that she called, "home." She knew, in fact, that the place had always only been an indication that she had no home, that she was alone, so alone she felt most comfortable up here on the very top of the knob, on a cold stone, her bare breasts pressed against the warm sky. And she found herself singing the song, inside her mind, *I aint got no home in this world anymore.*

But all that was pointless since she had to worry about Johns.

And Morgan. She knew, somehow, that Morgan would come up this way, this morning, looking to go down and watch the Morelock homestead, watching for her. Of course he would, after yesterday. At that, she rose and began to dress herself, hurriedly, as though he were just down the way, about to come over that round of granite and appear, from the other side. *I'll meet you over on the other side*, she sang to herself. It was a song she'd known from her mother, and now she heard her mother saying, "abide." So, warmer now, she stretched out on the rock and lay still, looking at the brightening sky.

And he did, in fact, appear, after the sun had come up fully, and she felt slightly dazed in the heat and light, as she watched him appear over the rounded hump of rock, head and shoulders and body, like he was rising from a sea, this man she had only spoken to last night, whom she felt had known her longer than she had known herself, and so, she believed, could give herself back, create some shimmering truth she would hear as though she had been waiting for this new sound all along, the way he made those sounds on the flat, trivial board over which he passed the steel bar like a diviner.

Yet the meeting itself was something of a letdown, at first, because he'd brought her back to earth, back from the night sky and her bared flesh against the moonlight. And here she was just a woman talking with a man, both trying to maintain decorum, to say less than they thought, or wanted. They conversed at first like acquaintances standing at a church supper, polite and friendly and untouchable, though he had been outraged by the sight of her beaten face. But she had hushed him, afraid of his anger, afraid for him: he didn't know how bad the Morelock men could be.

"You got hurt," he said, reaching out, now, and nearly touching her bruised face.

"Don't worry," she said. "I'll be okay. I come up here after he hit me. I got away from him and come up here." She spread her arms wide. "I believe I could stay here, right here, for the rest of my days."

"I don't like to see them bruises," he said.

"I'm okay," she said. "Let's just not talk about it." And that had stilled him, so they sat together on the knob and talked, as though the bruises had gone off somewhere, leaving her equally free of the hurt and the man who had hurt her.

"You been up here all night?" he said.

"Yes. I wanted to. I spent the night up here. It was wonderful, even..." She stopped talking, not wanting to mention the beating again.

"It's right pretty up here," he said, though he was looking at her.

"It came up dawn and I saw the sun pick its way under them ridges off yonder," she said. "Same as back home. We're high enough, here that them hills is lower and the sun kindly slants its way up here, so you know them folks is yet in the dark, while you watch it brighten over the top of their ridge. You know what I mean?"

"I guess I don't," he said. "But I can see it in your voice." They were standing side by side, looking across the hollow to the east, seeing the sun passing over mountain and ridge, the deep hollows in between still shadowed in deepest blue haze.

"They look like your eyes, them coves," she said, turning to him.

* * *

He resisted, at first, when she kissed him and drew him down to her. And she had no real idea what she was trying to do. She had never embraced a man in pleasure, when she might be as much the aggressor as the respondent—had never known that this act could be a matter of mutual response at all—and she was so surprised by her own impulsiveness that she stopped almost as soon as she had begun, so that the kiss and the embrace served more to throw them off balance, and, later, she would think of this first contact as more of a crash than a caress.

It had been passionate enough, their lips seeking and meeting, but then they'd rocked backward, his body too heavy over her, his thigh too strong between her opening legs, her teeth clacking on his when she tried to open her mouth to him, then her leg came up between his and he caught his breath, wincing.

She said, "Oh my Lord, I'm sorry," when he rolled away from her onto his back, saying nothing. It was a horrible failure, and she felt responsible, as if she'd spent the night on the mountain preparing for something she had no right to expect, no right to demand of him, and so she had made such a bad hash of it.

And then he had begun to laugh. He lay on his back, still breathless with pain and arousal, and laughed, his arms flung wide. She sat up, shocked, looking at him. Then she caught at her throat and she began laughing as well.

"Aint we a pair?" he said, as she lay down beside him, looking at the sky, hearing them laugh and feeling some burdensome weight sliding from her body and tumbling down the mountainside, down into the dark, rocky hollow, away from them.

Then she had turned toward him and brought her mouth slowly down to his, feeling her lips give way to him, and pressing herself upon his chest, sliding her thigh up over his legs, feeling him firm against her soft flesh. She opened his shirt and kissed down his body, finding herself doing things she'd never known to do, feeling his pleasure become her pleasure, undressing him, then laying back, passive, while he knelt over her and removed her clothes, sliding his hands over her breasts, as though he were worshipping her body, or drawing music from her with his hands, listening to her grow taut, and then liquid, like a gliding tone. And he bent and nuzzled her nipples, as she reached down and took him in her hand, guiding him down and into her, and she made love with a man, this man, for the very first time.

And so it began. She wondered how they would arrange to meet, until she came to realize that she was alone, on her own, most of the time. The Morelock men ignored her and were on the road making their runs a good part of every week. Johns appeared to be ashamed of the beating he had given her, so he avoided her even when he was around. She believed he still saw the woman he'd "won" at the dance hall. He stayed away often whole days and nights. So it wasn't so much a matter of arranging to meet. Instead, she began walking up the trail whenever she had the time. If Morgan appeared, she figured, that would be wonderful. If he didn't, she would still enjoy being by herself on the mountain. And, often enough, he would be there waiting for her.

It was harder on him, though, perhaps because he couldn't feel the same pleasure in climbing the trail and being alone, waiting for her, which, for her, was like going home. Since he worked weekends, he would worry those nights that she was up on the mountain while he played in some smoky dance hall. So she told him to expect her at one o'clock, Tuesday, Wednesday, and Thursday, when the men made their runs, and she would know, then, whether they could stay together overnight or not. On weekends, she said, they'd stay apart.

"And don't worry about me up here. I'm better off alone up here than anywheres else in the world," she said. "Except with you."

* * *

Later, when she was on the run, she blamed herself. *Why wasn't you more careful? Why didn't you just leave him alone? Let him be, instead of gettin him mixed up in something you should have known was a going to get him hurt?* But, at the time, it had all been so wondrous, such a pure relief to have this man holding her, his body against hers, feeling the excitement, the insistent pleasure and the waves of peace, afterward. She had never known such joy and it had convinced her that everything could be all right, that this could last, this wild abandonment, up in the high laurels, under the broad sky, the two of them, naked and loving on the mountaintop. She couldn't have stopped herself even if she'd known all along that it would end, that the sense of giddy anticipation each time she took herself up the trail, the feelings of adventure and escape, were actually marks of the futility of the entire affair, its impermanence, and its doom.

Because his father had forbidden it even before it began, telling Morgan to "stay away from that Morelock gal," on that first night, after they'd dropped her off. He talked as if his son were thirteen years old and needed managing. Morgan had ignored him, of course, not even bothering to say, "I'll do as I please," and had tossed and turned through the night, waiting for daytime and the chance to go up the mountain and down to her place, looking for her.

As the affair developed, though, his father appeared to have forgotten all about her, and so Morgan would even tell him, at times, that he was going up to the old place, where the trail began its sinuous way. His father had merely nodded, absently.

Then it had been Morgan's turn to warn the father. Because his dad had begun bootlegging, selling liquor to a barber in Glade, and had now begun to work some places over the other way, closer to Roalton. Morgan had found this out by having a customer come to him one night at the dance he was playing and trying to place an order for rye whiskey.

"I'm sorry," Morgan had said to the man. "I aint in that line of business."

"No need to get delicate with me," said the man. "I aint a going to blow no whistles on you."

Morgan protested that he had no connection to bootleggers around this area and the man scoffed at him, saying, "That's a mite particular, since I bought three quarts offen your daddy last week. Standin right here where I'm standin tonight."

When his father picked him up that night, Morgan was in a temper. "What in hell you doing runnin liquor into the same places I'm tryin to make music?"

His father brushed the anger aside, saying lightly, "Why not? I'm out thisaway anyhow. Why shouldn't I mix a little business with the pleasure of drivin you around ever weekend? Make a little easy cash whilst I'm out, kindly."

"This aint a barber shop in Glade is why," Morgan said. "These are some city boys, down here. You get involved in bootleg whiskey down here, you're mixin with some pert shady characters."

"I aint getting wrapped up in no big operation, don't worry about that," said his father. "I aint getting bold. Aint supplyin nobody wholesale, I'm just sellin to individual customers, outen the trunk of the car."

Morgan relaxed a little, watching the headlights bounce back from the wooded mountainsides. "I don't know, Daddy," he said. "It might could be bad enough if these boys found you cutting in on them even a wee mite. Besides," he said, "You know who the big operators is, don't you?"

"No," his father said, watching. "I aint even going to bother to find out, neither. Like I says, I'm just handling a few jugs at a time, just friendly like, to a few folks."

"Well, you might want to know that it's Morelocks is mixed up in all this," Morgan said. "Everybody in the dance halls knows who the big money boys is. And word is the Morelocks has got a booze-and-pills operation going all over this part of the country."

He had talked with Ellie about this very thing on Thursday. They'd been caught in a sudden rain and had run down the trail to the old Hampton place, where they found an old quilt and spread it on the floor of what had been the parlor of the old house. One end of the house was wrecked, crumpled by an enormous fallen oak, but, inside, there was still a scattering of crude, homemade furniture, even a big, walnut-framed mirror, next to which a pair of overalls hung from a nail. After they had made love, they lay listening to the rain drumming on the rusted tin roof, spooning, his hands clasped together around her small stomach, the curve of her soft buttocks pressed against the hollow of his groin. And then they turned to face one another, running their hands lightly across each other's body, looking into each other's eyes.

"You have eyes like the rain," she said, stroking his cheek.

"I thought they was like the coves," he said. He ran a finger along the notch of her collarbone.

"Like the coves in the rain," she said. "Like the big hollows up on Elk Creek, where I grew up. The big, deep coves in a rainstorm."

He asked her about Elk Creek and she told him her story, how she had come to be here on Shaleen, how she'd found herself married to Johns Morelock. And she told him about the four-state drug-running operation.

"They make a pile of money at it, I'll tell you that," she said. "And they aint afraid of the law, neither. They got a cousin into the sheriff's job and they got him in their hip pockets keeping him drunk on their liquor and hooked on their pills. Johns runs what he calls 'free samples' into him every week. Then for the real business, they take everything across different states, so if the Tennessee law is lookin for them for sellin bootleg whiskey, or the Virginia police want them for buyin pills, or Kentucky for sellin the same pills, well, they're just a settin here in Carolina, where none of the other states' law can come, in a county where the sheriff is on their own team, so to speak."

She told him she never saw any of the money, "But they's loads of it." She said the closest she came to seeing any of the details of the operation was counting pills. "They just keep it away from me. And I don't want to know no more than that," she said. "It's a mean old business."

He told her about his own family. How the Hamptons have always run whiskey, too, but never on a large scale. How they'd left this county and moved south, after the fighting with the Morelocks.

"My daddy was the youngest, so he didn't never get involved in the fight. He never could tell me about how it started. No more could his older brothers, the ones that was left, though they'd all had a hand in it. Even had a sister—she was the knee baby, just two years older than daddy—who got killed and the Morelocks, they somehow pinned even that on one of us Hamptons.

"But we still made white liquor, all along. My daddy stopped makin it and took to sellin store liquor in dry counties. Bootleggin. Still does a little. But, being the youngest, he kindly inherited the little piece of land we're on up here and he decided he wanted to come back. It was good for me because most of my work is down toward Roalton, and this is closer. So here we are." He kissed her. "Mighty glad of it, too."

He had wondered at first why Ellie stayed with these men, why she didn't just walk away. But gradually he came to realize the kind of hold they had on her, the fear and control, the feeling she had that they'd reach out and snatch her back from anywhere she went. He had thought about finding a way to bring the law down onto the Morelock men, to get Ellie away, get her for himself. But she had warned him off, saying, "Don't you tangle with them. They'd as soon kill you as shake your hand. And they'd kill anybody got in the way of their show. They already talk all the time about how they run the Hamptons out of the county, and they aint none too happy that you two come back here, no matter that you're just a musician and his daddy. You leave them alone. Sooner or later, I'll find a way to get away from them without you getting involved. I promise you." She kissed him, then folded herself onto him, nuzzling his belly.

* * *

So when Morgan discovered his father selling liquor in the Morelocks' territory, he was worried, and he warned his father, saying "They're dangerous boys, and they won't like to hear anybody, especially a Hampton, is sellin so much as a drop of whiskey down here."

His father snorted, "Hell, Morgan, they don't even notice me. I'm small enough potatoes, they won't even bother." He looked over at his son and said ruefully, "We aint nothing to them anymore. They done took care of us already."

FOUR

She would remember the last days in a chaotic swirl of emotion. She had met him as usual on the mountain, but this time she had to tell him about the new thing, problem or blessing, she didn't know which. Because she couldn't help but be thrilled to know that she would have his child—and she knew it would be his, since Johns had left her alone ever since that night after the dance hall, the night he'd beaten her and she had found some measure of escape by climbing up the dark mountain. So, for the entire affair with Morgan, she had been his, alone, and she felt a new kind of purity, or a return to the innocence of her childhood, so that she felt she could give herself to him in the most natural, loving way. The shame and the pain of the Morelocks dissolved and drained away on the mountaintop, and she had been able to come to Morgan as herself, alone: Eleanor Taylor, from Elk Creek.

Still, the joy was underscored by terror. Johns, too, would know this wasn't his child. She knew he would respond with a deadly rage, and would go looking for the father, and that he would destroy both of them, totally. And now she had to extend that fear to cover another—the coming child—as well. So she realized the degree of danger to herself, Morgan, the child, the entire world they had built, up on the mountaintop. And so the discovery of her pregnancy, as much as it had seemed a verification of her true self, the truth of her contact with Morgan, the erasure of Eleanor from the list of Morelock victims—as much as it represented escape—it also seemed a confirmation of the ethereality of the whole affair, the intrusion of reality upon what had been only fantasy: a love engendered and consummated on the curved surface of a mountain, where they could pretend that the world of Morelocks didn't exist, only because they could wash themselves in the insubstantiality of moon glow.

So she told him and tried to explain this mixture of joy and terror, beauty and horror, all of it represented by the life sprung within her womb. And he had embraced her, hushed her, reassured her.

"We'll run away," he said. "We'll go before he even knows it's happened. And we'll get beyond his reach."

"He's got a mighty long reach, Morgan. I fear for you. He'll not let us go without a huntin us down and tearin us apart. I know it." She began to cry.

"It aint none of his baby," said Morgan. "It's our'n. Our'n alone. And they aint no God in heaven that'd ever let him win."

"He's won for years," she said. "His granddaddy won, and his daddy won, and he'll win."

No," Morgan said. "Not this time."

So they had made their plan. There was another problem—the danger to Morgan's father because of his bootlegging, and Morgan worked out a way to take care of both problems at once.

"I'm a going to set the law on Johns, and I'm a going to clear my daddy at the same time," he told her.

"Don't do nothin to get at Johns," Ellie warned. "Let's just get on away from here and leave him be."

"Can't," Morgan said. "You said so yourself. He'll come after us. But if we get the law down on him, he aint a going to be able to come after us or Daddy, neither."

"The law is his cousin," she said. "And he's a drunk and a addict, who gets his fix from Johns. So he's tied right to him."

"I aint a goin to go to him," said Johns. "I'm a goin to the state boys, in Roalton.”

“Roalton aint in this state,” she said.

“No,” he agreed. “But iffen I can get Johns to stay in Roalton long enough, I can set the state boys on him before he can run back across the mountain.” He hugged her. “That’ll take care of him, and we’ll be free.”

Morgan explained to Eleanor that he would use his own identity as a musician—a man who worked all the big clubs on the Roalton side—to lure Johns into a partnership, of sorts. Johns knew nothing about Morgan and Ellie, so there was no reason for him to suspect an approach from Morgan. So Morgan would offer to take the risk of delivering and exchanging on the Tennessee side away from the Morelocks. He would show that he could do this because he could work the runs out under cover of being a musician, who crossed back and forth over the line to play his jobs—jobs that occurred in the very locations where the Morelocks did business. And so his father would no longer be an encroacher upon the Morelock empire, but a part of it, and so he, too, would be safe.

“I don’t reckon Johns Morelock would be able to resist it. It’d be a great plan, iffen I really was on his side,” Morgan said. “Of course, it’ll be him a takin advantage of me, not the other way around, the way I’ll offer it to him. He’ll see he can get a lot out of me and then take over the whole damn show, just like he always wants to do. But he’ll go along with me for a while, because he’ll want me to get it all started. It won’t be until it’s all set that he’ll try to shove me out. And by then it’ll be too late, because the law will come in and get him. Because I’ll go to the law right from the start and let them know what I’m a doing. And we’ll be all set.”

There was no choice, she believed. It was Johns or them—there was no room for any other alternative. And now, with the baby coming, she felt again the confirmation of escape, the reassertion of herself as a real person, able to live and love with this gentle man. The joy overcame the fear, so she forgot about the gauze-thin reality of their entire affair, a reality that might not survive the light of day, the heavy atmosphere below, down the mountain.

But what else could she do? She had to believe in the escape. Because there was nothing else.

She went back down the mountain to the Morelock house, and she waited, sitting on the long front porch, hearing her own foot tap the boards, timing the day, knowing Morgan would suggest a meeting to Johns, and Johns would determine the time and place.

Later, too late, she would decide that Johns had known all along, had already begun to look for ways to stop Morgan's father, the man who was encroaching on the liquor business, and to eliminate Morgan, the man who had reached into the Morelock prison and released Ellie. *I should've knowed it*, she would rail at herself, later, as she ran over the mountain. *I shouldn't have waited, or I should have done something else, not let Morgan give Johns the chance he'd been a waitin for all along.* She castigated herself for having closed her body to Johns, so that the pregnancy would be so clearly evidence of Morgan's "guilt." *Why not let Johns have me all along? What difference would it make? He'd done took me enough times that it didn't matter no more, and it would have been a mite of pleasure in knowin I was offerin myself to protect Morgan. Why didn't I do that?*

Or, she wondered, why had she allowed herself to endanger Morgan right from the start? Why had she let him help her that first night, in the dark, pebbled parking lot, where a man lay nearly at her feet crumpled and beaten by Johns Morelock—as clear an omen, or at least a warning, as she could have asked for. But she had tucked herself into the circle of Morgan's care, and it had doomed him. And why had she done so, when it would have been so easy simply to walk away from him? Because she had been already eradicated, she was already finished, her own self obliterated by the power of Morelocks. So she would have lost nothing by spurning Morgan because she had already lost everything.

And now she had not only assured the disaster but had allowed Morgan to recreate Eleanor Taylor as a real, free person, and so she would destroy herself, again. And worse, unpardonable, she had created a third victim: the child, the mark of the truth of everything, all the love and hope, despair and horror, the moon glow and the harsh light shining form the long porch on the front of the Morelock home place.

There had been nothing for her to do but to wait. Morgan had told her that he would meet her on the mountain on Thursday night, the night the trap would be set, the meeting, to be held up at the old sawmill ground—Johns's ground, whence Morgan would come up the trail and meet her at the fork, walk up to the top, the curved granite where they had first sat, and tell her they would soon be free.

She had spent that day counting pills for Johns and doing the usual work around the house. After supper, she sat out on the porch and watched the mountainside change color in the slanting shade of evening, the sun already well below the hump of the knob, the woods dark and deep, though the sky remained a bright, thin blue. She sat and waited for the blue to become gradually weighty, to sink down nearer, meeting the mountain and closing the night over the hollow.

Jessum came out at one point and stood, watching her. She felt a shiver of anxiety—*does he know, somehow, about Morgan?*—but she hushed her fear, telling herself, *abide, abide.*

"You wantin something?" Jessum asked her.

The question was so unusual that she flinched, nervously, and said, "What do you mean by that?"

"Just askin," Jessum said, "Iffen you want somethin. Iffen I could get you something."

She felt a rush of resistance, anger, at the life he had let her endure at the hands of his son, his family, this grotesque one-armed man who had never hurt her, directly—had, in fact, taken some sort of rough care of her—but who seemed to her, in his vague, negativism, to embody the entire principle of the darkness she named *Morelock*. She realized at that moment that hatred can become a principle, too, and can take its most dangerous form, perhaps, in impassivity, in the disconnected stare of Jessum Morelock.

"It's a mite late to be offerin to help me, wouldn't you say?" she said, letting all the bitterness show.

He looked at her with his glinting, narrow eyes. "I done told you once before," he said. "It aint help."

With that, he stepped off the porch and headed for the truck. "I'm a goin to town," he said. He stopped a moment and turned back to her.

"You just remember that," he said. "You remember what I told you all along." He lifted his one arm and pointed vaguely upward, up the mountain. "It aint help."

She would tell herself, later, that she'd heard the gunshots, though that was unlikely down in the cove, when they had come from the long twisting road leading up to the mill. It may have been that she at last recognized the baleful import of Jessum's behavior that night, the strange query about whether she "wanted" something, the finality of the last three words he repeated to her. At any rate, she jumped to her feet, sometime near midnight—she had been supposed to wait until deep night, two o'clock or so—and ran toward the mountain, toward the dark trail leading up the knob, knowing already she was too late.

She stumbled more than once, running in the dark. Once, she fell headlong and cut her hand on the rock, so that, after, she ran with the blood dripping from her.

At the fork, she turned back to the right and began to descend to the mill ground, still running, her breath coming in ragged heaves, the blood draining from her hand. She began to weep. When she reached the flats at the mill, she found it empty, soundless, the curve of the meadow looking vast, endless. She held her hand up, cupping her cheek, and felt her own blood, slickened by her tears, and alive, where it had somehow escaped her flesh, so that she felt as if she were touching her own, separate self.

And from here her memory became tangled and melded into a dream, where she was running, carrying some throbbing, breathing weight in her hands, pressing it against her tear-stained cheek as she fled endlessly across the immense, measureless meadow, knowing that she would fling herself down, soon, then rise and run again, back the same way, across the endless curve.

She found the bodies halfway down the mountain, near an old pullout lined with rotting saw logs. She knew it was Morgan, though she couldn't have recognized his face, and she saw the father, an unreal, bloody bulk, wrapped tightly in the rusted, barbed fence. She fell to her knees, soundlessly, and lifted her lover's beautiful, useless hand, kissing the dead fingers that had once made such lovely music.

And then she rose and began running again.

PART FIVE

BLOOD KIN

The window reaches out to me.
I surface the glass, smell the hedgeflower.
Scenes blur, balance,
Turn over a hill in a meadow's hum.
From my grassbed I rise in a trampled
place and live on my family's tongue…

Dovetails spread white and gray in the tilting,
whistle of wings, stop where drafts take yard-oaks to the stars.
Hens ruffle feathers under the doorstep, the sound
Rushing the sweet past, gone.
—Shelby Stephenson

ONE

So she had wept, holding the yellowed news clipping in one hand, touching Jim's face with the other, remembering Morgan Hampton, who had given her back to herself, had almost saved her from all of it, and had then disappeared, himself, beneath a cloud of the same violence and shame she had lived with for all these years.

Jim knelt beside her, while Sam and Leela waited impatiently to show him the clipping they'd found back in the old cells, Sam finally saying to Jim, "Okay. Okay. Look at the paper." And Jim reached carefully out, slowly, easily, the way you might try to capture a bird, and took the frail clipping from his mother.

It was indeed a news story. The headline said, "TWO SLAIN ON CHASTEEN CREEK." Below this, the smaller subheading said, "Sheriff Held in Liquor Killing." And there were two photographs, two faces, with one caption: "Hampton victims, father and son."

"See?" said Sam, eagerly. "Did you ever see any such a thing?"

"See what?" said Jim, feeling dazed. His mother's thin hand reached out. the index finger touching, tapping lightly at the photo on the right.

"That one," she said. And, just as before, she said, "Forgive me."

"What?" said Jim, and he felt fear rising. *I don't want to know, don't want to see what they insist that I see. But I am going to have to see it, aren't I? I'm going to have to recognize something else, some new version of myself, and then it will start again and it will never stop. I will never cease from looking, searching, trying to reconcile, when there is no reconciliation available, no peace, no ending to any of this.* And he suddenly felt inexpressibly tired.

"Look at him," Leela said. "Look at the young man in the picture." He heard that lilt in her voice, the soft tone of sadness, and comfort, we call *sympathy*. And so he looked, knowing already what he would see: the photograph faded and hazy but unmistakable, the big, deep eyes—his eyes—the broad forehead—his own brow—the line of his chin, his lips.

"He looks just like me," Jim said, very softly, looking up at Leela, who nodded, her eyes glistening.

"Yes," she said. She knelt beside him, putting her arm around his shoulders. "He must be your father. This man. Not the others. Not Johns Morelock, nor George Thorwait, neither. This man. Look at him."

But Jim remained looking at her, beseechingly.

"That's right, isn't it?" Leela said to Ellie.

"It's right," Ellie said, in a tone of inexpressible regret and defeat. "Yes."

"So what in hell?" Sam said, breaking the quiet pathos, "What in hell is all this about 'your father is your father'? What was that except a bunch of bullshit?"

"Never mind, Sam," said Leela. "Never mind." And now, one arm around Jim, she reached across to the woman, smoothing the wet cheek, brushing back the hair, looking at the weary, worn face. "She was trying to do right by her boy. Trying to give him one more gift. Weren't you, Ellie?"

Leela stood up. "We'll talk about it later," she said, taking charge, her voice suddenly decisive and upbeat. "Let's get this part straight, first. Come on," she said, reaching a hand down to help Ellie up, while Jim rose, too.

"Let's get some sleep," Leela said. "We'll talk about this in the morning."

Ellie looked alarmed. "But them boys, Johns and Paul, they're up to something. You got to stop them."

"Well, there aint a damn thing we can do tonight, is they?" said Sam. "Do you even know where they are? Where they're a fixin to do this terrible thing?"

"No," she said.

"Or even what it is. Really?"

"No."

"So we're about played out before we even start. And you," he said, pointing to Jim, "have wore yourself and your momma out, both, a tryin to tell each other who your daddy is. For an orphan boy, you sure got a plenty of fathers. So sister's right. It's time for some shut-eye."

That night, the dream changed. No longer formless, no longer the strange intimation of grief, the touch of his face to a wet cheek. This time he was there, a person he could see, in the dream itself, and around him, an entire world began to compose itself, the darkness congealing into shapes and surfaces, with a narrow band of bright sky overhead. And as the landscape came together, he began to realize that he wasn't one, but three, though he felt assured that he'd lost nothing of himself in the splitting, since he remained complete in each person, as though the separation were somehow a joining, a completion of the circle. And though he knew somehow this was a dream about the past, he felt that the past had become part and parcel of present and future, eternally recycling, reenacting, the three of him becoming single, then multiple, then single again.

They were on a pathway leading upward, and they were in a hurry, eager, going to meet someone. They reached the top and there was a passageway, down into the mountain. One went into the passage, while one went over the trail, down the other side of the mountain, and one remained, sitting on a curved rock. He could follow each person, as if he were present in all three places simultaneously, though he knew all the while he was the one sitting at the top. And then he was embracing Leela, or being embraced by his mother, or he was another man, being held by a stranger.

But then the strange, one-armed man rose out of the mountain and pointed his finger, which became a bright flame and Jim screamed and felt himself disappearing.

He awoke, trembling, and reached to switch on the light.

A storm was blowing hard across Roalton as Paul Morelock and Dicky Hampton stepped out of Paul's truck in front of Pink's Grill. Dicky threw an empty cheese puff bag to the street and turned up a beer can, finishing the last dregs. He crumpled the can and threw it into the gutter, then spit a gray wad of chewing tobacco into a puddle on the sidewalk, growling, "God damn it, it's a rainin."

"Well don't stand around, like a moonfaced idiot," said Paul. "Get in the goddamn door."

Dicky took a few quick steps and stopped again. "Don't forget, you said you'd buy me a drink." He'd already finished a six-pack on the way down the mountain.

"Buy you the whole fuckin bar," said Paul, "Iffen you'd just go on and get in it."

The rain slapped down harder and Dicky made an abrupt dash for the door, yelling, "Jeee-sus Christ" as he entered the dark smoky bar.

"Over here," said Paul, motioning to the two end stools, near the front wall. Trapper Mason sat at the third, his back to them, hunched over a beer and a shot glass.

"Ain't that your daddy down the way?" said Dicky.

"Over here," said Paul again. "You want a beer?"

"Tits on a bull," Dicky said, sitting down. Paul moved along behind Trapper, who had not yet noticed the newcomers, and motioned to the bartender. When he got the pale man's attention, Paul handed him a folded bill and said, "Give me two drafts."

"Get me a pickled egg," shouted Dicky. Trapper turned and looked at him, quizzically. He didn't know Dicky Hampton, and so the diversion had served the Morelocks' purpose, taking Trapper's attention away from Paul, now standing down the bar to his right.

When the barman set down two large glasses Paul took three small capsules out of his shirt pocket and emptied their contents into one of the beers. He brought the glasses down the bar and handed the adulterated glass to Dicky Hampton, who swallowed half of it in a gulp. Again, as though the timing had been scripted, Trapper had finished his puzzled look at Dicky, and had turned away.

"Damn good," Dicky said to his beer. He drew his knife from its sheath and began to pick his teeth. "Durn damn good," he said.

"What did you say?" shouted Paul, striking Trapper on the shoulder. "What?"

Trapper turned, confused, saying, "Whaa?" He had barely time to recognize the man who'd yelled at him, when Paul hit him in the chest, not too hard, but enough to knock him off the barstool to the floor.

"Nobody calls my friend a dirty sonofabitch," said Paul, loudly, as Trapper pulled himself to his feet. He was angry, and he wasn't going to be sucker-punched by Paul Morelock a second time. He swung a fist and Paul dodged him so that the punch glanced off Dicky Hampton's shoulder.

"Hot damn," said Dicky. "I'll get the sonofabitch." He leaped off his stool and headed straight for Trapper, arms swinging.

At that instant, another fight erupted down at the end of the bar, near the pool table. The pills hit Dicky in midswing and he tottered to the floor, just as the lights went out in the bar, and the two fights merged into a full-scale brawl.

* * *

Much later, the police arrived and the lights were put back on. There was no electrical problem. Someone had merely pulled the switches at the back of the room. Picking through the debris, the officers revived the three or four men who'd been knocked out— "cold cocked," the bartender called it—and then they found Trapper Mason. He was obviously dead, his belly torn open by a dark, gaping knife wound, shedding blood and viscera. Next to him lay Dicky Hampton, unconscious, the bloody knife gripped tightly in his right hand.

Paul, Johns, and Pierot Morelock were not there. They were in Paul's truck, already half the way back up the mountain.

In the morning, with the bright sun flecking through the windows, it all seemed better, and Jim joined the others in the office with the kind of eagerness he'd felt on earlier days, when it had seemed less a personal crisis than an interesting puzzle.

They all were similarly relieved by the change of tone and they gathered round Sam's desk, where Leela set the clipping, saying, "Okay. We looked to see what had happened in 1973, when all of this began. And Sam found your father."

"We must have scrammed our way through fifteen tons of papers back in the old cells," said Sam. "Every god damn arrest for drunk and disorderly, what have you. Turns out the sheriff was the town drunk, his own self, back around seventy-three. And then I found a little matter of a murder. On Shaleen, of all places. So I figured that was pert close to home, so to speak. And then I took a good look at the photos and what did I see but Jim, here, a starin back at me out of a news clip forty years old."

"It is amazing how much he looks like you, Jim," Leela said. "Can you see that?"

"Yes, I can see it," Jim said. "I've tried not to see it, I guess because I had just decided I really did have my father's eyes—my adoptive father, that is—since Ellie just finished telling me all about how he was really my father. So I tried. But it couldn't be coincidence. It looks like me. It must be my father." He shook his head. "Dear God, what a night."

"So why tell him George Thorwait was his father?" Sam asked, looking at Ellie.

Ellie said nothing.

"I don't think she needs to answer that," said Leela. "Just say it was a mother's love that made her tell that lie. Still trying to give her boy a good home." She looked softly at Ellie. "Something like that?"

Ellie dropped her eyes and said nothing.

"Wait," said Sam. Then he rubbed his forehead and said, "Have you noticed how many times somebody winds up hollerin 'Wait,' in all this business? But wait, anyway. I want to know about this murder." He looked at Ellie. "We're right, of course. This Hampton boy is Jim's father."

"Yes," said Ellie. "Morgan. Morgan Hampton."

"You and he had a, had a..."

"Yes," said Ellie.

"While you were livin with Johns Morelock. Married to him," Sam said.

"Yes," said Ellie.

"And you got pregnant with the child that would turn out to be cousin Jim, here."

"Yes."

"Okay," Sam said. "And me and Leela, we was lookin to find what happened in seventy-three that got you either hopeful enough or scared enough or despairing enough to take off and run out of this country, when before you'd been too scared or despairing anyway—and maybe even hopeful, too, since this nice Hampton boy was around, now, too—to think you could get away. But then, BANG, you found out that the new fear or hope or despair was away more than the old, and so you just knew you had to go, run off, even if you didn't know where you were a runnin to."

"Yes," she said.

"And it was this murder, of course," Sam said. "The killin of your boyfriend." He stopped and looked at Leela. "I aint trying to be frivolous. I just don't know what to call him but 'boyfriend.' That all right?"

Leela didn't answer.

"He was the only one in the world," Ellie said. "The only man who ever…"

"Okay," Sam said. "I'm sorry. But we're right, aren't we? It was this that made you run, wasn't it?"

"Yes," she said. "We was fixin to run off, together. He had a plan that he thought would get Johns outen the way, clear the way for us. But it was too late. And so he got killed, and I just lit out, kindly. Not knowin what to do, where to go. But I had a slip of paper with my sister's address on it. I just kept showin that to folks. I couldn't read it, myself.

"Grabbed up your things and head for a place you'd never even dreamed of," said Sam, "Where you probably had no idea even how to get there, much less what you were going to do when you did. Get there, that is."

"Yes."

"With a child growin in your belly and nobody to help and no reason to believe that Johns Morelock wouldn't just hunt you down and bring you back just like you had believed he would do any other time you thought about runnin and decided you couldn't."

"I should have," she said.

"What?"

"Should have gone before. We should have gone. He wanted me to go, but I didn't believe it, didn't believe we could. I was afraid for him. It didn't matter what happened to me, not then, not before the baby. But I thought they'd kill him, and so I wouldn't let him try to get us away." She shook her head. "And then they killed him anyway."

"The sheriff," Sam corrected. "It says here the sheriff done it. Wrapped them up in barb wire and shot them both. Says they found the gun and the bloody gloves and all in the sheriff's office, where he was passed out drunk the next morning after the murder. Had witnesses saw him go out, late at night, a carryin the shotgun and come back a hour or two later carryin the same gun. They got him dead to rights.”

Ellie shook her head.

“No,” she said. “Johns killed him. Weren’t no sheriff done it. And I knowed it. And so, just when I found out he was dead, and it didn’t matter, gettin away, no more, because now there weren’t nothin to get away for. But now I had to or they was a going to kill me, too. And I didn’t care about that, neither. They could kill me three times over and I’d only thank them for doin me the favor.” She shook her head.

“But the child,” she said. “I was a growin the child. His child. And I didn’t want to let them get to the child, not by killin me, nor by a claimin him whenever he was born under their own roof. And that wouldn’t happen, anyway, because I knowed what they’d done. In the murder. And so they would’ve killed me before I had the child anyways. So I had to go. And I had to find somewheres to put the child, so they couldn’t never get him. It tore my heart out to give him up, but I knew I had to do it. Because it was too late for me.”

“So you went to Roalton and found your way, somehow,” Leela said.

“My sister’s,” she said. “I had a sister in Roalton I didn’t hardly know, but I figured would be good enough at least to take me in until I could get some work and find my way, like you say. They was a paper, like I said, with her name and address on it that I still had from the old home place. Somebody steered me to her.”

“Wait. Wait,” shouted Sam. Then he smiled, saying, “There’s that word, again: ‘wait.’ But wait, dammit.” He pointed to the clip. “You’re telling us Johns Morelock did it, killed your boyfriend, when the paper says all the evidence was found on the sheriff.”

“He done it,” she said. “Johns and his Pawp, Jessum. The one-armed man. They done it and kindly set it all up for the sheriff to be picked up for it. That sheriff was a drunk. And they drugged him, put some pills into his drink. 'Goof balls,' they called them. And they took his shotgun and his uniform, and his police car. And went up and killed Morgan and his daddy. And come back and put everything into the sheriff's office whilst he was kindly sleepin off the drug. And so after the bodies had got found, people naturally went to the sheriffs. But they found him passed out, with the murder gun and all that a settin there. Bloody gloves, they'd used to wrap barb wire around Morgan's daddy." She shuddered. "They wrapped him up in barb wire and shot them both. One at a time. So one of them had to watch them kill the other, knowin what was comin next."

"Jesus," said Sam. "So not only did they kill the two men, they set up another one to take the fall for the killing."

"Morgan's daddy's car had a trunkful of bootleg whiskey, I reckon. And Johns must have put a load more down in the sheriff's office. So it all looked like a whisky feud between the sheriff and the Hamptons."

"When it was Morelocks all along," Sam said. He whistled.

"It weren't the first time," Ellie said. "They'd set up something years before, Jessum and his brothers had, or the old old man, Cuddy. They kindly have a tradition of gettin away with murder."

"So I think we've done it, haven't we?" said Jim, some moments later. "Solved the mystery?" He sipped his coffee and winced. "God, Sam, you made it stronger than ever, today."

"Yes I did," Sam said. "I'm a going to try to cut back a mite on the alcohol, today. I thought maybe I ought to start by gouging my innards out with some extry-solid coffee."

"You might see whether we think our own innards need scouring before you pour that stuff our way," Leela said. She made a face. "What did you do, run it through twice?"

"No," Sam said. "Just threw a little bit more in the hopper." He offered a cup Ellie's way.

"I don't believe I'd care for any," she said.

They were interrupted by a furious knocking at the door.

"Now who's that?" said Sam. "That bear's head door knocker is takin a beatin these days." He went to answer the door.

Jim heard her before he saw her.

"My God, let me in," said a frantic voice, vivid with fear and grief.

A moment later, Lindee burst into the room, carrying her very scared little girl, and sobbing, "They killed him. They took and killed him. And they'll kill me." Lindee looked wildly about the room, taking in Jim, Ellie, Leela, then turning back to Sam, pleading. "You've got to help me. They'll kill me." The little girl began to cry.

"Here, honey," said Ellie, reaching out for the child. "Let me take your girl." Lindee surrendered her frightened daughter and Ellie turned away, smoothing the little girl's hair and saying, "Let's let these folks talk about them things on their own, honey pie. We'll just go into the kitchen and see can't we find us a cookie, okay?" The child curled into the older woman's breast, sniffling, and Ellie took her away from her mother's terrifying cries.

"Okay. Let's settle down just a little," said Sam. "Who's killed? Who's fixin to kill you?" He looked at Leela and added, "As if I didn't know."

"Trapper," Lindee sobbed. "Trapper's dead. They killed him."

So she told them. She'd gotten a phone call from Paul Morelock, early this morning, telling her Dicky Hampton had killed Trapper in a fight at Pink's Grill, outside of Roalton. That Dicky had been arrested and was locked up in the Sullivan County jail. "I'll see to it he fries for this," Paul had said.

Lindee had sat up in her bed, naked, the phone to her ear, her eyes wide with shock. She said, "This aint no joke, is it?"

Paul said, "No joke about it. Trapper's deader'n a pullet. I aint surprised, the way he was carryin on, I'll tell you that much."

Lindee knew what he meant, knew the unspoken message was intended to be understood: *Dicky didn't kill your man. I did. And I'm going to come after you next, if I find out you've been goin around me.* She felt a rush of fright and this set off all the emotions that had been checked by the initial paralysis of the shock. She began to moan, rocking on the bed, the phone still clutched to her ear.

"What's wrong, Mommy?" said Caroline, standing in the doorway, gripping her worn stuffed bear. "What's wrong?"

Lindee's moaning shifted tone, becoming strident, and she began to breathe in ragged, harsh huffs. Paul said something else to her, but she didn't hear him. She dropped the phone to the floor, frantically grabbing at clothes. When she was dressed, still moaning and sobbing, she snatched Caroline into her arms and ran out the door.

In Sam's office, Leela took over the task of settling Lindee down, and gradually the scared woman calmed enough to be led to the couch, where Sam handed her a glass half full of whiskey, saying, "Toss it down. You'll feel better when that grabs hold."

She drank the bourbon off, and almost immediately seemed more composed. "Where's my baby?" she said.

"She's fine," said Leela. "She's in the kitchen having some cookies."

"Paul Morelock," Lindee said, looking at Sam. "He got Trapper for running product on his own. And he'll get us, too, you and me, for tryin to tell anybody about the Morelocks and their operation. You got to stop writin that story."

Jim turned to Sam. "That's where you've been going. You've been writing the story about drug running."

Sam nodded. "Me and Lindee, here, we been puttin the facts together. I promised her I'd not identify her or Trapper in any way. But I reckon Trapper was already marked out as soon as he started sellin on his own."

"It was my fault," Lindee said, beginning to cry again, softly, this time, the tears sliding down her bruised face. "I thought we could get it done, get the money and get out of here. Have ourselves our own place, before Paul or anyone else would bother to find out. We was small-timers, not enough for him to even notice."

Sam patted her shoulder awkwardly. She turned her tear-marked face to him.

"But you got to stop writin that story."

"Too late," Sam said. "I called it in to Roalton, yesterday. The first installment. They're going to print it."

"Jesus," Leela said. "Sam."

"Well, I wanted to be a newsman. I guess I am, now," Sam said. "I believe I'll have a drink. Whilst I still can."

An hour later, they all sat around the desk: Leela, Sam, Jim, Ellie. Lindee remained on the couch, holding her daughter on her lap. Sam had been trying to sum up the situation.

"Well," he continued, "they don't know where Lindee is right now. Likely they don't know you been talkin to me."

"They know we've been poking around, though," said Leela. "All of us. We weren't poking into their drug operation—we were looking for Jim's mom—but they never believed it, did they?"

"It doesn't matter," Jim said. "There were two things they needed to hide: the whole drug operation, yes. But they also had a murder set up forty years ago. And they knew I'd walk right smack into that if I had any success finding my mother and father. Right?"

"Did Johns know about you and Morgan?" Sam asked Ellie.

"And the baby? The pregnancy? Or was it all just coincidence? They might have just killed him because of his daddy's bootleg business, regardless of whether they knew he was carryin on with you, mightn't they?"

"I don't know," Ellie said. "I'd always thought they didn't know while I was with Morgan. And then I decided they'd known all along, after I found him dead. But just like now, like you say, it didn't make no difference. They would've killed him anyways."

"Just like now, just like now. Good God," Sam said. "Do you all realize how much this all seems like some sort of family blueprint? Like a god damn outline? Or like one of them tape loops that just keeps a playin over and over and over? You get drug runnin and wife beatin and bring in some poor Hampton bastard who winds up in bed with a Morelock's wife. That'd be you, Ellie," Sam said, pointing his finger. "And that'd be you, too, Leela," he said, turning his finger toward her. The two women looked at each other.

"I reckon you're right," Leela said. "History repeating itself."

"Well let's hope not," Sam said. "Because the poor Hampton bastard, the one who's a going to wind up wrapped in barb wire with a bullet through his head? That'd be Morgan, back then. But that'd be our Jim, here, this time. Wouldn't it? Same old story."

"Except I'm not involved in bootlegging," said Jim. "They've got no reason to go after me."

"Sure they do. You just said so. You got a reason to hunt up that sheriff who's still in the pen for killin your daddy, that he didn't do, and is probably just achin for somebody who gives a damn—who might have a connection with a newspaperman, by the way—to start makin noise about a miscarriage of justice. Besides, it don't matter if you're runnin drugs. You got into that by proxy the minute you set foot in Gracie's motel. Because Lindee thought you were snoopin after drugs, and I bet she told both Trapper and Paul. Hey?" Sam looked at Lindee.

"Yes," she said. "I told them."

"And there aint no reason for them to think otherwise than that you're some sort of federal drug agent or what have you under cover of huntin for his long lost mom. All they know about you is you aint from around here, and you're askin questions."

"Until they started to recognize him," Leela said. "The old ones, Johns and his Pawp...who is it..."

"Jessum" said Ellie.

"Jessum," Sam said. "And they saw that he was the breathin image of Morgan Hampton that they'd thought they got out of the way forty year ago. Jesus. Might *that* have been a shock to these fellers, to look up and see a dead man? Which brings us full circle, again, don't it, since the mom-huntin is all they need to get worried about you. And you are a Hampton, after all. So they might could just want to shoot you for old times' sake."

"What you're saying," Jim said, "is that I came down here to find my true family and I stepped right into the middle of three generations worth of family feud. And we're reenacting the same old patterns, time after time, aren't we?"

"Complete with Juliet," said Sam. "In every damn generation."

"And at last I find out I'm a Hampton, just in time to realize the Morelocks are gunning for me."

"They're gunnin for all of us," Sam said. "One thing I can't figure out, though. Why didn't they kill Ellie, while they were at it? Or Leela, too, for that matter?"

"I didn't matter," Ellie said. "They got enough use out of me just havin me around. And I didn't know much. You'd be surprised to find out what a family can keep secret from one another, iffen they want to."

Jim and Leela looked across at one another and nodded.

"And they had me scared to set foot outside," Ellie said. "I bet Leela, too. They tie you to them, somehow, so you don't think you could get away, even if you wanted to. And they got me hooked on them pills soon as I come back. Put me up the creek to take care of the old man and give me pills, ever day."

"I don't believe this," Leela said. "They tried that with me, too. The pills. I reckon I was lucky because that's the one thing they didn't succeed in doin."

"So I had to stay," Ellie continued. "Because I had to have them pills." She looked at her hands. "I still do."

"What?" said Jim. "What do you mean, 'still do'?"

Ellie reached into her pocket and pulled out a bottle. "I been takin them all along. Oxycontins. Pain killers. They help. I come back and Johns, he got me hooked on the pills. I know that. It was a way of keepin me tied to them, keepin me from tellin about the past or snoopin around too much in the present. I was there to take care of the old man and take my pills and that's all. But then I found the pills, they helped me."

"That's what every addict says," Jim said.

"Says it because it's true," said Sam. "Let her be. She's probably right: they put her to work for them and gave her the pills to keep her happy. Got themselves a indentured servant, so to speak."

"What I don't understand is why you came back," said Leela. "You got away from them, got to Roalton, even got a job and a family you liked, that took your child. Why turn around and come back to these people?"

"You might want to ask yourself that question once and again, sister," said Sam. Leela looked at him. He shrugged.

"I didn't have no place to go," said Ellie. "He—the doctor— wouldn't have me to stay around there. I can't blame him for that," she said, looking to Jim. "Once you was his, he couldn't have me a hangin around lookin after my boy, could he? When I give you up, I had to give up Roalton. Which weren't much to give up, anyhow." She wiped a sleeve across her brow and sighed. "And I knowed that Johns Morelock had won. I knowed the only thing for me was to give up the child and get on back. I was a Morelock because there weren't nothin else left for me to be."

"That's why you signed the adoption paper with a big M, isn't it?" Jim said. "I was wondering about that, about why it wasn't

T, for Taylor. That was your real name."

"Yes," Ellie said. "But not no more. There weren't no more Ellie Taylor, not after Morgan got killed. Not after I give you up to the doctor. Nothin left for me but Morelocks. So I wrote a M on the note and I come back." She sighed. "It's a mean world, is what it is. Here I was, a gal from away up the mountain, on Elk Crick. Where I always loved to be, and where I should've stayed and lived all my life. And how did I come to have the life I did? It just kindly seems to be what's happened. Like I didn't have no choice in the matter, at all."

"I think maybe we all know something about feeling that way," Jim said.

"So you came back," Leela said.

"I come back. And found Johns and asked iffen he'd take me in. Something or other. And he grabbed me up, like I was a something somebody'd stolen, or borrowed, like a saw or a pair of pliers. Grabbed me up and made sure nobody'd never borrow me again. Sent me up the mountain to take care of his Pawp. Where I been ever since. I weren't his wife no more, he said. He'd always said I weren't his wife by law, anyways. Said he could throw me out any time he wanted to, because all it was was a mountain preacher that had married us, didn't have no standin nowhere but in the sky. Said if I mispleased him, he'd just take and throw me out. That was before everything happened. But he did take me in, when I come back. I got to say that." She looked at Jim, cocking her head, sizing him up. "You don't understand it, do you?"

"Don't understand how you can let a man brutalize you for thirty years and act like he's done you a favor. Taken you in, you say."

"I didn't have nowhere else to go. You don't know about it: you aint lived it, so how could you know, growin up like you did, where weren't nobody had to hit nobody else, nobody down on they hands and knees because you can hire it done. No. You can't understand it."

"Because you gave me away." He felt the hot flush of tears and struggled to hold them back, restrain the emotion.

"Jim," Leela said. "She handed you a family and a home and a future. It's something she never had."

"Leastways I tried to get you into a safe spot," Ellie said. "I worked for the doctor and I liked him. Liked his wife, Nancy, and they wanted a child. I said, here's where I can do one thing right, get my baby into the lifeboat, kindly. So I give you to them. Son."

"All right," Sam interrupted. "Look. We aint got time for all this love makin right now. Let's save it for later and you all can work it out then. Let's get back to Lindee, here. As I was sayin a while back, I don't think they know she's here or know she's been talkin to me. In fact, I reckon they think she's on the other side, another drug runner tryin to keep the news from the nosey news guy. Right?"

"Probably," Lindee said. She began to cry, saying, "Trapper was the only man who ever was good to me."

"I know it, honey," Sam said. "And I know you need to find a way to do some cryin. They aint goin to be a hell of a lot of time for it until we straighten all this out, but you try and take what you need." He sighed. "So as long as you stay here, they won't find you, since this is the last place they'd expect to find you. Right?"

Jim and Leela nodded.

"So we may as well add child care center to the list." Sam looked at Ellie. "And maybe Betty Ford Clinic? That is, if Jim can talk you into getting off them pills. And…and what?" He looked around the group. "Battered wives' shelter…I said that a few days back. Missing persons bureau…What else has this place become in the last few days?"

"Newspaper," said Leela. "It's become a newspaper."

Sam grinned.

TWO

Sam and Jim went out and bought two folding cots while Leela and Lindee cleaned the papers and junk out of the jail cells in the back and Ellie tried to keep the child entertained in the office. In Sam's advertising files, Leela found some glossy stills from a few children's movies and put them up in what would be the child's room. "It'll make her feel a little more cheery," she said.

"I aint done right by my girl," Lindee said, abruptly.

Embarrassed at this outburst, this bid for confessional intimacy, Leela tried awkwardly to reassure the young woman, saying, "I'm sure you've done your best." But Lindee persisted.

"No," she said. "I've been bad to her. I've hit her."

Leela shook off the discomfited feeling. She stood up straight, looking directly at Lindee, and said, "I know. I can see the bruises."

"I don't mean to do it," said Lindee. "She hollers or cries and I feel ashamed or scared and then next thing I know I'm a hittin on her."

"Well, we're all of us bruised, here, aint we," Leela said. "You and me and Ellie and Jim. And your daughter. Only one aint been hit is Sam. And I reckon he's been shot at. So now we all got something in common."

"But you haven't hit anybody. None of you. I'm the only one that's done that."

"I bet you been hit a time or two yourself, aint you?" said Leela.

"Oh, my brother, my big brother, he used to whale me ever chance he got," Lindee said. "And Paul Morelock, he knocked me around; that's how I got these bruises on me now." She gazed at Leela, a pleading look. "But that don't change the fact that I hit my little girl, does it?"

"No," Leela said. "It don't. But it's a shame, either way. You know that old holiness hymn, 'Nobody's Fault But Mine'?"

"Yes," Lindee said. "I sure have seen folks sing that. And seen them weep and tear their hair and fall down on the ground. I seen folks. But then I think, they're a wallowin in shame for their sins but they aint never beat their kids. Trapper, he hated it when I'd hit her, and beg me to stop it. And now it's him dead, instead of me."

"Is that what this is all about?" Leela said. "You feelin sorry for yourself, thinkin, 'Why aint I the one that's dead?'"

"It's just that I don't think you can tell me you and me is the same."

"I think you're wrong," Leela said. "Because we both of us got the same thing to be ashamed of," Leela said. "You hittin your kid and me lettin Paul Morelock beat me. Either way, smackin someone or being smacked by someone, either way it's a shame and a sin. And I've only just come to see it, only just now. But you aint no worse than me." Leela shook her head, sadly. "No worse."

"I don't believe you," said Lindee.

"Okay," said Leela. "You don't have to. But let's turn it around: you're just as guilty from the beatings your brother gave you as you are for the beatings you're givin your kid. Because it's the same thing, misuse. Either way. The same thing. And I'm comin to believe that you got to fight it in the same way. It all started because you let him do it."

"No. I run away from my brother," Lindee said. "Got away from him."

"No you didn't," Leela said. "Any more than I got away from a man who abused me, when I was little. I just found that out, just this week. If I'd gotten away, I wouldn't have wound up finding a husband to beat me, like Paul Morelock. And if you had gotten away from your brother—really gotten away—you wouldn't have to hit your own kid, to bring back the same shame you always felt. If I'd had a child, I reckon I'd have hit her, too. But I don't have one. So, I figured out this week, it don't matter: I just let him hit me, instead. It's the same thing. I seen this all, finally, watching Jim look for some person he thought he must've been if only he'd grown up with his own maw."

Leela felt weary, and she sat down on a box. "Sam's right, too, though. Jim just walked into the same old thing. The same thing, generation after generation, all down through a family, two families, whatever. Jim, who could have walked away from all this, because his mother tried to spare him the grief—tried even up to last night, lying to him even then about his father, just to protect him from it, try and get him to just walk away. Because he'd stepped right into it, not even ready to see it. So blind he didn't know enough to stay away. The hurt and the grief, one generation to the next." Leela touched her face, the fading discoloration of the bruise. Then she reached out and touched Lindee's.

"So it don't matter," Leela said. "It's all just shamefulness. Until you can really walk out of it."

"How?" cried Lindee. "How walk out? I don't even know I'm fixin to hit her until I find myself doin it. And it grieves me so. How do I walk out of it then?"

"I don't know," Leela said. "Maybe you need to walk into it. Into the grief. That's the key, somehow. I think you need to let it grieve you until you can start learnin to grieve for your little girl. Something like that. Something I learned just this week: I learned I needed to see that I'm a going to lose anything I come to love. That we all are. That love and loss are the same thing. That all my life I've been around people who tried to own their world— that's what an abuser is, someone who tries to own you—and I grew up trying to save everything I loved, trying to own it enough that I could keep it—that's what a victim is, too. But I just learned that love is the opposite: love is the hurting and the losing. Saying,

'I agree to lose you. I agree to grieve for you.' Because we're all a going to die. We're all a going to lose each other.

"So you see? You can't *have* your daughter. She's gone the minute you try. That's why you find yourself hitting her: you're trying to *have* her. And there's nothing you can have but the worthless flesh, the pointless blood and hair. And you hit that, or yank on that. Or you let it hit you. When you can't have anything you love until you're able to lose it, able to say, 'I know you are lovely and you are going to be gone in a heartbeat. And so I would never dare to hurt you or let you hurt me.'"

"I don't know what you're talkin about," Lindee said. "But I wished I did. And I hope to God I will."

"Well," Leela said, "I hope to God I'm right."

Sam and Jim left again, driving through town in Jim's car, heading, this time, for the grocery to do what Sam called *vittlin the troops*.

"Best hope we don't run into Morelocks a drivin round here," Sam said.

"Let me get some of this straight," said Jim. "Lindee says Paul Morelock killed Trapper, even though they found Dickie with the bloody knife gripped in his hand."

"Lying right next to him, with a rip in Trapper's gut that was made by the same knife. Like somebody thought they was cleanin a jackfish."

"So how is it she knows Paul did it?"

"She says it was the way he told her on the phone," Sam said.

"A veiled threat as a confession?"

"Well, something like. Maybe the other way round." Sam made a sudden left turn, swerving the truck onto a crossing street. "Let's go talk to Glen, right quick," he said. "I want to know more about this old time murder, too. The one your new momma says Morelocks done, when everybody else says the drunk sheriff done it."

"It's the same, isn't it?" said Jim.

"Same either way," Sam said. "We got two women that've been kindly took in, or took over, by Morelocks that now say it was Morelocks killed their boyfriends. So either Morelocks has a tradition about treatin women so bad they'll accuse em of a murder somebody else done, or Morelocks has a tradition of settin up other folks for murders Morelocks have done, their own selves. One or the other."

He skirled the truck into the gravel lot at Caray's. "Glen'll have the latest news on Dicky and the earlier news on the other un."

They found Glen already seated before the stove with Dave McCann across from her on another folding chair and a man in farm overalls leaning against the counter, who introduced himself as Orrie Joe.

"I reckon you all are safe from gettin beat up by Dicky Hampton anymore," said McCann, when they entered. He turned to Orrie Joe and said, "Dicky was all set to bust up Jim, here, on account of he was from Roalton."

"So I understand he decided to go into Roalton, instead, kill another newcomer," said Sam. "Trapper...what the hell was his last name?" He looked around the room. The men shrugged.

"Mason," said Glen. "Richard Mason. He was born over west of Roalton, across Clinch Mountain. He has a few folks over this way. His Aunt Gracie married a Shelton, run the motel til she got too old. Trapper come to town with a gal...I don't recollect her name."

"Lindee," said Sam. "That'd be Lindee Macleen. She come from up yonder, in the coal fields. Run away from her brother's place a few years back. She didn't lose much getting away from there. Got herself a daughter named Caroline, sometime or other. Aint Trapper's daughter, but he kindly took care of the both of em."

They all stared at him. He winked at Glen. "Got one you didn't know?" he asked.

"It happens once in a blue moon," she said. She shook her head. "But I'll be rolled and cut if Dickie killed that fellow last night" She stood up and went to the cooler. "I don't believe it. You all want a Dr Pepper?"

"We aint got the time," Sam said. "But we was wonderin if he could've done that, ourselves. Thought we'd holler at you and see what you knew."

"I was there," said Orrie Joe. "Right on the spot."

"You can't beat that for information, can you?" said McCann. "Horse's mouth." He pulled a sack of Beech Nut out of his bib pocket, reached in, and carefully shook out a pinch of the scrap leaves, rolling them into a ball. He tucked it into his cheek, then offered the sack around. Orrie Joe reached across and got himself a wad. McCann rolled and sealed his sack, dropping it back into the pocket. Then he continued. "Iffen you got horse's mouth information around here, by god, you'd best bring it over to Glen. Aint that right?"

They all nodded. They waited patiently for Orrie Joe to finish tucking in his chaw.

Glen grabbed two Styrofoam cups from the coffee counter and returned to her chair, handing the cups to McCann, who leaned one over to Orrie Joe.

"Thankee," said Orrie Joe. He spat into his cup and then raised it in a toasting gesture to Glen and McCann. "Thankee both."

"Well," Sam said, "like I said, we aint got a whole lot of time."

"Seems like they aint time to do nothin these days," said Orrie Joe. "Everbody's in such a rush all the damn while."

"Aint that a fact," said McCann. "Nothing but hurry hurry hurry. Make a little money you're too damn wore out to enjoy the spending of it."

"I believe they'd like to hear what happened last night," said Glen, prodding. "I believe they aint got time to wait."

"Oh," said Orrie Joe. "Whyn't you all say so?" McCann gave a low laugh, and Jim wondered if they'd all been doing this for his benefit, playing some sort of slow-down game with the city boy. But he didn't know. *That's the point, I guess. That I don't know if they're putting me on or not.*

"Well, it was a hell of durn thing," said Orrie Joe. He spit into his cup again. "I didn't see much, mind you. Nobody did. Because about the time everthing started, the lights went out. But I saw Dicky come in with Paul Morelock. Saw them go to the bar. Strange thing, they never said nothing to Johns and the young un. Paul's brother…he's kindly backward. What's his name?"

"Pierot," said Glen.

"Pierot. Jesus Christ, who in hell would name a feller Pierot?"

"Anyway…" Sam urged.

"Anyways, two seconds later, I seen Dicky go after that Trapper feller, like you'd expect Dicky to do, iffen a fight starts."

"Seen him do fifty million times before," said McCann.

"And about the same time, damned if another fight don't start up at the back of the room. And pert soon everbody's a pushin and shovin everbody else. I like to get clobbered myself. And then the lights went out."

"Strange," said Jim.

"And when they got the lights crunk up, the place looked worse than a barnlot in a cyclone. And there's Trapper a layin in a pool of blood, with his belly tore open like a butchered hog. And Dicky's a layin next to him with a grip on that big ole knife of his'n. So they weren't much doubt, they says, and they arrested him and took him in. Paul Morelock, he weren't around, but I hear he gone down this morning and made a statement."

"I bet he did," said McCann. "I bet he was a eyewitness."

"So why don't you think Dicky did it?" said Jim.

"Dicky Hampton?" said Glen. "He'd not hurt a butterfly."

"I thought he was a big barroom brawler," Jim said.

"Is," said McCann. "Like I told you. He'll start one ever chance he gets. Or he'll jump into anything that starts up. That's Dicky. He loves to fight." McCann spit. "But he don't win, for god's sake."

"And look here," said Glen. "How many fights does Dicky get into every month? And how many times has he ever stuck anybody with that knife of his'n? Even when he's a gettin his brains beat out, kindly?" She shook her head. "No sir."

They sat in silence a moment, while Orrie Joe examined his boot.

"So you think they set him up," said Jim.

"What else?" said Glen. "You got Paul comes in a while after his Daddy and brother, who're down to the end of the bar. And Paul, he steers Dickie up to this end, right next to Trapper. And then Paul starts up a fight that Dicky jumps into."

"Because Paul knows goddamn well that's just what Dicky'll do," said McCann.

"And then, down the other way, Johns and the boy start a row. Because that'll get the bar all riled up and get things confused. And then one of em cuts off the lights."

"And Paul grabs up Dicky's knife and kills Trapper," said Sam. "Okay. But how does Paul get Dicky to grab hold of the knife and fall down unconscious?"

They all sat still.

"Somehow," McCann said. "Some kind of how."

Sam and Jim had "made their manners," as Sam said, and had left. They tried to work it all out on their way back home.

"So let's say everybody's right, and the Morelocks killed Trapper, and set up Dicky. Does that mean Ellie's right? That this is what Morelocks do? That they killed her boyfriend, too?"

"No. It doesn't necessarily mean it," Jim said. "But we know, too, that Leela and Ellie both talk about the way the Morelocks laugh about getting away with things. So it might be."

"So somehow they shoot two Hamptons up in the woods, right below the Hamptons' place. And the next day, folks tryin to report the murder find the sheriff out cold from having got good and drunk the night before. He probably don't remember much himself. He's likely in a pretty good haze when they start to askin questions. They find his sheriff's coat with blood all on the sleeves, and a rusty tear in it that they'll figure was made by the barb wire."

"Where he wouldn't have left it to be found if he was really the killer," said Jim.

"Unless he was too drunk by then to worry about it," said Sam. "Killed them boys up on the mountain and drank his way all the way back down and passed out before he'd got things cleaned up, kindly. And later, they find his gun in Shaleen Creek—which they can tell, later than that, is the murder weapon—and all the other paraphernalia, the gloves he used to drag the barb wire around, and the tools, all that. Find them tucked into the woods. Never do find one glove, actually. And he's in his office a sayin he don't remember nothin. He was just a settin there drinkin, as usual, he says, next thing he knows, it's daylight and all these state police is all over him with the evidence they found that ties him kindly to the scene."

"But you don't know any of this, really," said Jim. "Do you?"

"No," said Sam. "I'm just figurin. But I figure that's about how it would be."

"And we do know there's a witness who saw him leave his office late at night, with the gun and the gloves and all. And saw him drive off toward Shaleen."

"And up on the mountain, they got tire prints and footprints and spent shells and every damn thing else. And it's all matchin the sheriff's," said Sam. "So, goddammit, he must have done it."

"But Ellie—my mother—says that the Morelocks did it all, themselves. So how could that be?"

"Well, I don't know," said Sam. "Maybe she just hates Morelocks enough to pin everything that goes wrong onto them. Couldn't blame her for that." They rode along in silence, musing, while the headlights picked out the swerving turns, switching back down the east mountain toward town.

"Wait a minute," said Sam, slapping his forehead. "Of course they did. Just like they did it with Dicky."

"What do you mean?" said Jim.

"Spiked his booze," Sam said. "That's the answer to both of em. Spike your booze, and put the knife in your hand. Did it with Dicky, right on the spot. Did it to the sheriff forty years ago, and put on his things and went and killed them boys." He whistled. "Jesus."

They were silent. Jim looked out across the bowl of the town, at the looming mountains, thinking, *Jesus is right*. And he saw the men, the two Morelocks, their gleaming narrow eyes. They were on the dark hillside, wrapping their victims in wire; the Hamptons, their deep blue eyes—Jim's eyes—wide with terror, about to die. *And one of them, the Morelocks, would be dressed like the sheriff, in the sheriff's coat and boots and gloves, that he'd taken from the unconscious man after he'd drugged the liquor, put the man out.*

Jim said, "Okay. They spiked his booze and knocked him out. One of them, anyway. It would have to be only one." *So he could leave carrying the sheriff's gun, looking like the sheriff, driving the sheriff's car, all of it for the witnesses to see, at night, when they'd only see the hat and the uniform and the car, and they'd think they'd seen the sheriff. They'd swear to it.* Jim looked across again at the high, bulging mountains, too dark, under the still-blue sky, seeing that it was dusk already up in the hollows, up on the twisting, rocky creek, and seeing the grizzled one-armed man, waiting by the narrow lane, as the police car drew up, driven by his son. And the old man climbing aboard, motioning eagerly, hatefully, up the mountain, saying something like, "Let's git." As Johns Hampton steered the car up into the brooding woods, up the trail to where they'd prepared the ambush. *Or maybe not. Maybe the old man would insist on driving, on dressing up in the police outfit. Because he was the senior Morelock. So he'd be the one in charge. Either way. That's how they did it.* And then the vision came crashing.

"Wait," he said. "If there were two of them, how did they only leave the one set of boot prints? The sheriff's boots must have been the only prints that were found. And they couldn't both have worn the sheriff's boots."

"You're thinking the same as me," Sam said. He whistled, again. "Jesus Christ," he said. "You got to be cold-blooded to wrap up a man in wire and shoot him. That's bad. But then to plan it out so careful, so that you could just drive the car back down, go back into the sheriff's, just like you come out, so anybody lookin will think they see the sheriff comin back. And unload a mess of whiskey from out of the Hamptons' car. Let's say you maybe broke a bottle back at the scene, so they'd find that too, and could match what's in your office to the same brand and all."

"But how did they only leave one set of prints?"

"Who cares?" said Sam. "If they done this much, that part would be easy enough. Maybe the one wore moccasins, or they…" He whistled again. "How's this? The Hamptons, one of them was barefoot, let's say. Wouldn't be so unusual back then. So one of the Morelocks is barefoot, too. The law is just going to assume that they're lookin at three sets of tracks: one barefoot and the other two shod. And they're worried about identifyin the prints that walked away from the place, since the other two belong to the dead men. And it'd be easy enough to put your shoes back on, if you're the barefoot killer, and get away through the woods. Just be careful not to leave no track, while your daddy goes back out, makin sheriff's tracks."

"But how would they know the Hamptons would show up with one of them barefoot?" said Jim.

"They wouldn't have to. All they have to do is make one of the Hamptons take his shoes off before they get out of the car. Then they got the barefoot victim all set up."

"It sounds far-fetched," Jim said.

"Well, they done it somehow," Sam said. "Or maybe with all the other evidence, nobody even bothered to go up and look too close."

"Unless the sheriff did it after all."

"Unless he done it," Sam said. "Let's get home and eat."

THREE

When Jim and Sam returned, the atmosphere became almost festive, in spite of the grief and the threat. They came in with three big bags of groceries, setting Lindee and her daughter to work on their "cells," while Sam tried to contact the Roalton paper to see about putting a hold on his story. Meanwhile, Jim, Leela, and Ellie put supper together in the kitchen. This was Jim's first experience with real corn bread, not to mention beans and ham hocks, and he found the whole process—especially working together with his mother and Leela—invigorating.

"I never could understand why folks would eat ham hocks," he said, pouring water into the kettle of dried peas. "What is a ham hock, anyway?"

"Ham hock is a ham hock," his mother said. She dropped two of the smoky-smelling shanks into the water. "And you're about to change your mind and start tryin to understand how in the world folks like you could ever get along without eatin them."

"That good?"

"Good is right," she said. "Now just let that cook up for a few hours." She sniffed at the kettle. "Put a little pepper in there, honey," she said to Leela. A moment later, she turned quietly to the sink and got a glass of water. She reached quickly into her pocket and, ducking her head, put a pill into her mouth. Leela looked at Jim, wrinkling her brow.

"You think maybe we could talk about getting you off them pills?" Leela said.

"Maybe," she said. "Someday." She came back to the stove. "It aint as bad as it was. I cut back a whole mite on my own. I was gettin so I didn't care about nothin. Not about eatin or keepin myself right. Nothin. I just sat up there in that dugout with the old man and the kid, makin product and spending my time takin these pills. And one day Paul Morelock come up to pick up a run and drop off some pills, and he got into a squabble with the old man. Old Jessum. He aint got but the one arm and he's not such a bad feller, I don't think, inside."

"He killed my father," Jim reminded her.

"He did. He and Johns. But you look at Jessum and you see somethin different than plain meanness. Johns and his boy, they aint nothin but mean. Jessum, though, he's got something in his eyes, like he's in mournin and can't get away from it. Can't do nothing about it, but can't stop tryin, neither. I think that's what made him to hate the Hamptons, made him to shoot Morgan and his Daddy. Like he saw something he had to get rid of when he looked at Morgan, maybe. Not like Johns. Johns just wanted to kill somebody. And that day you walked in up there, first time I saw you, he recognized something in you, too. He saw them Hampton eyes of your'n and it threw him right to the ground. He weren't angry or hateful about you: he was grieving. I seen it. And I knew it, too, because I'd felt the same thing. I got to thinking on why he reacted that way, and you know what? I believe we both, Jessum and me, lost somebody who looks like you. It was Morgan, your daddy, I lost. But Jessum, he's got somebody in his mind, too. I could see it when he looked at them eyes of your'n. They aint no other explanation."

"Okay," said Jim. "Maybe yes, maybe no. I'm not ready to start thinking he's a sweet old guy, though."

"No," Ellie said. "I wouldn't never make that mistake. All I'm a sayin is there's something more to him than pure meanness. He's the only one of all them boys that never…never laid a hand on me.”

“Fair enough,” Jim said.

“But you were talking about the pills,” Leela said, reaching a big wooden spoon into the pot and giving the bubbling liquid a stir.

“Oh. Yes.” Ellie reached a hand to her brow, brushing her hair back. “Well, I was up there just feelin nothing, takin them pills and workin, you know. Nothin mattered but gettin another handful of pills whenever Paul come up. Then one day he got in a argument with the old man, and knocked him down. Just reached out and hit him right in the face.”

“He does that,” said Jim, pointing to his own bruised face.

“Yes, he does,” agreed Leela, pointing to hers.

“Well, he took and hit that old man. And I don’t care how bad Jessum might be, he’s ninety five years old and aint got but the one arm, and his own grandson reaches out and knocks him down. And you know what? It didn’t matter a lick to me what he done. He could have killed the old man and I wouldn’t have blinked a eye. But they was something inside me that could see that, could see that I didn’t care two shakes about it. So at that instant, I could see that as long as I got them pills from Paul, it didn’t matter to me no more what he did to anybody. And they was something deep down inside me that knew it and didn’t like it. And something said, *That don’t fit my pocket.* Like they was a part of me that really did care, at least enough to see that them pills had took something away from me. That I wouldn’t care if he went back and killed Morgan again.

“So I tried to give them things up. I cut down and down and down. Threw some of them out, so Paul wouldn’t find out that I weren’t takin them. And now I still got to have them, some. But I’m better. I can tell where I am. And what matters. At least some.”

“Let’s see if we can’t get you off them entirely,” said Jim.

“I’ll see,” Ellie said. “Maybe.” She sighed deeply. “They help is all.”

***

Later they all sat in the office, balancing bowls on their laps, eating the peas and ham, sopping the bean liquor with chunks of corn bread.

"This here is eatin," said Sam.

"I never thought I'd say it, but I believe ham hocks are pretty good" Jim said. "I never would have even considered eating ham hocks before."

"Looks like you're turning into a hillbilly," Sam said. "Tomorrow let's try him on some pickled pigs' feet."

"Not a chance," said Jim.

"I bet you've eaten some things we'd never touch. Hey?"

"Probably," Jim said.

"Snails," said Lindee. "You ever eat snails?"

"I have," said Jim.

"Lord help," said his mother. "Where did you ever wind up eatin a snail?"

"He was abducted by space aliens," said Sam. "Can't you tell by the way he talks?"

"In Paris," said Jim. "I ate them in Paris. In graduate school."

"You see what I mean?" said Sam.

"Lord, who in the world would think to eat a snail?" said Ellie.

"Frenchmen, I reckon," Leela said. "I reckon they're just different folks from us."

Sam arose and went into the kitchen. When he returned, he was gnawing on the hock bone and carrying a can of beer. He sat back down, wiped his mouth.

"I don't know how different they are," he said. "I reckon I could tell you how Frenchmen got to eatin snails."

"What do you know about Frenchmen?" said Leela.

"Nothin," Sam said. "But I know about folks." He gnawed on the ham bone. "I reckon it happened about like you'd figure. I reckon they's two feller, French fellers, a settin around whittlin, doin nothin, you know. And they look over on the simmon tree and see a mess of snails a crawlin up the trunk, maybe."

Jim recognized Sam's switch into the same tones and timing he'd used at Crary's the other day. Once again, Jim wondered whether Sam's ability to switch from one voice to another—from ironic cynic, to good old boy, to mountain storyteller—was a mark of Sam's genuineness or his fraudulence. Did it mean he had these older voices stored deep within, a true inheritance from a true family tradition? Or did it mean he'd found a series of good poses, so that he could construct a vocal identity to suit the ear of whoever he wanted to address? Jim wondered whether there was any difference, and decided, yes, there was. But he couldn't tell which version he was hearing, right now. *I suppose I couldn't judge unless I had those voices inside me, too. So the people at Crary's would know whether they were hearing the real thing or not. But I'd never be able to tell. Not yet, anyway.* And then he wondered whether this was something you could learn, an "ear" you could develop.

"So one of them fellers reaches over and grabs him a snail and opens him up with the whittling knife, the way folks'll do, just to see what's inside. And they both of em look in at this slimy black critter, a twistin around inside the shell, kindly.

"And they sets and watches the snail for a while. And you can see they're both of em thinking the same thing. Until one of em finally speaks up and says, 'Whyn't you eat him?'

"And the other feller shakes his head and says, 'I aint a goin to eat him.'

"So they sets and watches that snail for a mite more. Then the first feller, he says, 'I'll give you a dollar iffen you'll eat him.'

"And the other guy says, 'I told you, I aint a goin to eat him. Wouldn't eat him for a sock full of dollars.'

"So they sets there for a while longer, both of em watchin that snail kindly oozing around in his shell. Until at last the first feller speaks up again and says, 'I reckon you're afraid to eat him.'

"And number two feller, he gets a little hot. And he says, 'I aint afraid to eat him, goddammit. You don't have to be afraid of a critter to not want to eat him.'

"And number one, he kindly says, 'Hmmmph,' like one of them laughs where you know the feller aint really laughin so much as he's a sayin, 'Yeah, sure.' And they go back to watchin the thing movin around in that shell. Until number one says, 'I reckon your brother Gerald wouldn't have been afraid to eat him.' And I reckon that does the trick, because number two jumps up and grabs up that snail. 'All right, goddammit, I'll eat the sonofabitch,' he hollers, and he throws that thing into his mouth and chews him up and swallers him."

Sam cracked open his beer and took a long swallow.

"Five minutes later, they're in a fist fight over that dollar," he said. "And number one, he loses the fistfight, but he aint got no dollar, actually. So he has to eat two of them snails to make up for the one the other feller eat and the dollar he didn't have."

Sam looked around the room. "And I'd say that's about how it got started, eatin snails."

"You think so, huh?" said Leela.

"Yes, indeed," Sam said. "But the important thing aint that first snail that got eat." He took another chew on the bone and gulped at his beer. "No ma'am. It's them two the other feller had to eat. Because most anything in the world has likely been eat by somebody once. That's just a accident. But you eat something twice, by god, and it's food."

Suddenly the room seemed to disintegrate. The sound was deafening, as the front window exploded inward, crashing glass laying a thin treble resonance over the deep boom of the gunshot. They all dropped to the floor amid their own shouts and screams, Lindee and Ellie both trying to cover the child, the bowls of peas and ham upturned, china breaking, soup slopping across them as they hugged the floor.

The silence that followed was wide and eerie. Gradually, one by one, they raised their heads, looking around, staring wide-eyed at one another.

It took several minutes for things to settle down enough that they could pick themselves out of the mess and consider what to do. Ellie appeared to be unrattled by the shooting, going into the kitchen to find a broom and cleaning supplies, "Get this here mess took care of," while the others stood in the office, talking nervously about the incident.

"That was a pretty sure-fire warning," said Sam. "I'd say."

"I think it's time to call the police," said Leela.

"Police?" scoffed Lindee, who'd just finished hushing Caroline, settling her down. "The police is as likely to be the ones who pointed out the right address to Paul Morelock as anybody else."

"She's right," Sam said. "Police, here, would just make for more problems."

"Well, perhaps they were just trying to scare us," said Jim. "And maybe that's all there will be to it."

"I think you're right," said Leela. "They'll not do anything they could get caught for, even if they do have the police in their hands. I think it's just a scare. They still don't know Lindee's here. Or Ellie, neither. So they're tryin to intimidate Jim, scare him out of town. That's all."

"Well, let's get this picked up and get that window boarded up," said Sam. "I'll go out back and fetch some plywood." He turned and went through the kitchen door, as Ellie came the other way, carrying a mop and a bucket.

They all set into cleaning the broken china and spilled food. Working together, they found the tension again begin to drain away, and again began to feel almost festive about being there together, as though this new household of displaced persons had become something that afforded a new kind of strength, confidence, at least, to each of them.

Sam returned a few minutes later, saying, "Jim, you may not

believe this, but we're fixin to go out shoppin a third time tonight." He shook his head. "I got plywood. Got a saw. Got nails. Aint got a god damn hammer."

Sam and Jim drove off again, back to Crary's, to buy a hammer. They didn't stay to talk, except to report that their front window had been shot out, "by fellers unknown," Sam said.

"I reckon I could tell you who them fellers are," said Glen. "Not that it'd do a whole lot of good if everybody in the state knowed it. Aint nothin nobody is a going to do about it, is they?"

"We believe they're just trying to scare us," Jim said. "You think so?"

"I reckon so," said Glen. "Fightin you out in the open aint dezactly their way of doin things. But I'd stay out away from Shaleen, I believe. You don't know. Them are dangerous folks."

"We'll do that," said Sam, and he ushered Jim out the door.

As they drove home, they discussed their choices, Sam asserting that they had no real choice except to "wait and see." But Jim demurred.

"I think it's time to go back to Roalton," he said.

"Now, you might have a point, there," said Sam. "That's what they want. You go on back, and it might quiet them down. At least for now. After all, things was pert quiet here before you came along in the first place."

"Except Leela was getting beaten up, Lindee was hitting her kid, Paul and Johns were running the whole damn county."

"Well, sure," Sam said.

"Anyway, I didn't mean just me," Jim said. "Didn't mean I should go back to Roalton; I meant *we* should go. Get everybody out of here: you, Leela, Lindee and Caorline, Ellie…everybody out of this town and down to Roalton, where there's some law and order, and where the Morelocks can't just wiggle their fingers and control everybody."

"I got a paper to put out," said Sam. "I aint goin nowhere."

"You can't put a paper out if you're dead," said Jim.

"Hell," Sam said, "I aint afraid of them boys."

"Yes you are," said Jim. "Either that or you're crazy."

Jim turned his car onto Blackberry Lane and rolled down toward the house. As he pulled up in front, he heard Sam's sharp intake of breath.

"What's the hell is up, here?" said Sam.

The front door was wide open.

Jim and Sam stared at the gaping door, then back at each other.

"I don't know," said Jim.

They got out of Jim's car, slowly, feeling the eeriness of the doorway, an odd presentiment that the open square of light was shining out from an empty house.

"I don't like this," he said, watching the curtains flap desultorily in the open space of the shattered window. His stomach tightened.

"Let's you and I just kindly walk in, slow and easy. We won't announce nothin," said Sam. He reached out to Jim's arm. "Wait," he said. "Let's go round back, get the pistol out from the truck."

They skirted the house, heading toward the dark alley. When they had turned the last corner, they stood for a moment, staring. Since they'd both already accepted the plan, already made the movement, neither was able to merge his expectations with the scene he finally saw. They looked at one another, and then back at the vacant alley.

"Where's your truck?" said Jim.

"Shit," Sam said. "Where is my god damned truck?"

FOUR

A second later, they were both turning and running again for the front of the house. When they reached the front door, they slowed, moving carefully through the open square, into the light of the vestibule. Sam led the way, easing himself slowly around the corner, through the doorway, into the office.

Nothing appeared amiss.

Both men had been unconsciously bending forward, sneaking. Now, together, in the normalized surroundings, they both straightened, expelling long breaths.

A bumping sound came from the kitchen, then a small whine. The men tensed, again. Sam pulled Jim's sleeve, drawing him downward, the two men curling themselves into a crouch on the far side of the desk. Slowly, the kitchen door opened and a figure emerged.

It was Ellie. She was carrying the child, her hand held close to the little girl's mouth, as if ready to muffle any cry. She stepped carefully into the office.

Sam and Jim rose and the woman gave a start, clapping her hand over Caroline's mouth and making a small, tight shriek, herself.

"It's okay," Sam said. "It's us."

"Oh my Lord," Ellie said. She lowered the child, letting her stand, holding her hand. "They come here," Ellie said. "They went through the house. I hid in the cell with the child. Oh Lord, what a fright." She shuddered. "Leela, she and Lindee…"

"O my God," said Jim. He turned and began to run up the stairs, shouting, "Leela! Leela!"

"They aint here," said Ellie. "Thank the Lord. They went over to fetch things. So them fellers, they didn't find nothin." She turned to Sam.

"They found my truck," said Sam.

"How do you mean?" Ellie said.

"They stole my truck. It was Johns and Paul, I reckon," Sam said, his voice tight.

"Who else would it be?" Ellie said, looking strangely at Jim. "Anyways, I heard them. It was them."

Jim descended the stairs, wringing his hands. "Not a sign of Leela," he said, as though he hadn't heard any of Ellie's story. "She's gone."

"I told you, they went out. Went back to Gracie's. They's getting things, clothes and things."

"Settle down, cousin," Sam said, laying a hand on Jim's shoulder.

"All right," Jim said, taking a deep breath. "Sorry. I got a bit rattled is all. This isn't exactly my line of work."

"You seem to be pretty good at rilin it up, though," said Sam. "So okay," he said to Ellie. "What happened?"

"I was back in the back, a tellin the child a story," Ellie said. "I heard a commotion out front, and I was fixin to go see what was the matter, when I heard Johns's voice. Then I heard one of em a goin up the stairs. I heard him clompin around, back to Sam's room, scramblin around, then into the other room. Then he come back down."

"What was the sonofabitch doin in my room?" said Sam. "Lookin for me?"

"I don't believe so," said Ellie. "He was up there too long, a rustlin about."

"Looking for something," said Jim.

"Then he come down and I heard the two of em mumbling out in the office. I had to grab the child and clap my hand over her mouth, lest she'd holler. They done some things for a while in there. You could hear them movin around in the office. Then Johns he said, 'Let's go,' and I heard two of em goin out the door. But then Paul went into the kitchen and come right by here, and out the back hall. I reckon he was gettin your truck," she said to Sam. "And then it was quiet."

"When did this happen?" said Jim.

"A hour ago, maybe," she said. "I been stayin in the back, for fear they'd come back a lookin for you, or the other uns."

"Okay," said Sam. "We got to think this out." He started toward the stairs. "Let's see if we can figure out what they're after up here."

Upstairs, the two men looked through Sam's room. Nothing appeared to be missing.

"Whatever it was, they aint took it, I reckon. Or aint found it," Sam said. "Let's go back down."

"Let's check the other," Jim said, heading into the guest room.

Again nothing appeared to have been disturbed.

"Ellie's wrong. They was just lookin for us," Sam said. "Let's go."

Jim said, "Maybe they were looking for something that belongs to Leela or Lindee. Or were looking for my mother."

"They couldn't know your mother is here," said Sam. "They'll think she just run off. Whatever it was, we're wastin time. Let's go."

The two men turned to leave, when Jim stopped abruptly. "My pen," he said, swiveling back toward the bedside. "My pen's gone."

"What pen?" said Sam.

"I have a green onyx fountain pen. It's Italian. It's a kind of a special pen. I was showing it to Leela, and I brought it up here and put it on the table. Right here. It's gone." His deep eyes looked at Sam, puzzling.

"Why in hell would he come up here, in the middle of every-thing, just to steal your fancy ink pen?" said Sam.

The men stood, eyeing one another. At last, Sam spoke.

"You got to be mistaken. You must've misplaced it. It don't make sense he'd take your pen. Let's go."

Again the men turned to leave. In the hallway, Jim stopped once more.

"No," he said. "Go back. Look and see if anything's gone from your room. Something trivial, something you wouldn't even have thought about the first time you looked. Something the Mo-relocks couldn't possibly want to take."

"What in the world are you gettin at?" said Sam. "Time's a wastin."

"Little things you might carry in your pocket, maybe. Like my pen. I'll be downstairs, checking," Jim said.

"No goddammit, wait," Sam said. "I got to say it again for Chrissakes? Wait!" He gave Jim an angry, frustrated glare. "Just tell me, what you're thinking. So as I have some idea what I'm after."

Jim took a deep breath and expelled it slowly.

"They're fixing a setup," he said. "That's why he took my pen. So he can drop it somewhere."

Sam looked at Jim uncomprehendingly. Then he got it, his eyes widening. "Son of a bitch," he said.

"Just look," said Jim.

And he turned and headed down, taking two stairs at a time.

A few minutes later, they stood in the office.

"Your boots are gone," Jim said. "You had them on the back step, didn't you?"

Sam nodded.

"They took my dirty laundry," he said. "A whole outfit: pants, underwear, shirt, socks." He nodded. "You were right," he said. "They're settin us up. They're fixin to kill somebody and set us up for it."

"Lord help," said Ellie. She stood alone now. She had put the child to bed, trying to soothe her, telling her Lindee would be there when she awoke. Now Ellie lowered herself to the couch, saying, again, "Lord help."

The phone rang loudly.

"Jesus," said Sam. "Scared me halfway to heaven." He leaned over his desk and grabbed the receiver. He held it at his ear, saying nothing. Jim could hear the crinkle of a voice speaking sharply on the other end. Sam turned pale. He looked at Jim, then at Ellie, eyes wide. Jim heard the click as the line went dead.

Sam stood, still holding the phone to his ear, looking wild and frightened.

"What?" cried Jim. "What?"

"They got Leela and Lindee," Sam said hoarsely, lowering the phone. "They said 'too late for Lindee.'" He swallowed hard. "Said Leela's next unless we stay put and don't make a move. That's what they said. 'You want to see your sister ever again, you just stay put, til you hear from us. Don't move a god damn muscle.'"

"We've got to call the police," Jim said.

"Call the police?" Sam said. He sounded bemused, as if he'd never heard these words before. "Police?" He put a hand to his forehead, sliding it over his brow, across the top of his head. "Wait. No," he said.

"What else can we do?" Jim said.

"Wait," Sam said, bringing his hand down and turning it, palm outward, like a man stopping a car. "Wait. The police, these police, they aint going to help us. We already know that. The Morelocks got them right in their hip pocket. We already found that out."

"So call the state police. God damn it, what else can we do?" Jim said, his voice rising into a cry. "If you can't call the police, what the hell are you supposed to do?"

Ellie grabbed his wrist. Her eyes blazed. "Go there," she hissed. "Kill them. Like I done told you to once before."

"Jesus!" Jim shouted. "What kind of place is this!" He turned a full circle, his large eyes wild, panicky.

Sam grabbed Jim and shook him roughly. "It's a little too late to start askin that again, aint it?" Letting Jim go, Sam seemed to catch himself up, mastering himself, an act of will. He took a deep breath. "Ellie's right," he said. "We got to go get them women." He turned to her. "You got to help us find the best way to get up there, where they won't see us."

"They's a back way up over the knob," Ellie said.

"No," Jim said. "There aren't two women to get anymore. They said, 'It's too late for Lindee.' So they've killed her, already. This isn't a game, or a job for a city boy and somebody who wants to prove he's a news reporter. They're not messing around. And they said stay put or they'll kill Leela. We need to do that, stay here, at least find out what they want. We can't go running up there and break in on those people. They'd kill us before we could draw a breath."

"We don't know Lindee's dead," said Sam. "They didn't say that, exactly. And even if they did, why should we believe them? Anyway, why do they want us to sit around here? They going to make a ransom demand? No. There's something going on that we can't stop if we do what they say. Do as they say, they win."

Ellie gave a little scream when the phone rang again. Sam grabbed the receiver and shouted into it, "Listen you sonofabitch…" Then he stood, listening. He slammed the receiver down. "Shit!" he said. And again, more softly: "Shit."

"What?" said Jim, impatient.

"He said he was just checkin to see was we still here. Said if he calls and we don't answer, he'll kill Leela."

"So we have to stay here," said Jim.

"What is it they want?" said Ellie. "What is it they want you all a settin here for?"

"Jesus," breathed Sam. "You think there's a bomb in the house, somewhere? Think they planted a damn bomb?" His eyes darted, looking around the room.

"Stop it," Jim said. "There's no bomb. We already know what

they're up to. They're setting us up for the murder of Lindee Macleen. They took my pen and your boots and clothes. Probably some things we haven't discovered. Even took your dirty clothes. Who knows? Nowadays the police might know you'd worn them; they'd have maybe some trace evidence or something. And took your truck. And they're going to kill Lindee, anyway, sometime tonight, I'll bet you. They'll do it like they did the other, way back, Ellie's...my father. They'll do the murder just as if we were trying to get away with it: throw the gun in the creek, ditch the clothes."

"They got my pistol, too," said Sam.

"And they'll just count on the law to do its job, find the evidence. And convict us."

The phone rang again. This time, Sam reached slowly across the desk, raising the receiver slowly to his ear. "What," he said, quietly, tonelessly. He listened a moment, then hung up.

"Same thing?" Ellie said. Sam nodded.

"So even if we do call the police," Jim said, "We'd be calling them in to find evidence against us."

They stood in silence a moment.

"I got a question," Sam said. "Why would they want us a waitin here, for them to set up for the crime? Why sneak in here and get them things, only to call us and tell us to stay here? Why not just keep their mouths shut in the first place?"

"Maybe they don't expect us to notice the missing things. Or figure out why they took them. Remember, they don't know Ellie is here; they probably think she just ran away. They didn't know Lindee was, either, as far as we know. So they won't know that we know all the details of those other murders. Won't know we know they've set folks up before. They think we're in the dark. We're scared of them, and we know they're coming for us—they did shoot out the front window—but they don't think we know how they operate."

"But they'd sure as hell know that I knew my truck was gone," said Sam. "And if we're a settin here, because that's what they told us to do, how are they a going to get the truck back down here? Likely they aint a goin to run up there and shoot them girls dead and run back down here with the truck, park it out back, and bring back some of the evidence to plant, whilst we're a standin here chattin with Ellie. Right?"

"Well, what choice do we have?" said Jim. "They want us here for some reason. And they'll keep calling to make sure we're here. And I'm not going to call their bluff about killing Leela."

"I reckon we better sit and think this through," said Sam. He turned and walked around his desk, leaning over the liquor cabinet and pulling out the jug of stumpblower. "I need me a drink," he said. "Let's slow down just a second and think this over."

He whorled open the lid and poured them each a full glass, sliding Jim's across the desktop. Lifting his own glass, he said, "Let's hope to God we can figure this out." He tipped the glass up.

"Stop!" Ellie shouted wildly. "Don't drink that! Don't you drink that!" She leaped toward Jim, slapping at his hand, knocking the glass away. It fell, splashing the brown drink across desk, the glass shattering on the floor at his feet. Jim jerked away from her, incredulous.

Behind the desk, Sam stood frozen, glass still held against his lips. Then he lowered his hand, drawing the glass slowly away from his mouth, and tipping it, letting the contents run out onto the floor.

"I'll be god damned," he said, awed.

They were sitting now, Ellie on the couch, Sam behind the desk, and Jim in the folding chair, when the phone rang the third time.

"It'd be about time not to answer it, I believe," Sam said. "Wouldn't it, Ellie?"

"No," she said. "Answer it once more, and then we'll go. That'll buy us the time until the next call."

"Good," said Sam, picking up the phone. He said, "yes," then listened a moment, and hung up. "Okay. Let's go."

"Would you both care to fill me in on this?" said Jim.

Sam stood up and came around the desk. "Next time it'll ring and we won't answer it. Just like they figure. So they'll be happy. And we can get moving, now."

"What?" said Jim, worried. "I told you not to call their bluff. Not with Leela…"

"It aint Leela it's about," said Ellie. "And they weren't callin to find out was you still here. At least not after the first couple."

"Let's just get rollin," said Sam. "We'll explain it in the car, Jim. There's no time to lose." He moved quickly toward the kitchen, saying, "I've got a rifle back here in the jail closet. They's some shells in the desk drawer. Don't know how many but grab all you can find." He came back a few seconds later, carrying the weapons.

"Maybe your momma can show you how to shoot this thing on the way up there," Sam said, handing Jim the rifle. "Just in case you wind up havin to. You think?"

"I'll show him," said Ellie.

They drove out into a deep, drizzly night, the clouds settling low, wrapping into the hollows in the mountains above.

"No, I don't know what we're going to do," said Sam as he turned Jim's car down the East Main, heading toward the looming black wall of the mountain, darker than the overcast night sky, the road beginning to rise, gradually, at first, then steeply, up into the mountain, twisting back on itself, winding into the first cove.

Ellie was leaning over Jim's shoulder from the back seat, pointing to the action on the rifle. "It's loaded," she said. "You just pull back the hammers and fire. You got a magazine with eight rounds." She showed him.

"You need any more than that, we're already a goin to be dead," said Sam.

"You shot a lot of people?" Jim asked her.

"I was a hunter since I was a girl. I shot one of these almost as big as I was."

Jim leaned the rifle into the seat well. "Okay," he said. "Now what about all this with the phone calls, not answering the phone?"

"It's the stumpblower. Your momma's right," Sam said. He was leaning forward, peering, as the road began to rise into hard fog. "They called once or twice to scare us into stayin there. After that, they were callin to see could we still answer the phone. Because they knew me well enough, I reckon, to know I wouldn't just set there on my hands. I'd have me a snort of stumpblower. And they figured you would, too."

"How would they know about the liquor even being there?" said Jim.

"Where you think I got the liquor from in the first place?" said Sam.

"You're joking," Jim said, stunned. "You buy your liquor from the Morelocks?"

"Son, iffen you buy liquor up here," Ellie said from the back seat, "you buy it from Morelocks. One way or the other."

"Momma's right again," said Sam. He threw a glance back over his shoulder at Ellie. "I can see where he gets his brains from."

"So anyway…" Jim prompted.

"So when they come to the house, they loaded up the liquor with pills," Sam said. "Spiked it, just like forty years ago. And like again, with Dicky. And took everything they needed. The clothes and whatever. Picked up Lindee and Leela, somehow. Or already had them. And called us to say we'd best sit still. So we did.

"And then they called every now and again to check and see would we answer the phone. Or had we drunk enough of that spiked liquor so we can't hear the thing a ringin and couldn't answer it if we did hear it? Once we don't answer that phone, they know we're knocked out good and can have a idea how long that good'll last. I imagine they're countin on a long time, seven or eight hours, before they has to worry about us. So they'll know we're a going to stay that way while they carry out all their plans. Kill Lindee, or maybe Leela. Though I think it's Lindee they're after. Then bring back the truck and my boots, what have you. Set everything where they want it while we're out cold on the floor. And then the both of us, well, we'll get arrested for doin the killin."

"Just same as they done with the sheriff, away back when," said Ellie.

"It's the Morelock family way," Sam said. "Just like some folks celebrates Christmas the same way every year." He slowed the car. "This fog's getting thicker'n a bear's hide." He drove more carefully, taking the turns in slow sweeps.

"So now we got the element of surprise, kindly," Sam said. "Since they think we're a snoozin the night away. They think they've got plenty of time, don't they? So they'll slow down. And they don't know we got the secret weapon: your momma, here. Who's a going to tell us how to get up in there without them knowin it."

Sam jerked his head toward the back seat again.

"You said there's a way up in there over the top?"

They drove by the turnoff to the Morelock place, Jim having to roll down his window and peer through the rainy fog to see it. Around the next turn, Sam said, "We're by the turn out up to Shaleen. The way we went up last time."

"Now keep on a going," said Ellie, "And when you cross the bridge, start to lookin out for a track. It aint going to be easy to see in this fog."

Sam took the car through the next round bend and over the narrow bridge. He slowed to a crawl. In the creek hollow, the fog had thickened almost to the same consistency as the rain. "There aint no fog like up-mountain fog, I tell you that," Sam said grimly. "You can't see out front because all it does is shine your headlights back at you. And you can't see out the side because you're so damn blind from starin into your own headlamps." He drew the car to a stop.

"Hell, I can't find it. Can't hardly tell if we're on the road," he said.

"I'll find it," Ellie said, opening the rear door and stepping out. "You give me thirty seconds and then come a crawlin. I'll point your way in to it." She disappeared into the white haze.

"That's one hell of a mother you got," said Sam.

"What good is it going to do to find the turn out?" Jim said. "It'll be worse once we turn back into the woods."

"No, it won't," said Sam. He started the car into a slow roll, both of them leaning toward the right, straining to see Ellie. "Get back under some trees and bushes, it'll clear out some. And we'll climb up out of this hollow, some time. It gathers itself into the hollows. There she is."

The figure of Ellie loomed up nearly in front of them, blurred and formless, like a figure in a dream. She pointed with her hand and Sam swung the car to the right, Ellie trotting along beside his window.

"Just straight on in," she said. "They's a little dip and then you'll come uphill, all in a rush. Then you swing left a mite, to the old house." The car moved on ahead of her.

"I bet you she hasn't been here in forty years," said Sam, quietly. "I'll bet she remembers all this from old times, times with Morgan, your daddy."

Jim felt the car drop and then surge. At the top of the rise, Sam stopped and killed the engine.

"Now I reckon we'd best figure out what in the hell we're a goin to do."

They sat together in the car, hearing the smatters of rain on the roof. The drops struck irregularly because they were falling through treetops, now, sliding off leaves, falling in misty droplets

and big splashes, so the noise took on a syncopated sound, a complex rhythmic counterpoint. Their windows were rolled down
and Jim could feel the light splashes that occasionally reached
his face. They carried with them the aroma of the woods, the
deep sweet-rotty odor of wet leaf, humous, and big rocks, the
invisible mountains hulked all around them. The rain increased
its volume and a breeze began to shush through the trees.

"All right," Sam said. "Ellie, where's that trail and where does
it go?"

"The house yonder is what Morgan's daddy built when he
come back here. Inherited what was left of the land. Don't know
what's left of it. But out behind the house, they was a lane run up
to the old Hampton home place. I don't know if the place is there
yet, but I reckon we can find the lane."

"There's a flashlight in the trunk," said Jim.

"I brought a dern flashlight," Sam said.

"Two might be good, iffen we get separated or need to signal," said Ellie. "Anyways, once we get on up there, they's a big
rock, looks like a giant stairstep, out to the side of the old home
place. The trail rises up right beside the rock, goes up behind it,
switches back all the way up the side of the knob, and comes up
over a curved rock near the top."

"You can find the way up there?" Jim said.

"I believe I could," Ellie said. "I've walked it many a time in
my memories and dreams."

"Okay, what about down the other side?" said Sam.

"It comes down pert straight for a mite, kindly in a gully of its
own. Then you're into the woods. Presently it splits. The right
fork goes on down to the Morelock home place. The left goes
over to the sawmill, Shaleen Prong. To this day, the Morelocks
will tell you they's from Shaleen Prong, even though they live on
down the crick a good ways."

"So which fork do we take?" said Jim.

"We go to the sawmill," said Sam. "That's where they'll take
Lindee and Leela. They wouldn't want them around the house.

Wouldn't want no sign of them left there. Right?" He looked at Ellie.

"I believe that's right," she said. "They'll keep em in the dugout."

The rain picked up its volume another notch, and they could feel the light breeze through the car windows.

"This fog might clear off in two seconds," said Sam. "This breeze might pick up and take it. It'll stay steamy down here in the woods, but we'll be able to see."

"Be almost clear, up on the prong," said Ellie. "Iffen that happens. By the time we get there."

"Yes," said Sam. "But we don't know. It could settle right back in. The weather up here is so local, who the hell knows? I've been up here when the fog would lift up like a curtain, show you the whole view, and then fall right back down, all in about two minutes' time.

"So we got to figure all this into it. I was thinking, why don't we just use the fog to help us come up on the place, bust in, shoot whoever we need to, and grab the women?"

"My God," Jim said. "Hostage rescue. People train for years to learn how to do that. How can we expect to get it right the first time? We'll just get everybody killed."

"Depend on the element of surprise," Sam said. "Jump in and make a lot of noise, one of us focused on nothing else but getting the women and running them out of there. The other two of us covering the bastards, make sure they can't shoot nobody."

"Well, I suppose that sounds reasonable." said Jim. "I reckon there's no other way, now that we're up here. It might be an idea."

"I think it's a good un," said Ellie. "Except they's likely to have Pierot on guard somewheres. Usually out to the head of the meadow."

"Where he picked me up the other day," Jim said.

"We'd have to snatch him first. Get him out of the way. Then go in."

"They'd still not be a lookin for nobody the way we'll come in," said Ellie. "Least they never have. The old man, sometimes he'll climb a little ways up the trail, like he's fixin to find something up there. But he never gets too far. He wouldn't be doing it in this rain, I don't reckon."

"So," Sam said, letting out a deep breath. "Let's come down the back. Where does the trail let out?"

"Just at the steam engine," said Ellie.

"Good," Sam said. "I come around there the other day, got the drop on young Pierot. It'll be a place we can set and gather ourselves up. Then I figure we can decide on what we're doing dep、endin on the fog. If it's heavy enough, let's leave Pierot out there, and try to get everything done before he can pick his way back. Last one out of the dugout can look for him." He paused a moment. "Dugout's the only place they'll be, aint it?"

"I believe so," Ellie said. "Lessen they stake em out on the mountain, somewhere. They done that to me once."

"Jesus," Jim said. "You know, these are a very bad bunch. Maybe we ought to forget this and go get some help. Go down and call the FBI or someone."

"Well, if they're not inside," Sam said, "we'll have to lean on one of them Morelocks to tell us where. We'll have to bring one along, or hold em all at gunpoint. March them out, down the road, I reckon."

"I believe they'll be in there," Ellie said.

"Did anybody hear me?" said Jim. "We can't take these guys on. They'll kill us all."

"Son," Ellie said, "it's here and now, in front of us. It aint Roalton and it aint a place where we're goin to get no help. Here we are, just us." She reached up and stroked his shoulder. "We'd best do it."

Jim sat in silence, hearing the rain beating its convoluted pattern on the car. He took a deep breath and let it slowly out.

"Let's git," he said.

The Hampton house loomed out of the mist like a melting berg, its worn and discolored white paint sleek in the wet air. They walked by, intent on finding the lane, their flashlight beam looking solid, like a swath of gray satin, in the fog.

"It's here," Ellie said, and pointed them the way up a grass grown strip barely holding its place in the encroaching undergrowth. They headed up the slope in silence, shedding rain, soaked through. As they rose, the fog began to slip away in rags, showing wet tree trunks, the deep, dank gloom of the night woods. The rain was letting up, too, still dropping its big globes of water from the leaves overhead, but not drumming as before. It might even have stopped.

Twenty minutes later, after climbing over a big deadfall, the bark slippery with rot and rain, they came upon an opening, the lane tipping over a small bulge in the mountain and dropping downward slightly to a wide flat.

"This is where the old home was," Ellie said. Her voice sounded grainy, like old wood, in the gray darkness and drizzle.

"Let's get on up to it and go over things," said Sam.

"It'd be over to the right a piece, I believe," said Ellie, and Sam slid his flashlight accordingly. The beam swept across trees and brush and then gleamed, too brightly, off red metal.

"That's my truck!" Sam said.

"Hush," Jim said. "Get down. Douse the light."

They crouched in darkness, waiting.

"What do we do?" Sam murmured.

"Let's sit tight for a minute," Jim whispered.

They waited. There was no movement, no light to be seen. Nothing but the red truck standing now, out of sight, in front of them. The leaf-drops of water sounded too loud, now, and Jim tensed, ears perked, at each creak and rustle of the woods. At one point, a small crashing sound made him grab at Sam's arm.

"Just a critter," whispered Sam.

They returned to waiting.

After what had been probably five minutes, Jim spoke aloud.

"There's nobody here. They'd have seen our flashlight. Or there'd be some sound. We're okay."

"Let's go easy, anyhow," said Sam.

So they moved slowly, groping through the darkness, until they came to the truck. Jim touched the cold, wet steel and sighed.

"May as well switch the light on. If they're here, they know we are, and if they aren't, we're wasting time."

Sam swept the flashlight across the scene. From the front of the truck, a straight track like a driveway led to a ramshackle pile of wood.

"That was the house," Ellie said. "It's gone."

The beam picked up a few bright swashes of graffiti scrawled on a half-standing wall.

"Looks like some kids come up here," Sam said. "Probably smokin pot and noodlin, once in a while. It's a long way to come to get high, I reckon."

"I suppose once you got here, you'd know you could do anything you want," Jim said.

Sam humphed a laugh. "Everybody's dream, I reckon," he said.

"Let's go on," Jim said.

"Wait," Sam said. "Let me see." He turned to the truck and wrenched open the side door, leaning into the cab. When he straightened up, he held a small silver pistol. He turned back into the cab again, leaning the seat forward and drew out the sawed-off shotgun they'd taken from Pierot.

"Better armament, anyways," he said. "We aint a goin to have to bust in there with nothing but one rifle; we might have to kindly hand back and forth."

"But why is the truck here?" said Jim.

"I don't know," Sam said. "Scene of the crime, maybe. They've parked it here in the rain, it'll leave tracks and everything else."

"Well, they won't have to worry about leaving our boot prints around," said Jim. "We've done that part for them."

Sam gave another humph. "Where to, Ellie?" he said.

"Find the rock," she said. "It looks like a big stair step. Off yonder, beyond the house."

Some time later, they crested the top of the knob, coming up over the big, curved rock face and onto the arch of the summit. They stopped and sat on a rounded granite stone at the very top, flecked with quartz, and fringed with laurel and rhododendron bushes. Once they cleared the trees, they could tell that the rain had ceased. The air, too, had cleared and they could see holes in the dark clouds overhead, through which blacker sky shone like patches of glossy lacquer on a flat gray canvas.

"It's incredible up here," said Jim. He let the effect of the place soak up the hours of tension and the strain of the climb, the anxiety about what was about to come.

"It's a lovin place," said Ellie, her voice quavering. "It's where Morgan and I become…become what we was to become." Her breath caught, a sudden realization. "My lord," she said, softly. She reached across to Jim and touched his hand.

"I believe you've found what you was lookin for," she said.

"Found it?" he said.

"Where you come from."

FIVE

They'd forgotten to bring water, and the exertion and fear had created an enormous thirst. So Ellie showed them where there was a good spring, a ways back down the trail, the way they'd come, into a small hollow, fringed with laurel and ferns. Drinking in the cold, sharp water, Jim believed he'd never experienced such pleasure before.

"It tastes like drinking the coldest air in the world," he said.

They looked at one another, smiling, until Sam said, "We'd better get this worked out."

So they went back up to the top of the knob, sat on the rock, and made their final plans. They would make the descent without the flashlight, which Ellie said would not be much of a problem. When they reached bottom, Jim and Ellie would huddle behind the steam engine, covering Sam as he made a wide sweep along the edge of the clearing, looking for Pierot.

"And I hope to God he aint there," Sam said. "But if he is, I'll try to come down on him quick, get his gun, and get him out of the way."

"Couldn't you just knock him out, iffen you're going to sneak up behind him anyway?" said Ellie.

"Good," Sam said. "Much better. I'll get in behind him and take him down with the rifle butt. Put him out. Then I'll come back to you all. If I don't, or if you hear any kind of disturbance, go straight into the dugout without me. I'll get there if I can. If not, get them women the hell out and head up the trail. If I'm able to, I'll make a lot of distraction."

"Okay," Jim said. "So, when you come back, we head into the house."

"We'll group at the door," Sam said. "I'll kick it in, and I'll jump in first, firing one barrel of the sawed-off into the air." He smiled. "That ought to startle them a plenty, give us the time we need." He held up a hand. "We won't shoot to hit nobody. Not at first. If they aint got guns in their hands, let's try to hold em at rifle point, grab any weapons we see and get out. I'll have that sawed-off and won't be able to shoot it anywhere but in the air, until you get the women out, Ellie. If I try to shoot it at anyone, I'll kill everybody in the goddamn room. It'll make a noise like all thunder, though. Ought to scare even Morelocks."

"I think as long as we know to expect it, we should be all right," Jim said. "Just remember there will be lots of noise. Let them be confused by it, not us." He paused. "And what about if they're holding guns?"

"That's your job," Sam said. "As soon as you get in the door, you look for guns. You see anyone pointing a weapon, shoot him. If he's just standin there, slack jawed, I'll be hollerin 'drop your guns' anyhow. Give him two seconds. Then shoot him if he aint dropped it." He looked closely at Jim. "You think you can do that?"

Jim nodded grimly. "I can do it," he said.

"If they're unarmed or have dropped em, then we'll just hold em at gunpoint until Ellie's in and out of there with the girls. After that, my shotgun can cover em all. You grab up the guns, go outdoors, toss em into the field, and start to runnin after Ellie.

"Ellie you go in right next to me. Jim will kindly step in behind and cover all of us. You try to forget anything else that's happenin and find them women. Just get them the hell out of there and get em runnin up the trail. Don't stop for nothing. If one of them gets hit, just keep runnin. Jim'll be behind you and can pick up the pieces."

"All right," Ellie said, calmly. She looked at Jim. His deep blue eyes glowed like pools in the night sky. She thought of Morgan, the two of them on the mountain, the last good things. "I'll do whatever needs doin." She reached out a hand. "Give me the pistol in case it gets tight. I don't reckon there's much to firin a pistol, is there? I aint never done it."

"If you're close enough, you can hit something," Sam said. "And you'll mostly be a runnin."

The three of them paused, their eyes glowing with excitement, or fear, or some new feeling that was better and worse than either.

"Okay," Sam said. "Once Ellie's out of there, we'll grab whatever's to grab, and get out. You go first, and I'll back out holdin them with the shotgun. Once we're out, I'll fire another blast in the air, slow them down, and then one of us has got to head out across the meadow, whilst the other un goes after Ellie and the women. Which one you want to be?"

Jim considered a moment. "I'm in better shape than you," he said. "I'll cut over the clearing."

"Good," Sam said. "I was a hopin you'd say that. You head away from the trail, straight out through the clearing. By the time they get out, they'll only see you, a hopskipperin out the other way. So they'll try and collect up the guns and go after you. You can cut back once you're over the brow of the ridge, where they can't see. Just double back around the edge and find the trail. We'll all just keep a hoppin, Ellie in front with the gals, and me rear guardin with that old sawed-off. You catch up to me, make sure you let me know it's you, or the undertaker'll be pickin shot out of you for a week."

Sam took another deep breath. "Everybody got it?" he said.

"One thing," Jim said. "If anyone gets shot." He heard his voice quaver. "We'll have to switch roles."

"Right enough," said Sam. "Ellie gets hit, you grab the gals and run. I get hit, you start shootin Morelocks, give Ellie some time." He winked at Jim. "You get hit, it won't matter so much. We'll all just do like we planned, except I'll just blast away with the sawed-off."

"Good," said Jim. "I'll try to be the one gets hit, okay?"

"Generous of you."

They checked their weapons and hugged one another. Ellie stared at Jim, saying nothing, watching his eyes. Sam slung the shotgun and said, "Jim. I'm mighty glad I got to know you."

Jim simply said, "Let's go get Leela."

They took the descent as carefully as they could, though the rush of adrenaline made them all want to run down. They kept reminding each other to take it easy, watch their step, mind the slick, wet spots, go quietly, watch the branches. At one point, passing through a moss bed, Jim smelled a sweet, fruity odor and wondered what it was. The sky had continued to clear, and now there was a sliver of moonlight, so finding the trail wasn't difficult. Ellie led the way, pausing a moment on a wide stretch of rock, then moving steadily on, into the dense woods, stopping again to let her eyes adjust to the darker way. As they approached a sharp switch back, she stopped and turned to them, holding up her hand.

"This here is it," she whispered. "Once we round the switch, it'll drop steep for twenty yards and spill out into the meadow."

"We all set?" whispered Jim. "Set on what we do?"

Sam and Ellie nodded. She turned back and led the way. At the switchback, they slowed, then eased themselves down the steep curve, holding roots, trying to stop their feet from sliding, trying not to make noise. At the bottom there was about ten feet of scrub growth through which they could see the sky over the clearing. They paused, then almost on signal, rushed the short gap to the huffing steam engine, and crouched together.

Sam tapped them on the shoulder, gave an *okay* sign with his thumb and forefinger, and slid off, heading around the edge of the mill ground, going after Pierot. Jim and Ellie turned and sat, their backs to the engine, which vibrated against them, shuddering and wheezing like an asthmatic. This close, the huffing seemed to be made up of several different sounds, high hisses and deep moans. Jim felt something touch him, realized it was Ellie, and clasped her hand. They waited, straining eyes and ears, seeing nothing but the grainy curve of the meadow's edge and hearing only the multitudinous throbs of the engine.

Now that they were sitting still, Jim could feel how cold and wet they were. He found that he was shivering steadily, without knowing when he had started. He leaned toward his mother, she toward him, sharing what remained of each other's warmth. His mouth had gone bone dry again. He was afraid.

He found himself thinking of home, his work: the shimmering spruce tops of old guitars reflecting licks of flame from the fireplace. The tools and clamps that he knew how to handle the way an artist handles a brush. Home.

And here I am, sitting on the ground by an ancient steam engine on a mountain, in a place where oak paneling and the kind of instruments people think of as "investments" are as incongruous as an elephant would be. And myself? Am I an elephant who has wandered into this place? So out of my place? Preparing to break through the door of an outlandish dwelling, half cabin, half cave, in order to rescue a woman I had never even seen two weeks ago? When I should be sitting in front of a computer screen, looking up serial numbers, matching up some old mandolin to its history? Risking my life for this woman, this Leela? And maybe killing someone, myself. And, oddest implausibility of all: doing all this with my mother. My mother! The mother I met…yesterday, was it? Came here to seek her out and stepped into the middle of this swirl of families, loves, murders, all of it circling back upon itself, like Sam said, the past repeating itself, Morelocks and Hamptons, bound together in one unchangeable pattern, like the rain tonight, random drops and splashes making some terrible, unaccountable rhythm, again and again and again. And so now I'll act out my fated role, my family heritage, in a struggle with the Morelocks, who want to kill me, whose destiny is to want to kill me? Well, I suppose I asked for it, didn't I? He laughed quietly.

His mother squeezed his hand, leaning in closer.

"It's all right, you know?" she whispered, as though she had heard his thoughts. "I'm glad I've seen you. Seen my son. Glad you was willing to find me, no matter what it cost. Glad I could see them eyes. One more time."

He heard a scuffling sound and caught at his rifle, seeing a figure rise up from the ground not twenty feet away. It was Sam, running, now, crouched, and dropping to his knees in front of them.

"Got him," he whispered, breathing hard. His eyes were shining. "Come up behind him and knocked him colder'n a dead trout. I'll be damned." He put his hands on his thighs and drew three hard, long breaths. "Just let me catch my wind and we'll go in there."

Jim listened to Sam's breath as it gradually slowed, grew quieter, thinking, *My heart's hammering like a drumbeat.* He clutched at the rifle, and tried to work his hands, stiff now and awkward with the cold. He found himself trying to will the time to slow, putting off the inevitable moment when he would have to stand and walk around the engine to the dugout, thinking, *not yet not yet not yet.* And then his heart seemed to settle a moment and he knew it had to be *now now* and, with one pulsing effort, he stood up.

"Let's go," he said to Sam.

"Why not?" said Sam.

They filed out from behind the chuffing engine and saw the dugout only a few yards away. There was a pale light in the front window, making the place seem almost warm, almost comforting, like a real home, instead of the bizarre, atavistic lair he knew it to be.

They walked slowly, almost strolling toward the closed door,

Jim and Sam moving apart now, holding their weapons at slant. Ellie walked between them and a few steps behind, the pistol held straight down at her side. When they reached the door, the two men pressed their backs against the harsh wood on either side, and looked across at one another, then at Ellie, then back at each other.

It will be loud and confusing, Jim remembered, telling himself to expect it, to let the surprise be theirs, not his.

His eyes met Sam's. The two men nodded at each other and Sam stepped back a few feet in front of the door, motioning at the hasp. Jim reached down and pressed the latch, and Sam began to run, giving the door a tremendous kick, letting his momentum carry him into the room. Jim dove in after him, already shouting, "Drop your weapons."

Sam's shotgun went off with a tremendous roar. In the dimness of the room, the muzzle flash was blinding, something Jim had not told himself to expect. His eyes stunned for a moment, he began trying to identify the men in the room. Johns Morelock was standing to his right, toward the back of the room, a rifle in his hands, held slack at his waist. To the left, in a chair, was the old man, his eyes looking vacant, as though the noise and flash had erased his senses completely. The two women were standing near Johns, to the right, closer to Jim. There was no one else in the room.

Sam was yelling as the top of his lungs. He fired another roaring shot as Ellie came by Jim and grabbed at the women, shouting at them, pulling them toward the door. Jim stepped laterally to the left, trying to keeping a clear view of Johns. He saw the man begin to raise his weapon, and then Lindee stepped in front of Jim, blocking his aim, just as Johns fired.

Everything seemed to slow down, in the swirl of noise, the muzzle flash. Lindee seemed to leap toward Jim, her arms floating outward, her upper torso disappearing, in a slow blooming of blood and flesh. She fell into Jim, who staggered, his rifle caught between himself and the dying woman.

Leela was frozen in horror, watching Lindee's body slide

down to the floor, while Ellie yanked at Leela's arm, trying to drag her in the direction of the door. Suddenly she appeared to understand and began to move, going by Jim, everything moving quickly, again, Leela heading out the doorway. Ellie turned to follow, when Johns reached out a hand and grabbed her by the shirt, pulling her to a sudden stop. She turned, bringing her free arm across her own body and pointing it at Johns. Jim saw the flash of the pistol as the man dropped to the ground, motionless. And then Ellie disappeared, running by him, out the door.

Sam was standing with his shotgun trained at the old man, who, Jim now saw, had a rifle cradled in his lap. He showed no sign of using it, still wearing that bemused, vacant expression, as if he'd been struck blind and deaf by the pandemonium.

"Leave him be," Jim shouted. "Let's go."

Sam backed away from the old man, while Jim stepped laterally over Lindee's body and turned himself out the door.

Outside, the two men turned and pressed their backs against the log wall, just as they had before. Both were breathing hard.

"Where the fuck is Paul?" said Sam. "What do we do?"

"Let's just keep on as planned," Jim said. "He's out the meadow way, somewhere, or he'd have stopped the women going up behind. You go after Ellie, and I'll go out across the meadow. Maybe I'll draw fire from him, if he's out there somewhere, and we can at least know where he is."

"Good," said Sam. He drew a breath and said, "Go!"

Jim headed straight into the clearing, running, though he felt slow and lame in his heavy, wet clothes. He heard the blood throbbing in his ears, and his throat felt scraped, his lungs flayed. He kept running, feeling the dark mountain, the deep sky, his own solitude, a model of futility, this lone man running from nowhere to nowhere, a useless rifle in his hands; his objective, to have a murderer spot him and fire at him. The meadow seemed to be an endless curve, reaching across the rest of time.

Suddenly he remembered that he had tripped on a root, or some piece of mill machinery, last time, and he began frantically to lift his knees, running in an absurd, high-stepping stride, as if the ground were hot coals, still waiting any second to hear the shot, feel the bullet bite.

At last he was at the top of the curving meadow, and he flung himself down, face first, gasping for breath. He could hear nothing but the sounds coming from inside himself. He wondered if Pierot was still unconscious out here, wondered how close he was, thought again about Paul. *Where is he? Where is he?*

He jerked himself upright, as he suddenly heard his mind provide the answer. *He's down at the Hampton place. Setting up the murder scene. And Leela, Ellie, and Sam are going to be off their guard coming down that side of the knob. He'll hear them coming. They'll walk right into his sights.*

"Oh my God," he said aloud. He stood, and began to run straight back, the way he had come, feeling again the drag of his wet clothes, the breadth of meadow extending itself before him, the exhaustion from all of today's worry, and effort, and violence. Running, feeling his side ache, his feet so heavy with the water and the fatigue. *This must be what it feels like to drown,* he thought, gulping for air that wouldn't come deep enough, running as hard, as doggedly, as breathlessly, and as slowly, as he ever had.

He went by the dugout and saw the old man standing at the door, rifle in hand, still looking absent and unaware, but now clearly seeing Jim, following him with his eyes, his vacant, demented eyes, looking straight into Jim's. He was saying something, calling some name, "Larry," was it? Or "Laura"? And then Jim passed him and struck the dark trail, trying to run but flagging on the steep slope. Slowing, finally to a walk, feeling his thigh muscles jerk and burn, trying to get a good breath, to get the air all the way in, and finally giving up, stopping, and resting.

The sweat came, and he wiped it from his eyes, running his sleeve along his brow. He listened to his own breathing, feeling the air begin to cool. The desperate gulping stopped and he discovered a degree of control over the rhythm of his own lungs. He drew a long breath and released it in a slow, luxurious exhalation, trying to let the ache and fatigue out with the used up air. He took another full, sweet breath and let it go, in a long, measured outflow. He was ready.

He decided it would waste his time to try scaling this mountain at a run, figuring he'd have to stop and recover too many times, and he was likely to trip in the dark, which might put him out of the way for good. And he believed he could accomplish a steady walk in one long push. So he began, stepping evenly, trying to find a pace, letting his muscles relax when he raised a foot from the ground, letting himself find his own stride. This was better.

He realized with something of a shock that he'd stopped thinking about his three friends, who were somewhere up the trail, and Paul, down across the crest, at the old Hampton place. *An appropriate enough place to finish this*. Then he remembered Lindee, her body flung toward him by Johns's gunshot, the explosion of blood and bone, the weight against him. *I must be covered in blood. Her blood.* She had gotten in the way, so he hadn't been able to do his job, and he wondered, abruptly, whether Johns had been firing at him, whether Lindee's death had been a random outrage, a matter only of where she happened to move in her attempt to get out the door. And he felt a profound sorrow overtake him.

He was tiring, again, in spite of the slower pace, his legs burning again, his feet leaden. *What more do you want?* he asked some unknown being that he felt must be connected, somehow, to the elusive air, which wouldn't let him take in enough of itself. And so he stopped, again.

Rested, he pushed himself upward, as steadily as he could. His feet were beginning to feel awkward, to stumble over small rocks or roots. But he kept on, moving agonizingly slowly up the grade, assuring himself that he'd make up the time on the downward slope, where he believed he could run.

When he came to the split, where the path up from Morelocks' place joined this one, he felt a surge of what he hoped was a second wind. Freshened, he pressed onward.

A split-second before it happened, he had a vague presentiment that something had gone very wrong, that he had made some terrible mistake. He sensed a shadow rising up behind him and he tried to turn, but there was a sudden crash and he fell to the ground, knowing nothing but brightness and pain.

Paul Morelock stood over him, holding the oak club loosely in his hand. "What in hell are you doin here?" he said. "And where's your friend at?"

Later, as he was being led him back down toward the mill ground, Jim decided that Paul must have been at the Hampton place, parking the truck, then had come back over the knob some time before Jim, Sam, and Ellie had come up. Paul must have taken the left fork, down to his house, instead of coming to the mill ground, probably because he had forgotten something he needed at the "murder scene," and had gone back to pick it up. And now he was on his way back over to finish his job, when he heard Jim laboring up the hill and hid himself just beyond the fork, rising up and knocking Jim down with his oak club.

"What you doin here?" he had said.

He had dragged Jim to his feet, roughly, and pushed a pistol against his temple, saying, "You'd best tell me what the fuck is going on up here. You know I'd be happy to leave you dead, right here where we is a standin."

And Jim made a decision. Or perhaps he only found himself telling the story, without having made any willful choice at all. Perhaps it had all been reflex, the continuing attempt to carry out his role, cover his friends' escape, draw Paul's attention, as he had attempted to do in that ragged run across the clearing. And so now he turned Paul away from the Hampton place, telling

him Sam and Leela and Lindee—he knew not to mention Ellie—were down below, at the mill, saying they'd tried to free the
women, but Pierot had gotten the drop on them and that Paul's
brother and father were holding them captive.

Jim had a vague understanding that the decision to tell this lie
would involve nothing less than his own doom, that Paul would
kill him as soon as they got to the dugout and found Johns's
body, found that Sam and Leela had escaped. But this didn't seem
to frighten Jim, didn't even feel like any sort of momentous decision. Perhaps he was too exhausted to feel dread. Or perhaps the
blow on the head had short-circuited some self-preservation instinct. Or perhaps he just wanted all of this to be over. At any
rate, he told the lie, and let Paul march him at pistol point back
down the trail, back toward the dugout and death.

The sky had cleared completely by now, and the breeze had
become brisk, beginning to boom as it piled itself into the high
hollows. As they walked down the trail, Jim felt the clear sky
like some cooling stream, felt a kind of peace descend, felt the
anguish and terror and struggle wash away, like so much trivial
debris. He had done what he'd come to do, find his mother. Seen
her. Found his past. The stormy, terrible past of the Hampton
family, doomed to be slain by their neighbors, simply because
their neighbors couldn't abide encroachment on what they saw
as their own family right and monopoly. He laughed inwardly
when he thought this had all been about moonshine and pills. It
had never been a romantic feud over honor or love. Though
there had been love, enough, it had been an accidental distraction, and the lovers had suffered for having gotten in the way of
the main thing, the family destiny, the struggle for nothing more
important than money and power. And wasn't that always the
way, the way we invent legend and romance to keep us from
realizing that it's the wealth and power winning out, stronger
than life or desire or even memory?

And now there would be no Hamptons left, at least none of
the Shaleen Hamptons. The line had petered down to two

ridiculous last descendants, the moon-faced, stupid, ineffectual Dicky—who would now spend his life in a jail cell—and himself, the effete, cultured, stranger out of a wealthy physician's home in Roalton, who had been foolish enough, or fated enough, to join in the family fight, and who would now meet his death at the hands of old Cuddy Morelock's great-grandson.

Then he thought with a kind of peaceful yearning about Leela. And the two of them, bruised and abused by this same Paul Morelock, lying in the bed, laughing and comforting, and, finally, loving one another. *He hits pretty hard, don't he?* Leela had said. And Jim found himself nodding, as he stepped down the steep slope in the dark glow of the clear night, saying, "He sure does."

"You shut up," said Paul, "And get on down there good and quiet. I aint stupid enough to walk into no ambush, you hear? First gunshot I hear, I put a bullet through your fuckin head, you hear? Now let's go, nice and quiet, like."

They came to the final switch back and Paul grabbed Jim's collar, saying, "Easy now, down this steep. Don't you even think of gettin out ahead of me." So Jim went down the drop half sliding, Paul clutching at his collar, so that Jim finally fell backward and skidded to the bottom.

"Get up," hissed Paul. "Get up and you walk straight on to that dugout. Just walk on in the door. Don't say nothin, don't try nothin, hear? I'm a going to give your pals the surprise party of their lives, you hear?"

Jim walked slowly past the steam engine, toward the dugout, remembering Ellie, his mother, squeezing his hand, in the cold and the fear, saying something like, "It's all right." He still felt that full peace, the warm wash of the night sky, the surcease of wounds and exhaustion and fear. It would all be over, soon enough.

The old man still stood at the door, the rifle in his hand, his eyes immediately settling on Jim's, watching him approach as if mesmerized, beginning to murmur, saying that name again.

Paul prodded Jim past the man, who was now saying, quite

clearly, "They told me I had done killed you, but I aint killed you, has I? They said I had killed you, but here you are, them lyin bastards, here you are. Them lyin bastards."

"Shut up, old man," hissed Paul, reaching for the latch and kicking the door open, shoving Jim into the room hard so that he stumbled and fell over Lindee's outstretched body.

Paul stepped into the room.

He stood utterly still for a moment, trying to compose the scene into something understandable, trying to meet anticipation with reality, looking for Sam and Leela, trying to see Johns holding them captive, instead of the two torn bodies lying heaped on the floor. As the actual scene began to form itself, he let out a loud bellow, of grief, or rage. He ran to his father's body, dropping to his knees and turning the man face-up, cradling his slack head.

"They killed him. Killed him. You killed him," Paul bawled. He leapt up, swinging the pistol toward Jim, his hand shaking, and shouted, "You sonofabitch." He took a step toward Jim, trying to steady the pistol. "I'll send you to hell," he cried.

Jim was looking at the old man, who had come through the door, still mumbling, still seeking out Jim's deep blue eyes, saying "They said I'd done killed you, said I...they lied, didn't they? Didn't they, Laura? Laura?"

"Look at me," Paul Morelock screamed at Jim. "I want to see you die."

Jim turned his head toward Paul, still feeling that sweet drop of peace, the ease of it all. He curled himself inward, like a child sleeping, feeling at last that he had ended the search. He turned and gazed at the barrel of Paul's pistol, two feet away, and said, "Leela."

"Not this time, not this time, Laura," the old man cried, swinging his rifle upward with his one arm, pulling the trigger in the same motion.

Paul Morelock's body leapt into the air and crashed to the ground on top of his father's.

* * *

Jim lay curled into that fetal position, hugging his knees, as the gunshot echoed and rang in the room and through his own brain. He felt a disagreeable sensation, being tugged out of that peaceful stream, the bathing fluid of the night sky, and he didn't want to wake from it, didn't want to be pulled into life, into pain and the harsh ragged breathing. He heard vaguely the old man's mantra, "Laura, Laura," while he felt on his tongue the aftertone of his own last word: "Leela," the beautiful double softness of the syllables, tongue touching palate, "Leela."

He felt a hand on his cheek, and heard her voice, saying, "Here I am, Jim," and he realized he'd been saying her name aloud, a counterpoint to the old man's chant of "Laura," so that the room must have flowed back and forth, like taking in and expelling breath, "Laura, Leela, Laura, Leela."

She spoke again. "Here I am, Jim. Are you okay?" And he opened his eyes to see hers, shining down on him like the night sky.

Sam was standing by the old man, easing the rifle from his hands, saying, "It's all right, grandpaw, it's all right," until Ellie stepped in and said, "Let me. He knows me." She looked toward Jim and Leela for a moment, then led the old man out the door, where Pierot Morelock sat, his arms and legs tied, his eyes blurry and unfocused.

"Where the hell you been, cousin?" Sam said. "We waited on you a mite, then I decided you'd probably gone off on some fiddle collectin trip. But Leela here—her and momma—they insisted we had to come back and look for you. We picked up junior a wanderin around the wild moors, still tryin to get hisself woke up from the smackin I give him, and we tied him up for his own good, before he got run down by a tree."

Jim slowly sat up, Leela trying to steady him, until he said,

"I'm fine. I'm fine." She smiled and stood, watching him rise slowly to his feet.

"Let's get on over the mountain and get down home," said Sam. "We got to figure out how we're all going to stay out of jail for all this. Got to see if we can find some law that might believe us." He smiled at Jim. "Good thing we got a big city hotshot with us. I reckon you know one or two Philadelphia lawyers, don't you?"

"The best money can buy," Jim said.

EPILOGUE

Four days later they sat together again in the office, Sam standing in front of his desk, filling glasses with stumpblower, while Jim and Leela sat together on the couch, holding hands. Ellie rocked Lurlee in Sam's desk chair, singing softly to her:

> *What're we goin to do with the baby-o?*
> *She won't go to sleepy-o.*
> *Wrap her in corn shucks nice and soft,*
> *Throw her up in the fodder loft.*

Sam handed the glasses around, insisting, when she demurred, that Ellie take one, too.

He held his own glass high, saying, "Here's to Pierot—pronounced Pye-Rot—Morelock. And thank the Good Lord I didn't hit him too hard, so he still had enough sense left to confess the whole damn story." He swung his glass, pronouncing the toast: "To Pierot. Who kept us from rottin in jail."

"And may have gotten Dicky out," said Jim.

"And to Dicky, who may be back to fight again," said Sam.

They clinked glasses and drank.

"I got me another prisoner to get out of jail, too," said Sam. "Got to find out where that poor bastard is that they sent up for killin Morgan and his father. Get to work doin some real journalism and get him out of jail, too."

Leela raised her glass.

"And here's to Lindee," she said softly. "Poor girl."

"Mommie's in heaven, in the angel band," said Lurlee.

"Yes she is, honey," Ellie said, cuddling the child.

They sat in silence for a long minute.

"What about the old man?" said Sam. "Jessum Morelock."

"What a strange case," Leela said. "He killed your father. And your grandfather, too, come to think of it. And then looked at you and saw something he couldn't let die."

"And saved your life," Ellie said, looking at Jim. "After almost a hundred years of hatin Hamptons, in a matter of speakin."

"So what's to become of him?" said Sam.

"He's in the hospital, right now," said Jim. "And then we'll see. I'm going to put some money aside to make sure he's taken care of. He'll be okay, I think."

"Don't know how he'll do down here," said Ellie. "After all them years up on the mountain. Right back where he was born. I believe he forgot there even is a 'down here' to worry about." She looked away, into some place beyond the room. "I'll keep a eye over him, some ways," she said.

"One thing I wonder," Jim said at length. He turned to Ellie. "How did you know? When you knocked that glass out of my hand, how did you figure out that they had drugged it?"

"Know?" she said. "Didn't know. Just kindly felt." She smiled. "I saw you lift that glass up, and I thought, 'Lord God, it's the end of everything.' I can't say I even knowed it then. Didn't know dezactly why. I didn't want you to drink that stuff was all. Felt somehow it would be a terrible thing iffen you did. So I jumped at you. It weren't until then that I even begun to think about why. And when that glass busted on the floor, I saw it all clear as a spring day. But, come to think of it, none of us knows, even now, do we? Don't know for sure iffen it was drugged. Because you never drank that stuff. Only way we might've known was iffen you had. I reckon sometimes it's best not to know, but just to decide."

Next morning, the last morning, he'd knocked again on Ellie's room door. She was sitting on the bed, playing with Caroline.

"I wanted to say goodbye," he said. She reached up and took his hand.

"Good," she said. "And I reckon I'd like to say again I'm glad you come. Glad you worked so hard to find me."

"I think you should come back with me," he said. "I have money and a big house. I could take care of you. You're my mother. You've got a place to go, now."

She rocked the child, watching him, looking at his eyes.

"That's okay," she said. "You're my son, and I'm glad to know you. But you aint got a place for me. My place is up on Elk Creek, and that's been gone longer'n you'll ever know." She shook her head. "I aint got no place."

"Come with me," he said. "I'll take care of you."

She shook her head.

"You're my mother, damn it," he said, pleading. "I can get you out of all this, take you back with me, out of these forsaken hills, where these people, these Morelocks, have stolen your soul. I can care for you for once in your life."

She shook her head again.

"At least come and see it," he said. "See the place, see if it might be somewhere we both could make a way for ourselves."

"See it?" she said. She made a soft sound like a laugh. "I've seen it, son. And what makes you think I'd ever want to go back there? Back down to that place? Back to Roalton? What makes you think I want to get out of here?" She rocked the child, again. "I been there," she said. "I don't never want to go back."

"But what will you do?" he said. "What is it you want?"

"Aint a matter of wanting," she said. "Life aint a matter of wanting. I learnt that. I lost what I wanted a long time ago. And since them times, it's a matter of doing. Being where you got to be and doing what you got to do. I reckon I'm glad I learnt it so soon, maybe it didn't hurt as much as it could later on. So maybe I'm better off than you, even."

"How can you say that?" He appealed again with the mute, sweeping gesture, taking in the town of Glade, the looming mountains, all the terror and the grief and the pain she must have experienced in this strange, dark place. "How in the world can you say that?"

She cradled Caroline in her arms, nuzzling the little girl against her cheek.

"I got me a child to raise," she said, smiling gently.

Later, Sam helped Jim pack and put his things into the car for the trip back to Roalton.

"I reckon baby sister will see clear to come down there and join you, after she gets to thinking about it," said Sam.

"I don't know," Jim said. "She believes she belongs here. She says, 'This is my home,' and she doesn't seem to want to think otherwise."

"Well," Sam said, "you could come here. You can be a music expert up here as well as you could in Roalton, Tennessee, I reckon."

"I don't know," Jim said. He opened the trunk and they both hefted the bags inside. "I guess we'll have to wait and see. I guess I finally found out that I'm from here and I'm not from here. They're both true." He smiled ruefully. "Maybe I still haven't found a place."

"Well, you found us," Sam said. "And you belong to us, some kind of how, no matter what. And we're all Hamptons, some way or another, come to think of it."

"And we know how to make stumpblower." Jim smiled.

"I reckon Leela will come around," Sam said. "She aint a goin to let you go, I don't believe. Crazy if she did. I don't know why she aint standin out here waitin to climb into your car."

"We need to find a place where we can both be, I guess," Jim said. "And that's not so easy."

"You done okay, here," Sam said.

"Maybe," Jim said, slamming the trunk lid.

"You take care, cousin," Sam said, turning and walking slowly into the house. He didn't look back.

After Sam had returned to the house, Jim stood alone, pondering. He wondered what he would do, knowing he couldn't simply return to the wood-lined study in Roalton, the gallery and the books. He knew he'd found something here, and lost something, and he suddenly felt a desire to go back into Sam's house, go upstairs and find Leela, say "I love you," again, and ask what that meant he should do.

But he knew she wouldn't have an answer for him. He'd already asked.

Last night they had held each other, in the dark of the bedroom, after having made what Leela called "sweet, long love." And he asked her to come with him, tomorrow, and she shook her head, finally saying, "I think I need to wait. I think we should say our goodbye, tonight, and you should leave and go back tomorrow. And we'll wait and see."

"Why?" he asked her, pleading.

She touched his cheek. "I don't know," she said. "Don't know if I have a place there."

"But I love you," he said. "What should I do?"

"I don't know that, either," she said. "I know I love you, too."

"So, after all this, I'm to just go back, alone, back to where I started?"

"That isn't where you started, is it?" she said, softly. "You started here. Up on the mountain. You started with two lovers, trying to get away."

"Couldn't that be us?" he said.

"I don't know," she said. "They didn't get away, did they?"

"That doesn't mean we can't," he said.

"Maybe," she said. "But maybe we have to let it be for a little, let the two of us abide for a time. This has all been so fast, and so strange. We need to let it sit. Abide, like I said."

"We won't see each other?" he said, his voice breaking.

"Oh yes," she said. "I'd have to see you. You come see me, and I'll come see you, and maybe we can find a way. Maybe there's a place, somewhere. I don't know if I could belong there, in Roalton."

"I know," he said. "I don't know if I belong here."

She kissed him and held his face framed in her hands.

"You have eyes that belong here."

He swung open the door and climbed into his car. He'd said his farewells. And so now he pulled out into the main road and turned for the west, climbing one last time up the winding road, into the mountains. He would take the short drive up, past Shaleen, down into Tennessee, past Pink's Grill, into Roalton. A brief way that might as well be a thousand miles. Alone.

He felt the land rise, felt the road swing into the turns and rolls that would take him up into the hollows, into the dark mountains.

When he swerved into the high cove and across the bridge over the creek, he impulsively braked the car and slid into the turnoff, the way up to the old sawmill, where so much had happened, over so many years. *The place that made me who I am. A Hampton.* He stepped from the car and felt the cool waft of air rising from the rushing water, saw the rocks and trees rising into the high mountain. *Up here. So many times in one place.* And he remembered them, Sam and Leela, talking about how it had all come full circle, the generations repeating the old stories in their lives, Hamptons and Sheltons, love and struggle and death and memory. And he heard Sam, saying, "You take care, cousin." He stood still, for a long time, looking up toward the steep, dark rise, where he'd found his mother.

"All right," he said at last, speaking to the creek, to the mountain air, to all the times and all the people, the lovers and fighters, killers and kinfolks. "All right."

He climbed into the car, and swung it back onto the road, pulling it around in a broad turn, then backing, turning again.

Heading home.

Richard Hood is a musician, photographer, and writer, living in
Greene County, Tennessee.

HoodsBooks.com

On the following pages are a few
more great titles from the
Down & Out Books publishing family.

For a complete list of books and to
sign up for our newsletter,
go to DownAndOutBooks.com.

Badge Heavy
A Charlie-316 Novel
Colin Conway and Frank Zafiro

Down & Out Books
September 2020
978-1-64396-152-1

Officer Tyler Garrett's saga continues when he is assigned to the aggressive Anti-Crime Team.

The team's sterling success in battling crime is only matched by the dark agendas surrounding it. The team piles up arrests and seizures, but tension grows as competing goals and loyalties come into conflict.

Something has got to give.

Deep Red Cover
A Cover Thriller
Joel W. Barrows

Down & Out Books
September 2020
978-1-64396-117-0

A body is found on the shores of a Missouri lake, throat slashed. There are few clues, and the trail grows cold for Investigator Morgan Kern.

At the same time, ATF has become increasingly concerned about the growing militia movement. Special Agent David Ward goes undercover to investigate possible illegal weapons trafficking.

Their paths will intersect in a way that neither could have imagined.

Blood by Choice
Rob Pierce

All Due Respect, an imprint of
Down & Out Books
September 2020
978-1-64396-116-3

Two women and a child are murdered. Dust, who unknowingly set them up, returns to Berkeley to find the killer. With his old buddy Karma in tow, Dust discovers that one of the culprits was Vollmer, a ruthless hired gun working for Dust's former boss, Rico. When Vollmer finds out Dust is in town the hunt becomes mutual.

In this, the third book of the Uncle Dust series, old debts are paid and new ones incurred. Brutish, dangerous men lurk in every corner and slaughter runs rampant.

Deemer's Inlet
Stephen Burdick

Shotgun Honey, an imprint of
Down & Out Books
August 2020
978-1-64396-104-0

Far from the tourist meccas of Ft. Lauderdale and Miami Beach, a chief of police position in the quiet, picturesque town of Deemer's Inlet on the Gulf coast of Florida seemed ideal for Eldon Quick—until the first murder.

The crime and a subsequent killing force Quick to call upon his years of experience as a former homicide detective in Miami. Soon after, two more people are murdered and Quick believes a serial killer is on the loose. As Quick works to uncover the identity and motive of the killer, he must contend with an understaffed police force, small town politics, and curious residents.

www.ingramcontent.com/pod-product-compliance
Lightning Source LLC
Chambersburg PA
CBHW021223060726
47590CB00005B/1619